Visions of War

Visions of War

World War II in Popular Literature and Culture

Edited by

M. Paul Holsinger
and
Mary Anne Schofield

Bowling Green State University Popular Press
Bowling Green, Ohio 43403

Library of Congress Catalogue Card No.: 92-72577

ISBN: 0-87972-555-9 Clothbound
     0-87972-556-7 Paperback

Cover design by Laura Darnell Dumm

Dedicated to

The Women and Men

Who Have Served Their Country

and

Nancy—Who Else?

Contents

Acknowledgements

It is an obvious truism that no book is solely the product of its authors or, in this case, editors and contributors. No matter how much all of us might wish to take credit for the finished product of our labors, there are always many others, behind the scenes, whose efforts guarantee that a book-length manuscript such as *Visions of War* eventually sees the light of day.

The original idea for this volume grew out of the area sessions on World War II at the Popular Culture Association held in St. Louis, Missouri, in April 1989. World War II, as a separate area of study within the PCA, was brand new that spring when its first six sessions of nineteen different papers were presented in conjunction with the meetings held in St. Louis' downtown Clarion Hotel. Immediately after the convention, several of us, still filled with the enthusiasm of newness, began to talk about putting all the papers we had heard about the war years into a collection and trying to publish them "as is." It was a nice thought; it was also unworkable for any number of reasons. But the idea of creating a book of essays that would look closely at some of the more significant literature and popular culture of World War II seemed too important to give up, and, early in 1990, a call for original papers dealing with those two broad topics appeared in *PMLA*. We did not know what to expect from such a vague call, but the results were overwhelming. Far from having only a few potential essays to consider, we had dozens, and the job of picking and choosing from among many fine suggestive articles began. By the time that PCA met in Toronto in early 1990, the first cuts had been made and the first call for complete essays requested. Through 1990, the selection process became ever more intensified, and all the contributors found here need to receive special thanks for the many times we asked for, and received quickly from each of them, revised and then, re-revised copies of their works. The final essays are theirs but the gratitude for the efforts each made to help in the finalization of this book is ours.

As usual, there are far more individuals and groups who need to be recognized than space could ever allow. Realizing this, however, does not make it less traumatic. At the same time, there is a small, very select group who absolutely cannot be ignored. Nancy Holsinger not only provided an atmosphere at home that made the completion of the bulk of final editing possible, but she repeatedly brought her own critical eye to the various essays much to their, and our, good fortune. Many times when the project seemed to have come irretrievably to a standstill, she found a way not only to get it started again but also to guarantee that it would be better in the end. Words cannot repay such constant help.

ii   **Visions of War**

The "Two Sharons"—Sharon Foiles and Sharon Garee of the Department of History at Illinois State University—twice, and in several cases, three times, typed and re-typed, all the individual, edited essays and then, just when they thought they were finished, found themselves typing, still again, the entire manuscript in draft form. If we had waited until either of us, hunting and pecking our way across our keyboards, had had the time to type correctly, as they did, the hundreds of pages of typescript, there is no telling when this volume would have been completed.

Illinois State University provided time for research and editing during the Spring semester of 1991 that expedited the completion of this project and Helga Whitcomb, Carol Ruyle and the staff of the Interlibrary Load division of Illinois State's Milner Library constantly searched for resources that both personally and collectively helped.

Librarians are always high on any scholar's "thank-you list" and this is certainly true in the case of Francine Fisk at the McFarlane Library of the University of Tulsa as well as the entire Interlibrary Loan Staff at that institution. The students in the "Women and War" class at the University of Tulsa during the Spring semester of 1991 offered many incisive thoughts. Particular gratitude goes to Sandy Vice, Hazel Kight and Lynn Z. Bloom.

M. Paul Holsinger

Mary Anne Schofield

Introduction

Wars are fought to keep the peace; thus, war begins in a state of illogical yet somehow irrefutable irony. War texts are full of images which symbolize this inherent quality of conflict: death versus life, body parts versus the whole person, stolen youth versus forced maturity, entry into the world of war versus re-entry into the "civilized" world, fragmented texts versus continuous narratives. These ironies are the literary elements which all war texts have in common. They are linked by the historical reassurance of all war writings that what seems to be right in the world will be turned upside-down by the war experience.

Visions of War examines this topsy-turveydom as it is revealed in literature and popular culture that focuses on the era of the Second World War. This is not, however, a book that looks solely at the obvious male-dominated aspects of combat in the front lines. Though several of the essayists featured here do, indeed, look at that part of the war years as it has been captured on the written page and in film, the majority concern themselves with the ways that the war changed persons' lives, whether on the war fronts *or* the home fronts between 1939 and 1945. Featured in the eighteen original essays are accounts of fiction and non-fictional literature, poetry, music, cinematic drama and artistic imagery. Americans are the focus of nine of the essays, but there are also chapters dealing with Canada, Britain, France, Nazi Germany, Poland and the U.S.S.R.

As the years have passed since the end of the war, the world has never been free of conflict somewhere on the globe. In the United States, young American men and women have been involved in two bloody Asian conflagrations and in more than our share of "brush-fire" wars as well. But for all the bravery, the trauma, the bloodshed, it is World War II that, by its sheer magnitude, continues to fascinate us above all other foreign wars. The authors whose works have been collected in *Visions of War* provide a series of unique but clearly connected essays on the war years. In their perceptive examinations, they challenge us all to rethink our long-held views about World War II and the many individuals—men, women and children—whose lives were forever changed.

Part One focuses "On the War Fronts" and the massive amount of literature that has been produced over the last fifty years to commemorate the front lines of battle, the spies behind those lines and the men and women directly affected by the fighting. In the first essay, "Snapshots in the Book of War," David K. Vaughan critically examines *Rhymes of a Pfc*, a collection of poems which Paul Fussell suggests may make its author, Lincoln Kirstein, "the greatest poet of the Second World War." These 95 poems are "often comic, even incongruous" because "they exactly catch the rugged flavor of the wartime experience from the viewpoint of the soldier." Although few of the poems describe combat directly, the collection, as a whole, does "provide an accurate and unified vision of the

1

war." A private himself throughout his war years, Kirstein was "intrigued by the possible ways that poetry might mirror wartime experience." But he was totally disinterested in praising the already famous. His heroes were almost always average soldiers, "all a...little foolish, a little selfish, a little nervous, a lot like most of us." Because of Kirstein's gritty visual imagery, the lives of average GIs, Vaughan concludes, "remain fixed in our memory...snapshots in the book of war whose meaning we may ponder indefinitely."

The battlefield also provides the focus for Philip J. Landon's "New Heroes: Post-war Hollywood's Image of World War II," but his heroes are enshrined on film rather than in the stanzas of poetry. Examining motion pictures such as "Twelve O'Clock High," "The Sands of Iwo Jima" and "Command Decision," Landon studies the cultural myth that made movies about World War II so popular during the Cold War era. The "battlefield in these films became a metaphor for the increasingly bureaucratized America which emerged from World War II.... Armed conflict gave mythic expression to the tensions and conflicts underlying the political concensus of the new industrial state." Within less than a generation, however, "the genre which had evolved a myth of heroism...had become increasingly ironic and self-reflexive in the treatment of the hero-as-organization man." The United States became, Landon concludes, increasingly disillusioned with "a political accommodation at first welcomed as the end of ideology and ultimately rejected—by both right and left—for stifling individual freedoms."

The war front was, obviously, not confined to the land. Indeed, the war at sea during World War II, especially as it was fought by the British Navy, created legends of heroism and valor in the best tradition of Horatio Nelson at Trafalgar. Few better evocations of that bravery have ever been produced than Noel Coward's great propaganda film, "In Which We Serve." Margaret Wintersole, in her essay "Noel Coward's Vision of the British Navy at War," examines this brilliant cinematic masterpiece, which Coward released over the objections of the Navy, and finds that his commanding use of realism makes it a true "ode to the Navy" at war. The film, which won a special Academy Award for outstanding production achievement in 1943, was, Coward believed, his "most important work for his country." "In Which We Serve," Wintersole concludes, "proclaims that a fundamental and idealistic patriotism—love of family, home, country, and God, courage, endurance, unity, loyalty, self-sacrifice, indomitable spirit, magnamity, kindness, and mercy—abides in the British Navy and in the British people."

The Russian/Eastern Front during the years after the Nazi invasion of the U.S.S.R. in June, 1941, reveals horrifically the blood and gore that war can engender. No works capture those traumatic days better than Theodor Plievier's three harshly brilliant works: *Stalingrad, Moscow* and *Berlin*. Jennifer Michaels, in her essay "The War in the East," shows how that author used his trilogy to protest against the war—indeed, against all wars. He denounces both the Nazi and Bolshevik regimes for the enormity of wanton destruction that their totalitarian systems caused. Because scenes in all three books are based closely on voluminous interviews with captured German soldiers, Plievier's "film-like technique...enables him to capture the scope of the fighting and the magnitude of the suffering" on paper. Pictures are etched in acid and remain indelible in readers' memories. Though Plievier's philosophic view is overwhelmingly negative, his works, Michaels maintains, are "deeply moral" and "one of the major accomplishments of contemporary European fiction."

Sally Parry's "Learning to Fight the Nazis" looks closely at a different sort of war—that fought behind the front lines by the multitude of secret agents. She examines Upton Sinclair's fictional Lanny Budd, the hero of that author's award-winning eleven-volume "World's End" series. Sinclair "believed that art ought to serve history" and that fiction existed "for educating readers about social and economic injustice." In creating Lanny, he sought to show how World War II was caused by the schemings of fascist-supporting, dictator-loving industrial groups. In successive novels, Sinclair takes his readers into the seats of power as his erstwhile spy becomes involved with most of the major leaders on both sides of the great conflict—Churchill, Hitler, Franklin Delano Roosevelt. Parry concludes that the series "is in the great tradition of historical fiction," though she readily admits that long before they came to an end, the volumes had shifted from political and historical education to "a documentation of the evolving political consciousness of Upton Sinclair."

Mary Anne Schofield's "Telling the Truth" also looks at the lives of spies in literature, though her heroines—the hundreds of female British agents who helped carry out Winston Churchill's request to his secret service "to set Europe ablaze"—are very real. Having studied many of the biographies and autobiographies of these brave women, Schofield argues that telling one's story becomes the ultimate act of self-definition and self-assertion. For years, however, spy narratology denied this self-validation to women. Accounts written, for example, by R.J. Minney or H. Montgomery Hyde cast the female spy as romantic heroine, one who commodified herself as a tool of espionage. Fortunately stories based on such seduction have given way to accounts by women writers who, following Helene Cixous's dictum, "break out of the snare of silence." Unmarginalized at last, these women deny "the patristic language of men." No longer seduced behind a curtain of espionage, the women agents/authors address themselves to this very important issue of gender in wartime.

"Women's War Stories: The Legacy of South Pacific Internment" by Lynn Z. Bloom, explores still another kind of war front: the Japanese camps where hundreds of American women were held in captivity from the days after Pearl Harbor until mid-1945. War makes story-tellers, we know, of men; Bloom examines this process in the lives of a number of extraordinarily brave women. "The profundity of the cataclysmic, watershed experience of being interned away from their native land during wartime endows their lives with a significance that they are impelled to explain to those who remained, more or less, safely at home." The publication of these narratives is validation of this voice. These women, all of whom "attained a moral vision," not only survived but triumphed over the adversity of camp life and internment. Keeping diaries, at the risk of their lives, was a way to gain "some measure of freedom and independence in confinement." And, Bloom concludes, "as they wrote, they created themselves the heroines of their own stories."

War literature is not only for adults, Marilyn Fain Apseloff reminds us in her essay, "Survival! Polish Children During World War II." Increasing numbers of books for children dealing with World War II have been appearing with regularity during the last twenty years or so. Emphases on the drive to survive, "not for personal gain but as a lasting witness to the horrors of war" occur in children's literature as well as in that for adults. Apseloff has chosen to focus her attention exclusively on juvenile literature dealing with Poland and Polish children because that country was "perhaps the best example of how war so completely altered children's lives" during the years after 1939. Having examined the works of writers such as Chester Aaron, Uri Orlev, Christine Szambelin-Strevinsky and Ruth Sender, Apseloff points out that "each of the[se] four volumes shows contemporary children how other youngsters acted during the Nazi occupation fifty years ago." She concludes that "the children pictured in these books are among the many heroes of World War II."

Robert L. McLaughlin's "I.G. Farben's Synthetic War Crimes" ends the first section on war-related literature by recounting the story of the great German chemical conglomerate responsible for not only the development of the V-2 rockets that devastated England but also the Zyklon B gas used in the extermination camps. The IG, despite its war criminality, continued its influence unabated at war's end. McLaughlin looks at it through the focus of Thomas Pynchon's "encyclopedic narrative" *Gravity's Rainbow*. Pynchon "sees the IG's influence everywhere" and proclaims the corporation, "even more than Hitler, the villain of World War II." He "uses the corporation to represent Western Civilization's tendency to control and corrupt the natural and transform it from the purposes of life to the purposes of death." In the end, Pynchon "refuses to let us distance ourselves from I.G. Farben's world view. He shows us how it has shaped our understanding of our world, how it affects us as individuals and how we are its product, passing on to future generations its deadly effects."

The literature and popular culture of World War II should not, of course, be viewed only through accounts of military actions or secret spy rendezvous. As the essays in Part Two, "On the Home Fronts," point out, the Second World War affected the life of everyone who lived through it, no matter where they were or what they did. James Rodger Alexander's study, "The Art of Making War: The Political Poster in Global Conflict," examines closely the history of poster art as a propaganda tool during the twentieth century. Alexander's closest scrutiny is directed at perhaps the most successful attempt of any nation to mobilize its home front for the war effort: the United States' artistic triumph between 1942 and 1945. Often utilizing "haunting," images to make their point, American artists, backed strongly by the United States government, "designed, printed, and distributed posters which educated the public, recruited men to serve, implored women into the work force, encouraged greater productivity, discouraged waste, and warned citizens about dangers on the home front." Posters graphically reiterated policy. Their imagery could be subtle or shocking but, invariably, they "worked." By war's end, the many artists involved in the poster campaign had "produced visual images and political slogans which influenced the American people for half a decade and shaped American culture for a generation."

Patriotic visual images were not, of course, confined exclusively to posters. In "Madison Avenue Goes to War: Patriotism in Advertising during World War II," Sue Hart examines the massive campaign which, she maintains, "may well have been the American advertising industry's finest hour." Even as product supplies and personal services dwindled and Americans did without, ad companies devoted themselves to instilling—and sustaining—a patriotic attitude toward the war effort. "Glamour was replaced by gunnery sergeants, and emphasis on the advertiser's product was downplayed to play up the importance of a united stand on the home front." Almost every area of commercial life was involved: foodstuffs, utilities, appliances, medicines, transportation companies. "Whatever their wares...World War II-era advertisers were selling patriotism and promise first; their products second," Hart maintains. When victory finally arrived, "it was in no small part due to the call to patriotism that arrived weekly in American homes disguised as magazine advertisements."

Calls for patriotic action also encouraged more than 350,000 women to volunteer for, and eventually enlist in, one of the five branches of the United States military. In "If You're Nervous in the Service," Carol Burke examines many of the training songs of those women who joined the Women's Army Corps during the Second World War in the hope of serving their country in its time of need. The WACS, Burke notes, "adapted popular songs by inventing verses which defined them as military women, proclaimed their enthusiasm and eagerness to serve and voiced their frustration about the rigors of training." Through their lyrics, songs also became gender weapons, as women vented their disillusionment with military life. "Expecting action and excitement, recruits soon found themselves bound to the domestic drudgery they thought they had left behind." Ultimately these women, Burke concludes, became heroines on the home front, frustrated by their inability to do more for their country but fulfilling a vital and important function nonetheless.

In the United States, there were few changes during the war that were more monumental than the nationalization of day care for America's children. "Rosie the Riveter and the Eight-Hour Orphan" by Rose Kundanis looks closely at the events surrounding this change and shows how dramatically American attitudes toward day-care were altered after 1941. In the 1930s, poor women had had access to child care; now middle-class women also needed help, as they rushed off to work while their husbands were overseas. It was obvious that "the hand that holds the pneumatic riveter cannot rock the cradle at the same time." An artistic depiction of a woman worker with a baby strapped to her back that appeared in one magazine appalled many viewers. Within a few short months, day care as a solution had become an acceptable part of the national psyche. Kundanis perceptively notes that, though the recent growth of child care in this country "has been the result of different economic needs than those of World War II," that era's legacy remains—"informing and inspiring us today."

The North American home front, for all its signs of positive change, also witnessed one of the bleakest denials of civil liberties in the modern history of the free world: the forcible removal of tens of thousands of persons from their homes and their incarceration in "relocation centers" because of their Japanese ancestry. M. Paul Holsinger, in his essay, "Told Without Bitterness," studies ten autobiographical accounts that recapture those days of hatred. Ashamed and depressed at becoming "enemies in their own land," Japanese-Americans and Japanese-Canadians took years before each was able to "deal finally with his or her own personal suffering." In the 1970s, however, writers such as Shizuye Takashima, Jeanne Wakatsuki Houston and Yoshiko Uchida began to write about their experiences; these books became "a catharsis, a cleansing of the past." In examining their studies, Holsinger emphasizes not only the cruel racial bigotry that existed in North America during World War II but also the stoic bravery of a group of persons whose only crime was to be Japanese in the years following Pearl Harbor.

On the other side of the Atlantic, the British home front saw thousands of dedicated women doing all they could to aid their country. Laura Hapke's "An Absence of Soldiers" investigates some of the most expressive novels of the era that focus on such women—volumes by a group that she labels the "Mrs. Miniver" school of novelists: E.M. Delafield, Stella Gibbons, Betty Miller, Pamela Frankau, Mollie Panter-Downes and Elizabeth Bowen. These women, each in her own way, upend the traditional gender roles that extol "manliness as battleground heroism, womanliness as homefront self-sacrifice." Hapke finds that "in one way or another their heroines question the role of the cheerful helpmate awaiting her master's return.... What these novels did with the 'essential truth' of the Englishwoman doing her part for the war effort was not simply verisimilitude in the name of patriotism. Rather, these works integrated social-historical depictions of women's new roles into a critique of male behavior." These women, Hapke concludes, provide an important revisionist reading of the war.

Cecilia Macheski, in her essay "Some Classic Pattern," continues this investigation of wartime revisionism with her challenging reading of knitting and needlework tropes in the World War II British literature of such authors as Mary Lee Settle, Beryl Bainbridge and Mollie Panter-Downes. In 1915, during the First World War, Canadian feminist Nellie McClung observed that "women have not only been knitting—they have been thinking." That was no less true a generation later as the world faced another war. Like Hapke, Macheski's critical study makes clear that the traditional icon of a woman knitting as a symbol of "loyalty, patience, patriotism" is too simplistic. Instead, she argues, knitting connotes shrewdness, "a virtuous guise like Penelope's for subversive activity, such as thinking, and dreaming, or harboring less than patriotic notions." "To knit," as Macheski reminds us, "is to see possibilities, to explore new combinations." The seemingly innocent needles could, and often did, become weapons "to fight the effects of war."

The perspicaciousness of British women during World War II is further noted in Phyllis Lassner's study, "A Cry for Life: Storm Jameson, Stevie Smith and the Fate of Europe's Jews." In 1934, "years before Nazi Germany was officially recognized as a global threat, Jameson and Smith were assessing the costs of denying it." Lassner continues that what makes World War II a unique assault "on the human spirit" is the "unfettered blood lust and ferocity" of the Nazi siege on the Jews. The figure of the Jew functions like a Rorschach test in the fiction of both women, "an object waiting to be filled in with ink blot representations of the desires and the fears of his friends and enemies." Both writers, Lassner argues, call into question the ironies of war, but it was Jameson who, once the war began, best understood the ultimate result of British anti-Semitism: "Our enemies are not the men and women of another country. They are ourselves...they are all of us in those moments when, losing faith, we think of a war as something other than it is—a blasphemous betrayal of the future of man."

Michael West's essay, "Cannibalism and Anorexia, or Feast and Famine in French Occupation Narrative," looks at an area untouched by any of the previous authors: France under the Nazis from 1940 to 1945. Overrun by a vicious enemy, that nation suffered endlessly. Its starving citizens became obsessed with food. Though their lives centered around the quest for sustenance, it was not until many years later that authors like Simone de Beauvoir and Michael Tournier or film makers such as Louis Malle addressed the issue directly. Beauvoir's *La Force de l'age* is particularly moving as it discusses that author and her lover, Jean Paul Sartre's, constant battle to keep themselves from total deprivation. Ironically, West demonstrates that similar themes of virtual cannibalism (feast) and anorexia (famine) have been a part of modern French literature since at least the Franco-Prussian War of 1870 and the writings of Guy de Maupassant. Yet, as he also concludes, such images remain a haunting reminder of France and her citizens' struggle during the Second World War to live fully once again.

There are, of course, thousands of other pictures that could have been painted; hundreds of works of fiction that might have been explicated; still multitudes of film focusing on World War II that call for analysis. But there are, sadly, just so many pages in any book. The conflicting images that appear and re-appear in these essays, however, are clearly symbolic of nearly all that remains untouched. They offer mute testimony to the still unsettled picture of those halycon days between 1939 and 1945 when the entire world found itself at war.

Snapshots in the Book of War:
Lincoln Kirstein's *Rhymes of a Pfc*

David K. Vaughan

American literary critic Paul Fussell has said of Lincoln Kirstein: "It would be funny and splendid if he should ultimately be recognized as the greatest poet of the Second World War." It seems an unlikely mix of terms—funny, splendid— to describe a collection of poetry that could, in fact, establish Kirstein as one of the most important American poets of the mid-20th century. Yet these two terms accurately characterize his *Rhymes of a Pfc*; these poems *are* often comic, even incongruous, in their effect. They exactly catch the rugged flavor of the wartime experience from the viewpoint of the soldier. In one of the last poems in his collection, for instance, Kirstein describes a scene in which he and some fellow soldiers stand around a fire in the rain after learning that the war in Europe has finally ended:

> Rain runnels helmet, skips the neck,
> > Drops, spits and hisses in our fire;
> We shudder in each leaky coat,
> > Boots squelched to ankle-deep in mire;
> Really relieved despite the damp,
> > A dozen buddies here have come
> To pool our mutual luck and thanks
> > And sweat it out till we're shipped home.
>
> Burn fire, rain rain; love, buddies, love
> > Each other sure. It keeps us warm;
> Battles of braver joes than us
> > Have kept us clean of scar or harm.
> By good sports shared, the wet warmth steams:
> > A summer's done; a war is won;
> Our drizzle downpour's not so bad,
> > And slight discomfort's not unfun.
>
> Real rain is soothing, for it hums;
> > Though weather's wet, still pluck is dry,
> And not a fellow's near as mean
> > As I deemed you or you deemed I.
> Do not misprize our meager blaze
> > Snapping the short slant summer night;

Tinder love may still catch fire
　　To kindle on the next sunlight:
Keep if we can some tender trace
　　To carry back to bed again
Salvage of twenty piss-poor months,
　　Copper embers in the rain.
("Armistice" 190-1)[1]

In this brief sample one can identify those characteristics that make *Rhymes of a Pfc* so unique, so special, and so wonderfully representative of the World War II GI experience. There are the humor (the play on words in "to pool our luck"), the GI slang ("sweat it out"), the playful misuse of grammar to fit a rhyme ("I deemed you and you deemed I"), the hint of sexuality ("love each other, sure"), the details of GI life ("we shudder in each leaky coat"), the vague guilt of non-combatants depending on the combat successes of the front-line troops ("Battles of braver joes than us") and the ability to describe the lasting importance of a common incident (the symbolic significance of "Copper embers in the rain"—as the fire of the European war dies, the rain replenishes the summer earth). But more important than all of these is the visual impact of the poem—the image of the Armistice captured in a Bill Mauldin kind of verbal snapshot of men immobile in the rain realizing that they might live to return home after all.

Rhymes of a Pfc is a collection of 95 poems describing the poet's progress through the phases of preparation for and participation in the ground war in Europe. Although few describe combat directly—Kirstein was one of the support troops, not a foot soldier—the poems provide an accurate and unified vision of the war. They depict a variety of individuals and the scenes and events of the war experience. No two poems are exactly the same; each employs a different meter, rhyme scheme or verse development; each describes events from a new perspective, often in the words or thoughts of new and unique characters. Originally published by New Directions in 1964 as a collection of 65 poems, a second edition, containing 85 poems, appeared two years later. The final edition, with ten new poems, was published by David Godine in 1981. Twenty of the thirty new poems added between 1964 and 1981 are specifically about the effort to capture lived experience in poetic form. That he felt moved to add these poems demonstrates his concern for making *Rhymes* a complete poetic statement about the war.[2] These later poems added the element of philosophic assessment that the earlier editions lacked.

Kirstein was uniquely equipped to document the life of a soldier in World War II; raised in Boston, where his father was president of the Boston Public Library, he graduated from Harvard in 1930. There he made the acquaintance of fellow students James Agee and Walker Evans and studied under such distinguished teachers as Alfred North Whitehead and J.L. Lowes. While at Harvard, he was one of the founders of the *Hound & Horn*, a well-received literary quarterly. Many years later, after enlisting in the United States Army, Kirstein could write:

To me, already thirty-six, war was largely didactic. I'd had Harvard, spoke French, some German, and held no rank. Since I never sewed my single stripe on a sleeve, since duties were those of courier, driver or interpreter, external signs of authority were not obligatory. A sly fellow with determination could easily pass where disoriented superior officers might be hindered. In volatile areas there was often no occasion to brandish credentials, so one moved freely in restricted zones. (244)

The combination of age, education, experience, language skills and (ironically) low rank enabled Kirstein to move about behind the front lines with relative ease, encountering types and witnessing events that eventually formed the core episodes described in *Rhymes of a Pfc*. The poems in the *Rhymes* reflect Kirstein's license: they are varied, energetic, unpredictable, kaleidoscopic, full of army slang and describe a wide range of scenes and events.

Kirstein tells us in his introduction to the 1981 revised edition: "the one writing here is not he who jotted jingles in Normandy, Lorraine or Bavaria. The residue is a product of thirty-five years, dating from 1943, into the present decade" (243). The poems reflect and are based on the practices and achievements of poets in the American and English poetic tradition. Kirstein acknowledges sources whose poetry or poetic theory directly influenced him: Henry James, Gerard Manley Hopkins, T.S. Eliot, Walt Whitman, Marianne Moore, W.H. Auden and especially Rudyard Kipling. As Kirstein says, "for me, Kipling was a far more masterful model than Clough, Tennyson, or Browning. For metrical music,...[Kipling] stands with Hopkins and Auden as a lord of the English language" (241-2). Inspired by Kipling's model, Kirstein "aimed to compose a sequence of narrative verse, hopefully, neither careless nor monotonous, borrowing from common parlance its coarse-grained savor" (242). To Kirstein, the poetic mode of Kipling, whose poetry established the pattern for the poetry of World War I, was appropriate as a model for poetry of World War II as well; his challenge was to modify the model of Kipling to meet the requirements of a war waged in the world of a later generation.

To do so, he decided to rely heavily on the rhymed and metrical model of Kipling but to modify it according to others demonstrated by Auden and Hopkins, both masters of meter and rhyme. From Hopkins he learned to match metrical form to religious thought, and from Auden he borrowed intellectual action as a substitute for the physical action of Kipling. Of course he borrowed or incorporated the ideas of other poets as well, especially Eliot and Moore. The result of these modifications is a body of poetry that combines meter and rhyme with a process of meditation and introspection.

The particular nature of Kirstein's achievement can be more fully appreciated by briefly examining the design of the *Rhymes*, by assessing the subject matter as well as the form of the poems themselves. Kirstein's poems are typically told from one of three viewpoints: that of the poet himself, that of other individuals who share the poet's experiences, and that of an abstract, detached viewpoint. This last viewpoint is used much less often than the other two, probably because it is less engaging than those involving personal impressions. This is not to suggest that Kirstein developed the *Rhymes* according to some kind of mathematical formula, but that he was concerned about balancing three visions: one of himself as poet, one of others in the military or combat environment and one encompassing other general impressions. Generally, there is an equal division between those poems in which Kirstein appears (which include a reference to "I") and those poems in which other characters are either narrators or occupy the focal point of the action of the poem. The initial focus is on Kirstein as a recruit and novice in the army; once his initiation is complete, however, the poems include an increasing number of new narrative personas from whose point of view events along the path to combat are presented.

As Kirstein broadens the scope of experience as seen in the perceptions of others, the impressions become those of the full range of individuals caught up in the war, and the vision of the war takes on a universal perspective as opposed to the unique perspective of the poet. Of course the poems are entirely the result of Kirstein's mind, but the truth of the various viewpoints is validated by their variety, by their details, and by the fundamental human experiences they depict. Their believability is necessary if one is to trust them as representative pictures of the wartime experience, an effect Kirstein clearly desires.

And believable they are. Witness such poems as "Top Kick," which describes a First Sergeant who worries about his physical frailty:

> Now Sergeant learns he's losing weight;
> > suspects that glob in rheumish eye.
> Inspects his stool. Each night, in hell,
> > dreads lest some virus urge he die. (23)

In "4F," an individual working for the Luce publications (*Time* and *Life*) attempts to rationalize his non-participation as a soldier:

> Survive. So far, survived he has. Now, he needn't worry.
> > Secure on *Life*, his draft board knows the tale.
> Orphan since three; years of neglect; TB;
> > Weak lungs still. Poor risk. How can he fail? (25)

"Gloria" is a comic epic of a female impersonator who convinces the Navy brass that a Navy friend is not a homosexual:

> they let him resign for the good of old Glory.
> > Sooo...then what does this Fool do? Joins the Marines...(31)

"Syko" is a showpiece of poetic technique in which a distraught soldier describes his Section 8 discharge (discharged for psychiatric causes), managing to express his story in meter and rhyme even as his power of coherent expression erodes:

> All con flicx are with my self and atually may I sooon die
> > My big trubl alway sbin with III I
> > I never find no wors averseraye (35)

Other character sketches focus on a variety of men, officers as well as enlisted and their experiences of the war. One of the individuals described is a major from Mississippi who discovers to his surprise that the brick used in the construction of his personal fireplace is abandoned German dynamite

("Chimbly"). Other characters include a captain who finds it more difficult to communicate with a French lady than to parachute into German-held land ("Chateau"); a colonel who is caught up in an American brawl over scarce gasoline supplies ("Hijack"); black soldiers in a white man's war ("Black Joe"); and Red Cross workers providing an impersonal but touching glimpse of a far-away America ("Red Cross"):

> Standing in line, three hundred joes grin boylike and
>   self-consciously,
> Nudging the quicker ones ahead step up for doughnut and
>   coffee.
> Doughnuts are tender cakes with holes which Yankee maids of
>   standards pure
> Substitute symbolically for many acts they mayn't endure. (88)

Kirstein shows that all men share the disadvantage of lack of ability to deal adequately with the war. This trait is in evidence in nearly every poem in every section.

It is when focusing on the constant pressure of combat and front-line duty that Kirstein, the poet, excels. Here, for obvious reasons, perspectives of other characters outnumber those told from his own persona. Look at the poet's description of a night attack by German aircraft ("Bedcheck"), the harassing fire of a distant German gun ("Load") or his visit to a burned-out German tank ("Guts"):

> You can feature what can't help but happen
> When fire grills a thin-armored can,
> Such container containing live persons
> Who'd climbed in as enlisted men.
> If you think this pageant smelled holy
> Then you can say that again. (118)

The events and experiences are too varied and too unusual to be compassed within the purview of one individual. Kirstein witnesses the effects of the war: air strikes, dead animals, burned-out tanks, displaced persons. He most clearly depicts the action of the war that is surrounding him and of which he is most often an interested but essentially powerless observer. The best example of such a poem is "Air Strike," an effective combination of image and assessment:

> Abruptly from out our west, heralded by a droning hive,
> Swept over level throbbing air, the stinging squadrons,
>   death alive.
> Hand upon hip in proud amaze, soldiers dropped hatchet,
>   nail, and saw:
> Four thousand planes roared overhead. We all were
>   speechless in our awe
> Of Yaveh, Thunderer, Battle God, who in His just, avenging
>   wrath
> Hath lent us much material bigger and better than Jerry hath. (100)

Kirstein ponders the meaning of the vision of a sky full of bombers: the support personnel required, the cost of such a fleet, the morality of bombing, the politics of war. But the final meaning of the vision is most directly expressed in subsequent events:

> In any case, four thousand planes flew overhead and we were
>   there.
> That night, we listened for the news. It was not mentioned
>   on the air,
> But at the morrow's trumpet-sun, the big guns sounded strong
>   and slow.
> We'd cracked their salient, and we were some kilometers past
>   St. Lo. (101)

In "Germany," the fifth of seven separate sections in *Rhymes*, war is even closer and the effects more disturbing and complex. The action of the war itself is shown vividly and dramatically in "4th Armored," which was, Kirstein relates in his notes, told to him by an Iowa farmer who witnessed the events the poem describes. It is the central poem of the section, located in the center of the section, and the intensity and coarseness of its language matches the events it describes:

> Worse thing was the cold. Cold, cold; all the time, cold.
> I mind the cold most. Weeks we never git warm.
> Bastone. We have two K-rations a day. That's all. No warmth.
> Cold. Jeez-us. Particularly your fuckin feet.
> . . . .
> Them Hitler-youth kids. Was they fierce!
> We see one stand up with his girl, her about twelve, maybe
>   thirteen,
> Both of them with their type bazooka.
> Charlie have his Heinie P-38. Wasn used to it then neither.
> One hundred yards, a long shot fera pistol. Hell, long fera
>   carbeen.
> Hot damn. That kid drop like a hammer hit him.
> Later, went over fera look. Charlie plug him jus unner the
>   left eye. (176-7)

This poem represents the harshness and brutality of war, not especially the kind of war fought by the 4th Armored, but by any men in combat in Europe in the closing months of the war. Appropriately, it is the only unrhymed poem in the book. As Kirstein says, the impact of the story "knocked rhyme out of me" (242).

For all his interest in recording the horror of war, however, Kirstein was also intrigued by the possible ways that poetry might mirror wartime experience. At Harvard, he developed an appreciation for combat experiences as expressed in poetic form, especially through the concept of the ideal soldier-king as represented in Shakespeare's history plays, *Henry IV* and *Henry V*. Kirstein now sees an England in which war is real, and in which the ideas presented in

Shakespeare's plays can be compared with the actions and demeanor of the English people. He concludes his poem "Tudoresque" with an account of a visit to a London theater to see John Gielgud's *Hamlet*, in which Peggy Ashcroft plays Ophelia with a hand wounded by debris from a flying bomb. Kirstein's Harvard impressions have been significantly altered, and he sees, like Hamlet, the characters of Rosencrantz and Guildenstern as "schoolday chums" who represent "snapped links with a charmed lost youth" (69).

This long, loose poem establishes an important theme: the poet's attempt to synthesize the events and impressions of the war in terms of both personal experience and the poetic tradition. The poem "Inter-Service," for instance, begins as a complaint about the unhappy side effects of Eisenhower's directive to integrate soldiers of the British and American armies. Kirstein, as narrator of the poem, complains of the ways in which an upper-class British officer (actually a Scot) unfairly usurps the American enlisted men's water and bivouac area:

> So he's a Scotsman born and bathes each dawn, a marvel rare.
> Thrice he's cadged water from our fire....

This intruding British officer represents practically every injustice visited on the American enlisted men, and they are prepared to hate him wholeheartedly—until they (or at least Kirstein as narrator) see what the British officer reads for relaxation:

> We scarce can credit our sharp eyes when we behold his
>   precious book.
> In our vexation we ignore, though Britain share our General
>   Staff,
> She's enlisted Chaucer's weather, Hamlet's humors,
>   Falstaff's laugh.
> England condemned by boyhood gods; gave Wilde a jail, Byron
>   exile;
> Owen, David Jones, Sassoon, honored their General Staffs in
>   style.
> Indignant verses mayn't absolve the snob, the tyrant, or the
>   fool,
> But, peace or war, when foolish games the snob ordains by
>   tyrant rule,
> British poets have always purged the curse of class or pride
>   of purse.
> Pardon the sponge bath. Thank God for the *Oxford Book of
>   English Verse.* (95-6)

One impression of this description is that poetry is valuable for its own sake in a wartime environment. To Kirstein, the *Oxford Book of English Verse* summons the poems and achievements of those English poets who have most affected his poetic outlook, and it makes little difference to him which poems the Scots officer is reading.

"Siegfriedslage" is the crucial poem in the volume addressing the issue of poetry as a vehicle for the description of war. It describes the unusual meeting of Kirstein with poet W.H. Auden, who was working on behalf of the American forces in the preparation of the U.S. Strategic Bombing Survey, organized to study the "effects of bombing on Germany, in preparation for final attack on Japan, and to determine post-war defense" (259). Kirstein was able to accompany Auden to Tergensee, where Auden was to interview Martin Niemoller, World War I submarine captain hero and staunch opponent of Hitler, whom Hitler had interned during the war. Kirstein compares the forest setting to Siegfreidslage, the forest camp of Siegfreid, hero of Wagner's *Ring of the Nibelungs*. In this location, discussion turns to the nature of war and war poets. Auden (called Morden in the poem) delivers the opinion that "poetry's not in the pity" (an allusion to Wilfrid Owen) but "in the words. What words are wide enough?" In answer to this question, the poem provides a list of characteristics and opportunities that demonstrate the materials of war poetry, and—for purposes of illustrating the achievement of *Rhymes*—catalogues the moments of inspiration for the poems in the volume:

> Yet if one's greedy in our craft or art,
> Shrewd, apt, ambitious—here's a recipe
> To fix some blood-types for a wounded heart,
> Resecting style, or better, grafting tones
> Eavesdropped in anguish o'er field-telephones,
> Wise walky-talking through our murky mess,
> Rococo bingo, gangbang or deathdance,
> A microscopic keyhole on distress—
> Merciless, willful, exquisite, grim, frank.... (184)

The list Kirstein provides is essentially complete; we may not like each item, but we cannot dispute its necessity. A war poet—and poems about war—must be shrewd, apt, ambitious, merciless, willful, exquisite, grim and frank. These are characteristics of any poet who would write poetry of lasting appeal and value, but their possession is especially essential in wartime. The artist's task is to capture the moment as faithfully as possible, using the tools and materials at hand. Interpretation, if there is any, will follow in its own time. The poet's purpose is to take the pictures. Another eye will decide what value they possess.

In this poem, Kirstein answers the other question about war poetry, which is, Why write it at all? As he returns to his unit, Kirstein reflects;

> Dazed, do I meditate through forests passed:
> History's long hurtle, my precious part
> In decades left me and the health in rhyme;
> How one believes, nay, must believe in ART (185).

Kirstein, the poet, realizes he knows what "This is all About": "Our present victory's but our future rout" (185). That this is the key poem in the thematic exploration of the link of poetry and combat experience is indicated in the fact that this was one of the last poems to be added to the volume, and was in fact included only after the death of Auden in 1973. Auden was, to Kirstein, the most important living poet writing in English, so his accidental encounter shortly before the end of the war was as thematically appropriate as it was totally unpredictable.

The figure of Morden/Auden represents poetic tradition, poetic assessment and poetic authority. If Auden was less than an authority on war, he certainly was one of the masters of poetry and poetic theory, and his appearance lends credibility to Kirstein's effort to link poetry and wartime experience. His characterization in the poem as a comic figure of disorder and misrule lends validity to the issue of the purpose of poetry, that could not be derived from ideas expressed by the type of soldier or civilian who appears elsewhere. The war ends not in triumph but in weariness, as the poet continues his attempt to understand the larger meanings of the war.

Lincoln Kirstein is an exceptional poet as well as a lyrical historian of an era. He is also a philosophical analyst of the war itself. In "Truce," for example, he suggests that there is never a satisfactory answer to the problem of war; peace is usually only an interval before the next engagement:

> And thus our trusty braggart myths
>   play havoc with a next crop's youth
> and if one dares to doubt his dad
>   he can be conned by cunning truth.
> Tossed on soft linden's whispering
>   searchlights cat's-cradle unborn stars.
> We trace a truce by auguries,
>   chill windage of what next big wars. (227)

In "GI Bill," one of only four poems found in the volume's last section, Kirstein provides a moving and meaningful summary of the futility of the war effort and a profound questioning of the effectiveness of the lessons learned in the war. A history professor ("an idiot AWOL from their war") attempts to teach returning GIs "lessons" that can scarcely match those they learned out of school:

> Ex-pilot wires his bombardier
>   To hop out west and meet the folks—
> A fortnight off for fish and games,
>   Air Corps talk and GI jokes;
> Whips back to college to cram up,
>   Add or subtract what so far fails
> To keep his classmates at their sums
>   When fires freeze or scrap-iron hails. (233)
> . . . .
> Lo: the World Wars I, II, and III
>   Now test our homework's memory;
> Ten months ago what towns were tall
>   Whose wrecks date Modern History? (234)

The poems of *Rhymes of a Pfc* effectively summarize some of the more important lessons of World War II, presented in a form designed to stimulate and challenge those who would study them. In its total effect, Kirstein's *Rhymes* describes some of the personalities, major and minor, involved in the conduct of the war; it describes the equipment, events and moods of war; and it combines both personal and poetic perspectives to give a sense of the chaos and drive that characterize the conduct of war in any era.

But its most enduring legacy is the collection of images of the many characters who populate Kirstein's road to war, from the banks of the Potomac to the banks of the Rhine. They are all, like Kirstein the narrator, singularly ill-equipped to react to the war or to accommodate its pressures and meanings. They are all a little comic, a little foolish, a little selfish, a little nervous, a lot like most of us. They remain fixed in our memory, frozen in poses that catch their spirit exactly: Red Cross girls serving doughnuts, GIs watching bombers passing overhead, the narrator looking into a burned-out German tank, a foot soldier freezing with cold, Auden discussing poetry in the German forest—snapshots in the book of war, whose meaning we may ponder indefinitely.

Notes

[1] All textual references are to *Rhymes of a Pfc* (Boston: David Godine, 1981).

[2] Kirstein also provided in his third and final version a set of notes designed to explain some of the technical terms and army jargon found in the poems and to provide briefly the historical context of some of the events indicated in the poems. These notes are also helpful in giving a clearer understanding of Kirstein's purpose in creating his comprehensive poetic survey of the war in Europe.

New Heroes: Post-War Hollywood's
Image of World War II

Philip J. Landon

You and I are professionals. When the manager says sacrifice,
We lay down a bunt and let someone else hit the home run.

They Were Expendable (1945)

Nineteen-forty-nine marked the revival of the Hollywood war film. The box-office and critical success of Delmer Daves' *Task Force,* William Wellman's *Battleground,* Alan Dwan's *The Sands of Iwo Jima* and Henry King's *Twelve O'Clock High* revived the film industry's interest in the World War II dramas, and, for the next two decades, it proved to be one of the country's most popular and most controversial film genres.[1] The renewed interest in war features is generally attributed to the influence of the Cold War (and subsequently the hot war in Korea)[2] or to the genre's increasing realism and historical accuracy.[3] While both these explanations deserve attention, they tend to oversimplify the complex relationship between popular narratives and their cultural contexts. Like all the major film genres, the primary appeal of the war film lay in its informing cultural myth, not in its verisimilitude. The battlefield in these films became a metaphor for the increasingly bureaucratized America which emerged from World War II, and armed combat gave mythic expression to the tensions and conflicts underlying the political consensus of the new industrial state.

If *The Sands of Iwo Jima* and *Twelve O'Clock High* seemed realistic at the time of their release, it was not simply because they employed documentary techniques and included footage shot by combat cameramen. Scenes of the Marines landing on the beaches of Tarawa and Iwo Jima and of air raids over Germany served less to recreate battlefield realities than to lend credibility to highly stylized generic patterns. These patterns shape, interpret and thus create the mythic meanings which underlie the historical events being dramatized, and at the center of the narrative is a hero capable of transcending the cultural dilemmas embodied in the myth.

By briefly comparing the hero of the late 1940s war film to his immediate ancestor, the frontiersman, it is possible to see why the military man better mediates America's ambivalent response to the industrial age. As he was conceived by Owen Wister in the 1890s, the westerner—who would become the model for Hollywood's western hero—was able to reconcile a heritage of unfettered individualism attributed to Western culture with the civilizing and domesticating influence of the East: represented by farmers, bankers, clergymen and schoolmistresses. In *The Virginian* (1902), the hero does more than defend an outpost of civilization from the anarchic and destructive selfishness of Trampas and his band of rustlers. In addition, he allies himself with the civilized East by marrying the Vermont school teacher Molly Stark Wood and by joining forces with eastern money, an alliance which makes him a wealthy rancher and landowner. His strength and unshakable integrity not only tame the lawless nature of the western wilderness but also redeem an eastern society whose spirit is being sapped by commercial values and material comforts. The Virginian's mythic achievement has its origin in the progressive ideology of Theodore Roosevelt's New Nationalism, which Wister admired, and it is exemplified in the hero's alliance with a wealthy, well-bred elite—a natural aristocracy suited to guide America's destiny in the Twentieth Century. Later Hollywood versions of the frontiersman, such as Victor Fleming's 1929 adaptation of Wister's novel and John Ford's *Stagecoach* (1939), suggested more populist political sympathies. Ford's Ringo Kid, for example, acts to expose the pious and hypocritical representatives of Eastern culture. Like so many American films of the 1930s, *Stagecoach* is closer to another strain of the Progressive Movement which began with Woodrow Wilson's New Freedom and formed the political foundation of Franklin Roosevelt's New Deal.[4] What remains unchanged, however, is the self-sufficiency of the frontier hero. His skill, native intelligence and unshakable integrity overcome all obstacles; acting alone and in the cause of justice, both the Virginian and the Ringo Kid are inevitable victors.

The war films of that time shared a myth essentially similar to the western. Acts of individual heroism carry the day in Howard Hawks' *The Dawn Patrol* (1930), and these acts, as in Lloyd Bacon's *Devil Dogs of the Air* (1935) and Frank Borzage's *Flight Command* (1940), are often undertaken despite the criticism of their unimaginative and bureaucratic superiors. Howard Hawks' *Sergeant York* (1941) exemplifies the importance of individualism as the World War One hero Alvin York single-handedly captures what appear to be hundreds of German soldiers. The events recounted in the film were, in fact, true. But in transforming the historical York into the spirit of the American fighting man, Hawks provided a poor model for the 14 million Americans about to be inducted into a military organization created to fight the first fully industrialized, global war.

Dismissed as westerns in uniform for resorting to familiar Hollywood heroics, very few war features released during World War II won any critical respect until mid-1945, when films like William Wellman's *The Story of G.I. Joe*, Lewis Milestone's *A Walk in the Sun* and John Ford's *They Were Expendable* were released.[5] Although praised for their lifelike qualities, these films appear closer to reality only within their generic context. As Paul Fussell has pointed out, Hollywood shared the mass media's aversion to examining the actual horrors of the War's mechanized battle fronts.[6]

The nature of heroism exemplified in these films, however, had changed radically. Engaged amateurs had been replaced by experienced professionals, and the new heroism demanded that a romantic tradition of individual heroics give way to collective action directed by remote superiors. Incorporated into the war film formula, this emerging hero appears in a variety of war films, including John Farrow's *Wake Island* (1942), Howard Hawks' *Air Force* (1943), Edward Ludwig's *The Fighting Seabees* (1944) and Edward Dmytryk's *Back to Bataan*

(1945). Employing a metaphor which was more industrial than epic, war films repeatedly characterize the war as a "job," battlefields as "real estate," and soldiers as representatives of "the firm." The genre's new heroes became the on-site managers of this deadly enterprise.

Several months after the surrender of Japan, too late for active duty on the propaganda front, John Ford's *They Were Expendable* offered the definitive portrait of the American war film hero in transition. A young naval officer, Lt. Rusty Ryan (John Wayne), learns that the type of heroism necessary in modern warfare consists in his giving up the idea of being a "one-man band" and accepting the fact that he is "a professional" who, when a superior says sacrifice, "lays down a bunt and lets someone else hit the home run." Wayne's screen persona, developed in dozens of westerns, adds to the ideological significance of the officer's transformation, and Ryan's reluctant acceptance of his professional role in the film's final scene insures the audience that, beneath his professional exterior, Ryan remains committed to an older and perhaps more fundamentally American form of individualism.

Although the war film fell short of dramatizing actual experience, it succeeded in evolving a mythic hero remarkably well-suited to the mood and circumstances of post-war America. Owen Wister's *The Virginian* had provided a mythic version of an America whose economic, political and social tensions were temporarily resolved by a Progressive consensus in the age of Theodore Roosevelt and Woodrow Wilson; the hero of the American war film provided a mythic version of a different consensus that had been forged between New Deal reformers and big business during the War years. To most observers, it marked a crucial and lasting change in the nation's cultural values.[7] This consensus, which assumed that a rising tide raises all boats, saw agendas of corporate capitalism complementing those of democratic pluralism, social problems finding technological and administrative solutions, and industrial wealth underwriting the American Dream. Post-war America, the argument went, had even evolved a personality adapted to the managerial ethos. The "other-directed" organization man would replace the anachronistic, "inner-directed" individualist as the dominant American character type.[8]

Although the war film's hero-as-organization-man, like the westerner, continues to mediate between a threatened community and its enemies, the terms of signification have been reversed. The frontier setting pitted the anarchic forces of nature (Indians and renegade whites) against the civilizing forces of social order and technological progress (the frontier town and the railroad), and the western hero mediated between civilization and wilderness by employing the skills gained from his contact with a savage world in the service of a community struggling for existence on the edge of civilization. The battlefield, however, already linked metaphorically to modern industry, becomes a symbolic setting in which democratic values (embodied in memory of home and loved ones) are threatened by a technologically advanced enemy bent on reducing free individuals to obedient automatons. The military hero shares the westerner's willingness to place his knowledge of the enemy's nature in the service of civilization, but he defends democracy by matching his adversary's ruthless organizational competence on the modern battlefield. Moreover, the hero has gained his technological skills as the functionary of a military system which appears remarkably similar to the society of his totalitarian enemy. By the early 1950s, the organization-man hero—who can be seen evolving during the War years—had become the generic norm. Whether hard-bitten platoon sergeants and infantry squad leaders in *Battleground* and *The Sands of Iwo Jima,* officers of the middle ranks in Nicholas Ray's *The Flying Leathernecks* (1951) and George Waggner's *Operation Pacific* (1951), or generals and colonels in *Command Decision* (1948) and *Twelve O'Clock High,* these characters share the same mythic signification and perform the same narrative functions within their respective films. Neither a resolute outsider like the western hero, nor a "one-man band" who learns to accept the constraints imposed upon the loyal professional, the hero of the war film is now a professional from the outset. Formerly, the dramatic tension focused on assimilating an old-fashioned American individualist into the military hierarchy; by 1950, it focused on problems confronting the assimilated professional.

These tensions may vary in detail from film to film, but they originate in the protagonists' profoundly divided allegiances. This division, in turn, reveals the ideological paradox at the heart of the genre's informing myth. Although he is privately devoted to the ideals of democracy and individual freedom, the genre's hero must banish them from his public, professional life, because they can only render his country vulnerable to the enemy. Dissenting points of view, an inappropriate emphasis upon the welfare of individuals, and the humane affections which provide the communal harmony essential to a free and democratic society must be sacrificed in the interest of combat efficiency. No two heroes better exemplify the implications of this divided loyalty than Marine Sergeant John Stryker (John Wayne) in *The Sands of Iwo Jima* and Army Air Force General Frank Savage (Gregory Peck) in *Twelve O'Clock High.*

Both heroes face the common task of forging recalcitrant individuals into an efficient fighting unit. Stryker's harsh discipline prepares his young Marines in *The Sands of Iwo Jima* to fight and survive on the beaches of bloody Tarawa. The experienced squad leader impresses them as a martinet whose life is lived within the stringent limits of Marine regulations and who has only one aim: the creation of a military unit with individuals which, he claims, will "move like one man and think like one man." In *Twelve O'Clock High,* the appointment of Savage as the commander of the 918th Bomb Group goes further in emphasizing the relationship between the arrival of the hero and the necessary descent from individual autonomy into the impersonal and rigorous world of military discipline.

Savage has replaced Colonel Davenport (Gary Merrill), a decent and humane commander who was reluctant to push his air crews to greater efforts against German targets. As a result, Davenport is depicted as too easy-going, too tolerant of error and too ready to attribute failure to bad luck. He may have the affection of his fliers, but he has lost the confidence of his superiors, who conclude that he thinks about "his boys...instead of missions." He is relieved of his command because his "over identification with his men" has jeopardized the Group's institutional objectives. Savage's job is to remedy Davenport's errors. Shortly after assuming command, he humiliates one of his pilots for breaking formation and going to the aid of a friend whose aircraft has been crippled by enemy fire. "For the sake of your roommate," Savage charges as he assigns the flier to "The Leper Colony" (an aircraft manned by incompetents and misfits), "you violated group integrity."

Both Stryker and Savage succeed in creating more efficient fighting machines, but in doing so they drive their men to near rebellion. The opposition to Stryker's cold professionalism is personified in the character of Private Conway (John Agar), the disaffected son of a dead Marine colonel who had once been Stryker's commanding officer. Although Conway protests that the military is hostile to democratic values and that Stryker is little better than the totalitarian enemy they are fighting, it soon becomes clear that the source of his anger is psychological rather than political. The disturbing analogy between the squad leader and the Japanese awaiting them in the Pacific is thus devalued and marginalized. Locked in an oedipal battle with Stryker, whom he describes as a virtual foster father, Conway blinds himself to the Sergeant's virtues. When Stryker refuses to rescue a wounded squad member trapped behind the Japanese lines during the Tarawa invasion, Conway calls the act "inhuman," but subsequent events reveal that the Sergeant had actually prevented the remainder of his squad from falling prey to a Japanese ambush.

In contrast, the opposition to Air Force General Savage's relentless demand for a "maximum effort," regardless of the casualties suffered by his Group, is more overtly political in a manner which dramatizes another of the difficulties facing the organization man. Like Sgt. Stryker, Savage must assert his authority over naive inferiors who understand neither his policies nor the complex motives behind them. Facing a dilemma already anticipated in Sam Wood's *Command Decision*, Savage must resist political pressures which threaten to subvert his mission, even if this resistance ruins his career. Led by a skilled pilot, who has won the Medal of Honor, Savage's junior officers decide to carry their complaints to the Inspector General. Savage, however, refuses to compromise and continues his costly attacks on German shipyards and ball-bearing factories. The success of these raids raises the Group's morale, earns Savage the understanding loyalty of his air crews and quells the rebellion among his pilots. When the Inspector General arrives to hear their complaints, the fliers refuse to denounce their commander.

Having established his authority as a professional who allows neither personal emotions nor political pressures to deter him from carrying out his assigned mission, Savage and his Group prepare for a final raid which will presumably set the stage for an allied victory in Europe. *The Sands of Iwo Jima* concludes with a parallel sequence. The experience on Tarawa has taught Stryker's squad of infantrymen that in battle the aloof expertise of their leader is essential to survival and victory. Even the stubborn Conway begins to perceive a genuine humanity beneath Stryker's cold exterior by the time they prepare for the culminating assault on Iwo Jima.

Long before these concluding episodes, however, the audience has already been made aware of the hero's human qualities through a figure who is in a position to understand the hero's divided allegiances. In *Twelve O'Clock High* it is the mature and perceptive executive officer, Colonel Stovall (Dean Jagger), who shapes the audience's perspective. The entire narrative unfolds in the form of a flashback triggered by Stovall's post-war visit to England and the abandoned air base which had once served as headquarters to the 918th Bomb Group. Now a corporate lawyer with an international clientele, he is a model of rectitude whose interpretation of events and assessment of Savage's character may be accepted as the truth. Similarly, Corporal Bass (Arthur Franz), who serves as a unifying narrative voice telling the "story of a squad of Marines," establishes the film's ideological as well as its narrative perspective. Through Bass's eyes, we are able to see Sgt. Stryker's devotion to men who regard him as barely human.

As the films move toward their climactic battles, the opinions of the disgruntled Airmen or Marines gradually converge with those of the narrators (and, by implication, the audience) until, at the moment of victory, the nature of the hero and the price he has paid is fully revealed. Before the final raid on Schweinfurt gets under way, Savage suffers a mental breakdown which leaves him partially paralyzed and unable to fly. Stovall, however, realizes the Group has learned enough from their commanding general to be successful without him. Appropriately, the 918th is led into battle by an officer (Hugh Marlowe) once regarded as a shirker but redeemed through his obedience to Savage's professional standards. An even more dramatic fate awaits Stryker at the very moment when his men have proved themselves and a Japanese defeat on Iwo Jima seems certain. As he lights up a cigarette, a sniper shoots him dead. But, like Savage, Stryker's example has turned his squad into professionals. Conway, formerly a rebel, is now prepared to take the dead sergeant's place as squad leader.

Only after his death do the members of the squad discover the lasting emotional bond between Stryker and the family he lost when he chose to make a career of the Marines. Although they were aware that Stryker's wife and son had left him years earlier, his men assumed that it was the result of the sergeant's indifference to human sentiments and his chronic drunkenness. They finally realize that a harsh exterior and a weakness for whiskey have been his ways of fending off the pain of his isolation. A half-finished letter to his son, found after his death, affirms Stryker's devotion to his lost family, his sympathetic understanding of his wife's decision to reject the rigors of military life, and his belief in the very freedoms which he has sacrificed in order to fulfill his professional duties. The letter advises his son: "Always do what your heart tells you is right." The laconic Virginian could not have made a more succinct case for individual freedom.

The war film's generic formula confers on home and family an ideological as well as an emotional significance. Throughout the Second World War, American propaganda efforts regularly equated the defense of democratic values with preserving the American way of life, and that way of life found its film equivalent in the small-town America idealized by Frank Capra. Consequently, Stryker's enduring bond with his former wife and son are essential to his mythic function. However tenuously, Stryker achieves the balance between a tradition of democratic liberalism and the authoritarian institution capable of keeping that tradition secure from totalitarian predators.

Sgt. Stryker and Gen. Savage exemplify a dominant motif in the war films produced in the decade following the Second World War. While the manifest content of these films opens them to the charge of serving as propaganda for an imperial America, at a deeper level they provide an epic affirmation of the ideological consensus forged during the War years. Post-war America's expanding corporate hierarchies run by efficient managers were believed to sustain a private, domestic world where traditional values would continue to flourish. The connection between the genre and the corporate world was quickly recognized by management consulting firms. During the 1950s, they were fond of screening *Twelve O'Clock High* in seminars designed to improve the leadership abilities of businessmen and educational administrators.[9]

Within a generation, however, the consensus had crumbled, and, by the 1970s, the genre which had evolved a myth of heroism based upon that consensus had become increasingly ironic and self-reflexive in the treatment of the hero-as-organization-man. The fault lines along which the myth fragmented were visible from the beginning, for they constituted the "logical scandal" which Claude Levi-Strauss found at the heart of cultural myths. Neither the genre's hero, nor the political consensus he personified arrived at a stable accommodation between the demands of a corporate society and the ideology of individualism so deeply embedded in American culture. The consequences of this instability appear both in the psychic pressures bearing on the hero and in the social conflicts inherent in his professional status.

The potentially soul-destroying sense of alienation suffered by Stryker and the paralysis which nearly cripples Savage hint at military protagonists who find them themselves utterly divorced from the democratic ideals which they are supposed to defend, turning themselves—as Stanley Kubrick indicates as early as 1954 in *Fear and Desire*—into mirror images of their totalitarian adversaries. One version of this pairing appears in characters like General Cummings (Raymond Massey) in Raoul Walsh's *The Naked and the Dead* (1958), a commander who takes sadistic delight in exercising power; another can be found in the type portrayed by Steve McQueen in Don Siegel's *Hell Is for Heroes* (1962) and in Philip Leacock's *The War Lover* (1963), the figure for whom battle provides a respite from psychic desolation. The stoicism idealized in earlier war films proves inadequate to its task. Individualism is not transcended, only redirected into avenues of death and self-destruction, and the potential for inhumanity evident in Stryker and Savage is fully realized.

The second aspect of this instability is political and emerges from the conflict between Stryker and Conway and becomes more explicit in the organized opposition to Savage. The hero finds himself unappreciated by those he seeks to protect and betrayed by the military hierarchy he serves. In *The Sands of Iwo Jima*, the burden of understanding is placed upon Conway, an immature youngster so devoted to a peaceful, democratic community that he is unwilling to recognize that such a community continues to exist only because of professionals like Stryker and his father. By the mid-1950s, this conflict moves to the center of the war film, receiving its fullest treatment in Edward Dmytryk's *The Caine Mutiny* (1954). It also appears in the recurring and increasingly problematical divisions between the hero and the domestic life he has left behind. Despite all the difficulties posed in films such as John Farrow's *Submarine Command* (1952), families and loved ones come to their senses and accept the hero's divided allegiance. Two decades later, however, the hero finds himself rejected by a thankless civilian world in Ted Kotcheff's *First Blood* (1982) or, as in Michael

Cimino's *The Deer Hunter* (1978), learns that his ideals have devastated the very community they were supposed to protect.

Even more sinister is the betrayal of the hero by his own superiors whose lust for medals and promotions turn them into the political creatures scorned by General Savage. This variation of the generic formula, first introduced by Robert Aldrich in *Attack* (1956) and fully developed by Stanley Kubrick a year later in *Paths of Glory*, is employed more and more frequently during the 1970s. From Robert Altman's *M.A.S.H.* (1970) and Mike Nichols' *Catch-22* (1970) to Ted Post's *Go Tell the Spartans* (1978) and Francis Ford Coppola's *Apocalypse Now* (1979), the conflict between the skilled professional and his cravenly opportunistic superiors (and in some cases inferiors as well) is thrown into increasingly sharp relief.

At least Gen. Savage has the security of knowing that, however demanding they may be, orders from his superiors are based upon sound judgment and unimpeachable motives. As he points out with great confidence, "When the Old Man cuts a field order, he's thought about it." The battlefield surgeons in *M.A.S.H.* (Eliot Gould and Donald Sutherland) and the aging major in *Go Tell the Spartans* (Burt Lancaster)—whose signifying nickname is "Old World War Two"—have no such assurances. They are at the mercy of commanders all too willing to sacrifice their competent subordinates to politically expedient but dangerously unrealistic theories of warfare.

These films, which emphasize the alienation and betrayal of the "hero-as-organization-man," reflect the country's increasing disillusionment with a political accommodation at first welcomed as the end of ideology and ultimately rejected—by both left and right—for stifling individual freedoms. A generation after their creation, as America entered the Age of Reagan, Sgt. Stryker, Gen. Savage, and the heroic myth they embodied had become as anachronistic as frontiersmen who preceded them. Their fate is eloquently summed up in the final scene of *Go Tell the Spartans*: stripped of their uniforms by the Viet Cong, the bodies of "Old World War II" and his men lie dead and abandoned at the site of a forgotten battle.

Notes

[1]The theoretical issues surrounding the definition and classification of genre films are too complicated to be adequately explored in a brief essay. The term "war film," as it is commonly used by filmmakers, audiences and critics, refers to films dealing with industrialized mass warfare and in which, with few exceptions, combat is central to the action. "Classic" war films include those films in which the genre's informing myth is fully developed (as in the case of the war film for a decade following World War II) and is treated in an epic and heroic manner. Finally, the term cultural myth is used here in relation to popular narratives as it has been defined and employed by Richard Slotkin in *Regeneration Through Violence: The Mythology of the American Frontier, 1600-1860* (Middletown, Conn.: Wesleyan UP, 1973). See esp. Chapt. 1: "Myth and Literature in a New World," 3-24.

[2]It is very difficult to see any immediate connection between day-to-day political developments and the evolution of the war film. At the time, *Battleground* often seemed

more important than Korea in bringing the genre back to life. See, for example, "War over Hollywood." *Newsweek* 28 Aug. 1950: 76.

[3]See, for example, Steven Jay Rubin's, *Combat Films, 1945-1970* (Jefferson, NC: McFarland, 1981).

[4]In *The Eastern Establishment and the Western Experience: The West of Frederick Remington, Theodore Roosevelt, and Owen Wister* (Austin, Texas: U of Texas P, 1989), G. Edward White discusses the evolution of Wister's frontiersman as a cultural hero who reflects Theodore Roosevelt's Progressive political views. See Chapter VI, "The Cowboy as Cultural Hero" 122-48. In John Ford's *The Grapes of Wrath*, the Joad family recuperates from their misfortunes at a government-sponsored migrant camp whose director bears an unmistakable resemblance to FDR. Andrew Sinclair describes Ford's political sympathies as a "hatred of authority balanced by his respect for [Franklin] Roosevelt's New Deal." *John Ford* (New York: The Dial P/James Wade, 1979) 97.

[5]I have discussed the evolution of the "hero-as-organization-man" more fully in "From Cowboy to Organization Man, The Hollywood War Hero, 1940-1955." *Studies in Popular Culture* XII (1990): 28-41.

[6]*Wartime: Understanding and Behavior in the Second World War* (New York: Oxford UP, 1989). See esp. Chapter 18, "The Real War Will Never Get into the Books," 269-97.

[7]The Progressive political consensus which prevailed in the years preceding World War One is analyzed by Henry F. May in *The End of American Innocence: A Study of the First Years of Our Time* (New York: Alfred A. Knopf, 1959). For a description of the political consensus which coalesced during World War Two, see Geoffrey Perrett's *Days of Sadness, Years of Triumph: The American People, 1939-1945* (New York: Coward, McCann and Geohegan, 1973) *passim*.

[8]William H. Whyte's *The Organization Man* (New York: Simon and Schuster, 1956) popularized the term "organization man," but David Riesman offered a more influential description of the same character type, which he described as the "other-directed" personality in *The Lonely Crowd: A Study of Changing American Character* (New Haven, Conn.: Yale UP, 1950). Daniel Bell announced, approvingly, the demise of political debate in the United States in *The End of Ideology: On the Exhaustion of Political Ideas in the Fifties* (Glencoe, IL: The Free P, 1960).

[9]See Lawrence H. Suid, *Guts and Glory: Great American War Movies* (Reading, MA: Addison Wesley Publishing Co., 1978) 82.

In Which We Serve:
Noel Coward's Vision of
the British Navy At War

Margaret Wintersole

Here's a ship that doesn't achieve anything very much, doesn't sink any great ships and gets mined and bombed and torpedoed and finally sunk. Very bad propaganda.
—British Ministry of Information (Castle 174)

When Britain went to war in September, 1939, Noel Coward wanted to make a significant contribution to the war effort. When his friend, Lord Mountbatten, lost the HMS *Kelly*, sunk during the Battle of Crete in May, 1941, Coward found the story to inspire him to make what he considered his most important work for his country: the naval film *In Which We Serve*. With Mountbatten's support, Coward made the film; it showed in Britain and America, achieving popular success and critical acclaim, with Coward winning a special Academy Award in 1943 for outstanding production achievement. With *In Which We Serve*, Coward orchestrates an ode to the Navy. It works as such through Coward's forceful utilization of the flashback as the film's main structuring device, a filmic trope that significantly alters ordinary linear narrative. This narrative structure shapes its themes and develops a stylistic power that would clearly appeal to the British audience.

For the British, the Navy's history epitomized a heroic England. The defeat of the Spanish Armada in 1588 began a great naval tradition: by its prevention of a Spanish invasion, the government and the people recognized the vital necessity of sea power to an island nation. Britain established its empire in India and its trade in China on the basis of that power. It alone protected Britain from invasion by Napoleon, eventually bringing him to defeat with its blockades. In his *Commentaries*, William Blackstone describes it as "the floating bulwark of our island." As Britain's first line of defense, the Navy produced many of Britain's military heroes, including Drake, Anson and Nelson. Thus, the film works with a highly recognizable, authoritative symbol for heroism. The film evokes an already well established correspondence between the country and the Navy from its opening dedication to the Navy—"Whereon under the good providence of God, the wealth, safety, and strength of the Kingdom chiefly depend"—to its closing shot of flags waving. It gives us a positive protocol for its consumption as a tribute (Barthes 128). Framed between a beginning that explains the film as heroic and a non-ending (those left alive go on the

27

other ships to continue the fight) that models an enduring character, it renders a myth universal to the Navy and Britain as well (Lotman 209-217).

An assault on a symbol of the Navy in the destruction of the HMS *Torrin* initiates the drama after which the surviving crewmen cling to a much smaller, more fragile and more exposed float—a tiny island of relative safety in a vast, and dangerous sea, just as England has become in war.

In a publicity note for the film, Coward wrote this synopsis:

Among those of her survivors who are able to reach a Carley float are Captain Edward Kinross, R.N. (Captain 'D', Commanding the flotilla), Chief Petty Officer Walter Hardy, and Ordinary Seaman Shorty Blake. As they cling to the float exhausted, wounded and machine-gunned, we see, through the *memories* of these three characters, their families and their home lives interwoven and dominated by their ship. Through *their minds* we are shown the ordeals, the achievements, and the gallantry of H.M.S. *Torrin* from her commissioning as a unit of His Majesty's Fleet until she sinks in her last battle.

(Mander 356; emphasis added)

Coward's note indicates that he conceived the film as something other than a typical action war film; the film's flashbacks break away from the ship, recording several men's remembrances of past events and absent people. The ship's importance lies in its function as the object—highly regarded—that calls forth the memories.

Perhaps the film's most subtle and persuasive device is its use of multiple flashbacks. They profoundly affect the perception of the narrative because they 1) move the narrative from the level of action to the level of history and 2) change the perspective from an objective viewpoint to several subjective viewpoints. Thereby, the flashback changes the code of the narrator from the apersonal (the third person system made necessary by the camera) to the personal (made possible by the flashback structure) (Barthes 124). In doing so, they cause the audience to accompany the different crewmen's thoughts into the past. The flashback's rhetorical power lies in its use of the subjective viewpoint and history: Maureen Turim points out in *Flashbacks in Film* that the flashback produces a subjective memory in two forms: "the rendering of history as a subjective experience of a character in the fiction, and the formation of the Subject in history as the viewer of the film identifying with fictional characters positioned in a fictive social reality" (2). While the Subject, the subjective experience and the social reality, is film fiction, its syntagmatic organization forms a subjective history with an intense psychological quality achieved through its highly personal referential order, which encourages a psychological identification with the characters. At the same time, it achieves a high degree of paradigmatic correlation to the war at hand; dramatic impact develops from its dynamic integration into the existing discourses and codes of the war everpresent to the war-time audience— it borders on the extra-aesthetic (Mukarovsky 17), between art, history and reality.

On the syntagmatic level, the rearrangement of time in the flashback places the past and present side by side as experiences selectively coordinated for the audience. This placement ties them together as significantly related events: in the midst of war and the sinking of the ship, the memory of family and home dominates the men's present troubles; and, in the men's memory of family and home, the ship and the coming war dominate the families' interactions. Memory envelops the past in the present, making the present most significant in terms of those persons or things left behind, the memories acting as powerful indices of love and concern. Then, too, each man's memory-sequence gets broken into parts that alternate with parts from the other men's memories, producing a dystaxic effect: independent but related, the sequences take up, elaborate, and repeat the film's themes in succession as counterpoints to each other (Barthes 129). The structure also delays the sequences, disturbing them and threatening the completion of any one of or all of the sequences, echoing the men's suspended, fragile position.

In certain cases, *In Which We Serve* utilizes these past and present associations as "hinges of the narrative," implying cause and effect with what Roland Barthes describes as the "confusion of consecution and consequentiality, what comes *after* being read in the narrative as *caused by*" (108). We see this, for example, in the way the film builds up to Captain Kinross's commissioning speech and in the way it tells the stoker's story, constructing the Navy as resolute and valiant. At the same time, the flashback activates nostalgia through the antithesis of the destructive present and the more peaceful past: "the past is an object of desire, due to its personal, intense, and even liberating attributes" (Turim 12). We see this, for example, in the Christmas party toasts and other commemorative images dispersed throughout the film, constructing the characters as devoted to each other and to the ship.

In certain scenes of the past, *In Which We Serve* hints that the ship's present crisis develops out of the public's inability to read the political situation correctly. A headline "No War this Year" appears on the screen as a discarded *Daily Express* floats on the water among debris in the wake of ships getting ready for war. The camera emphasizes the paper's message by moving in on the headlines; the film cuts to a caption that announces a date, "Crete May 23, 1941," then a jump to that time, in which Kinross orders "Open fire!" accompanied by the sight and sound of guns blazing. Through the contrary information connected by these visual images, the film implies the absurdity of the newspaper headline and the severe miscalculation of Hitler's intentions. The caption and time shift introduce the sequence in which German bombers sink the *Torrin* and the men abandon the ship for the floats.

With a flashback, the film returns to the idea of the public's uncertainty about the real possibility of war in a domestic scene in which Kath Hardy prepares breakfast for her husband, who reads the morning paper's headlines before he leaves to join the *Torrin* for its commissioning:

'Doesn't look too good does it?' Hardy asks Kath.

'Oh, you can't believe anything they say. Look at all the fuss and fume we had last year. Everybody flying about in aeroplanes and making speeches. After all that nothing happened.... I don't believe that Hitler'd be so silly. What would he expect to gain by having a war?'

'World Domination, that's what that little rat's after. You mark my words.'

Kath replies, '...Well, if we have another war, I give up, see. After all we went through last time.'

Although this slight exchange is congenial banter between an affectionate couple, it conveys the dissonance that most of the British audience must have shared just prior to the war. On one hand, Kath expresses the disbelief and confusion people felt about the political situation, especially during the distressing period of Chamberlain's appeasement policy, and the people's reluctance to fight another war so relatively soon after World War I. On the other hand, the British had to take the possibility of war seriously. The Hardys' dialogue suggests the pull between a desire to avoid war and the probable reality of it. But the subjective state of Hardy's memory in which the scene is shot encourages the audience to identify with the fictive Hardy and his history, i.e. his self-assurance in his understanding of Hitler's aim. From the audience's double historical perspective in the film's past and their own present, the scene becomes significant to the film's emotional appeal, since history has already confirmed his (and thus the audience's) reading of Hitler; that is, *In Which We Serve* reframes the past in the ideology of the present for the audience but disguises that reframing with its subjective realism.[1] Such confirmation is important, for it gives substantial approbation to the actions of its heroes, a quality that the film exploits further along, building on the Hardys' scene.

In a following flashback of Kinross's commissioning speech, *In Which We Serve* links Hardy's attitude in the scene above to Kinross's command and, through these men, to the Navy using camera cuts, the last portion of the speech and an ellipsis. The sequence creates such a strong affirmation of naval authority by the assertion of the Navy's preparedness that it makes a compelling argument for the Navy's soundness and strength. This preparedness contrasts the Navy to the *Daily Express* and Kath Hardy's reluctance to believe in war set up in previous scenes. Kinross says:

(Camera on Kinross) Well, you've all read your papers, and you know that Ribbentrop signed a non-aggression pact with Stalin yesterday. As I see it, that means war next week, (Camera cuts to Hardy who gives a slight nod at Kinross) and so I will give you not three weeks but exactly three days to get this ship ready to sail (Camera returns to Kinross).... Then we'll send Hitler a telegram saying the *Torrin's* ready. You can start your war.

Kinross's vehement call to action to his men and his challenge to Hitler set up an emotional charge: Kinross's astuteness and certainty in his judgement of the political climate must reflect, in contrast, on the historical cause of the ship's present situation (and the audience's)—the shortsightedness and ineffectiveness of world leaders—a fault in which these men, and by association the whole Navy, do not share. The cut to Hardy gives occasion for a subtle approving nod to Kinross's view of events, and Kinross's view gives approval to Hardy's view. In addition, in the ellipsis that follows this scene, Ordinary Seaman Blake also validates their position when he wakes up a fellow worker with "Wake up England. You've had your hour." (In a subsequent flashback, Chamberlain's announcement of war on September 3, 1939, may make for the audience an extratextual association with Chamberlain's appeasement policy that so utterly failed in preventing a war with Germany. When in his speech Chamberlain states, "You can imagine what a bitter blow this is to me...," Blake's sarcastic reply, "It ain't exactly a bank holiday for us," marks this failure.

The film compounds the dramatic tension by changing the potential violence guaranteed by Chamberlain's announcement of war into an immediate reality with a cut to a plane strafing the men in the float.)

After Kinross's speech, suiting actions to his words, an ellipsis of three- to five-second shots each quickly superimposed on the next shot shows the ship being outfitted with supplies, beginning with an establishing shot of men loading the ship off the dock. The second shot returns to Hardy delegating the work. Images of uniforms, helmets, the Captain signing orders at his desk, ammunition being loaded, floats being put on, etc., pass in quick succession.[2] The rapid interchange of images connotes time passing rapidly and hard work being done quickly. The ellipsis suggests the men's readiness and willingness to work hard as a team for a common goal in which they believe and for the man that represents that goal, Captain Kinross.

By hinting at the public's weakness as a cause and war as an effect and contrasting the Navy to the public as an effective force, the film establishes naval authority, giving the Navy a commanding ethos. Part of that ethos, too, is a heroism defined by unity of purpose. *In Which We Serve* reflects these qualities in various ways, but the narrative that elaborates on the theme most penetratingly is the stoker's history. The story allows the audience to feel both cowardice and heroism in war. Heroism here is the will to remain united in action with one's fellow soldiers, particularly in the face of death. The flashback lets the audience accompany the stoker back to the cause of his cowardice and follow his thoughts from his momentary weakness, through the rise of his conscience beginning with Kinross's caution, to his ultimate reconciliation with the heroic ideal at his death. The stoker, a very young and inexperienced sailor, panics during an intense battle and abandons his post. Afterward, in a scene in which he gives the stoker a caution, Kinross mitigates the stoker's actions by speaking moderately, never mentioning the stoker by name or singling him out in any way, giving the young sailor only an anonymous caution. Kinross takes partial responsibility for the stoker's mistake, giving a caution to himself as well as the stoker. Kinross's cautioning becomes an exemplum of leniency, understanding and forgiveness, qualities of a good leader that should inspire a sailor. Because of Kinross's speech, then, for the stoker the scene becomes a reckoning with his social conscience, a quality that will lead to making a good sailor.

Shot by shot, the visuals in the cautioning scene play the most important part in setting up the pathos of the stoker's story. The establishing shot gathers the crew on deck with Kinross standing above the men so that they may see and hear him clearly. Kinross's placement in relation to the stoker and the crosscutting from one to the other as Kinross speaks create affective cues for the audience. As Kinross begins to speak, the camera moves in to a more intimate medium shot of him and the men standing just below him. Kinross's position is that of authority, and his men's position is that of subordinates, yet the scene is staged in a way that conveys the men's mental closeness to their captain, a devotion signaled by the tightness of the shot, the physical proximity of the men standing by him, their stillness and their quiet concentration as they listen to him.

When Kinross's talk turns to the stoker's desertion of his post, the camera reflects the seriousness of Kinross's subject by singling out and focusing on Kinross, emphasizing what he has to say. The camera then turns to the stoker. The film uses several visual techniques to bring attention to the stoker, distinguishing the stoker from the mass of other faces but without resorting to a close-up. A close-up would separate him from the other men. Instead, in trying to put into images the narrative intent, that he has failed his fellow men, it must keep the context of his relationship to the other men but still pose him as alienated from them. It achieves this separation with a medium shot that shows him centered in a circle of ten or eleven other faces. Contextually, the stoker stands among the other sailors but stands out visually from them as the face in the center of the shot, as the only man among the group wearing a hat, and as the only one whose bright HMS shines against the black of his hat. These techniques allow the viewer to pick him out of the group. Once the film directs attention toward the stoker, the stoker's recognition of his wrongdoing and the guilt written on his face can then be read: as all other eyes remain firmly fixed on the Captain, only the stoker's eyes waver downward and away.

Near death at the end of the film, the stoker finds final forgiveness and purification for the injury he has caused to the ship's inviolability, as he has persevered and done his duty "to the very end" without again faltering. While the film does not ground the stoker's tale in the family as are the others', in the hold of a ship that has rescued the *Torrin's* men, the Captain tells the stoker that his parents can be proud of him, so he dies with a shadow of a smile on his lips. The story suggests the cause of the cowardice to be an action that puts the individual before the group, an action that endangers the ship. In contrast, in the end he reunites with the other men, not by living, but by dying—by giving his life for them. Structurally, the film builds this lesson with its semantic fields of 'shipwreck' and 'survival,' in which 'survival' becomes a false semantic field, for the hero (Lotman 231-238). We would ordinarily assume that a character would need to overcome the barriers of strafing, wounds, exposure, thirst and exhaustion that form the border between the two fields in order to cross the border from shipwreck to survival and become a hero. With the stoker, we see that survival does not necessarily make a hero, but rather that fear determines the real boundary he must cross to unity, the true semantic field and heroism. The stoker's story portrays the personal growth of a hero, his story establishing the manly scale of heroic values based on the unifying force of selfless action.

Through the topic shift created by the flashback, the film's stories subtly communicate the idea that the ship is something intangible. The film distances the viewer from the material aspect of the ship, of which, in fact, very little is seen, so that *In Which We Serve*'s visual and verbal rhetoric produces a ship that is not actual but rather spiritual or conceptual, existing in the men's minds as a congeries of sacred qualities, suggesting that the ship be treated with reverence and respect. It stresses, especially through the memory of home, family and ship, the concept of dedication—dedication to duty, country and fellow sailors as the heroic enterprise. The film repeats this idea on a larger scale with Blake and his brother-in-law's toast to each other's branch of the service and with the Dunkirk evacuation.

The multiple perspective that the film's flashbacks create also adds to the sense of unity among the men. Although seemingly paradoxical, the multiple subjective viewpoints help create a consensus of experience rather than the diversity that one would expect because the film concerns itself with representing the characters' common essence. It integrates them by giving them the same humanity, dignity and integrity although they come from different social classes, from Captain Kinross's upper class to Chief Petty Officer Hardy's middle class to Ordinary Seaman Blake's and the stoker's lower class. It negates the condition of class distinction that would certainly, under other circumstances, create disunity among the viewpoints. Hence, despite Britain's highly structured class system, the film produces the idea of oneness among difference.

There exists a close connection between causality, as the origin of an effect, and nostalgia, which is nothing more than the longing for origins. Memory produces both simultaneously, and *In Which We Serve* takes advantage of both. In the case of nostalgia, Coward employs a memory that folds over upon itself; thus, the film doubles its ability to signify the absent, increasing its emotional intensity. The flashbacks belong only to the men, and, in these memories, Blake, Hardy and Kinross all return to some point of origination in family and home. One memory, for instance, recalls another through similarity when the shot of the ship's complement singing a Christmas hymn during church services matches the shot of children singing under Blake's window on the men's last Christmas at home. This memory leads to a series of domestic toasts at Blake's and Hardy's homes and on Kinross's ship that first draws the audience to the family and then the audience and the families together back to the ship through commemoration of it. The scene intricately knots family and ship together with the sentimental threads of Christmas, God, love and friendship. Alix Kinross, however, most vividly ties home and ship together with her toast:

the wife of a sailor is most profoundly to be pitied.... She moves through a succession of other people's houses, flats, and furnished rooms. She finds herself having to grapple with domestic problems in Bermuda, Malta, or Weymouth.... wherever she goes there is always in her life a permanent and undefeated rival, her husband's ship.... It comes before wife, home, children, everything.... Ladies and gentlemen, I give you my rival. It's extraordinary that anyone could be so fond and so proud of their most implacable enemy, this ship. God bless this ship and all who sail on it.

In such a manner, the flashback gives the film a sense of stories being told as memories—memories that always lead back to England, to homes and families. Love for home is predicated, however, upon love for the ship, an idea emphasized by Alix's "God bless this ship and all who sail on it," heard as a refrain. The memory-within-memory apparatus binds home and ship together in such a way that we see the men perceiving home as a place of refuge, a reservoir of strength and a cause for action.

For the women, Alix's speech eloquently articulates the more than charitable acceptance of her husband's love for his ship, the same acceptance we read in the expression on Kath Hardy's face after she realizes that Hardy is toasting the *Torrin* and not her. Stated in the form of a paradox, Alix both loves and hates the *Torrin*, which protects her home yet takes her husband away. Alix's contradictory feelings reveal a fascinating and attractive kind of female courageousness. Understanding the practical nature of naval life, she makes a virtue of practicality. Her enumeration of naval wives' hardships indirectly points out their fortitude, self-sacrifice and intelligence. Perhaps this is why Kinross chooses to keep on his desk his picture of Alix as a bride, a woman committed to a man, rather than his picture of her as a mother. Throughout the film there are similar images: Kath Hardy, Mrs. Lemon (Hardy's mother-in-law) and Freda (Blake's wife and Hardy's niece) knitting and sewing in Walter Hardy's home; Alix Kinross reading Lewis Carroll to her children. Such pictures act as icons of the woman at the homefront, stalwart and brave, patient and understanding. The Hardy women's refusal to leave their home in spite of the Blitz reveals their resistance to terror and their determination to keep the homefront going until the time their men return. Kath Hardy's concern for Walter's flower bulbs signifies steadfastness, a faithfulness for which she and Mrs. Lemon die. Their stories establish the womanly scale of heroic values. The women's nobleness of character parallels the men's, and everyone's willingness to sacrifice for one another solidifies the connection between men and women, country and Navy.

By using the flashback to structure the narrative and transform it into subjective memory, Coward brings to the audience a picture of the British Navy detailed not in the war but in an intense reliving of the men's eventful past from the perspective of their present crisis. The 'ship' does not "achieve anything very much" in the Ministry of Information's sense: it does not sink any very important ships, and, in fact, it gets sunk. But, by making the audience the Subject of history with the flashback, *In Which We Serve* incorporates the audience into the mental and moral processes of its heroes: their private memories of their homes and family.

The film's rhetorical style of accumulating figurative images and verbal praise around the symbol of a British ship—its always bringing the individual characters back to the central image of the group floating in the sea—emphasizes values that would encourage a feeling of identification and admiration with any audience that holds an ordinary person's sense of patriotism. *In Which We Serve* convincingly proclaims that a fundamental and idealistic patriotism—love of family, home, country, and God, courage, endurance, unity, loyalty, self-sacrifice, indomitable spirit, magnanimity, kindness and mercy—abides in the British Navy and in the British people.

Notes

[1]Hayden White's *Tropics of Discourse* and Michel Foucault's *The Archaeology of Knowledge* address the problem of the subject in history. White also addresses the historical text as a literary artifact. Coward could be said to give a poetic account of history in his fictional 'interpretation' of Mountbatten's experience.

[2]Deleuze points out that the whole set of shots in relation to the subsets that form the ellipsis is "never content to be elliptical" but always conveys a change in the whole (19). The ellipsis does not omit information without producing meaning.

Works Cited

Barthes, Roland. *The Semiotic Challenge*. Trans. Richard Howard. New York: Hill, 1988.

Castle, Charles. *Noel*. Garden City: Doubleday, 1973.

Deleuze, Gilles. *Cinema I: The Movement-Image*. Trans. Hugh Tomlinson. Minneapolis: U of Minnesota P, 1986.

Foucault, Michel. *The Archaeology of Knowledge*. Trans. M.M. Sheridan Smith. New York: Pantheon, 1972.

In Which We Serve. Dir. Noel Coward. With Noel Coward, John Mills, and Bernard Miles. Two Cities, 1942.

Lotman, Jurij. *The Structure of the Artistic Text*. Trans. Gail Lenhoff and Ronald Vroon. Ann Arbor: Michigan Slavic Contributions, 1977.

Mander, Raymond and Joe Mitchenson. *Theatrical Companion to Coward*. New York: Macmillan, 1957.

Mukarovsky, Jan. *Aesthetic Function, Norm and Value as Social Fact*. Trans. Mark E. Suino. Ann Arbor: Michigan Slavic Contributions, 1979.

Turim, Maureen. *Flashbacks in Film: Memory and History*. New York: Routledge, 1989.

White, Hayden. *Tropics of Discourse*. Baltimore: Johns Hopkins UP, 1978.

The War in the East:
Theodor Plievier's Novels
Moscow, Stalingrad and *Berlin*

Jennifer E. Michaels

In his trilogy *Moskau* (1952) (*Moscow*, 1953), *Stalingrad* (1945) (*Stalingrad*, 1948) and *Berlin* (1954) (*Berlin*, 1956), Theodor Plievier (1892-1955) gives a vivid and historically accurate panorama of the human misery caused by the fighting on the Eastern front in World War II, from the German attack on the Soviet Union in June 1941 until the last days of the Third Reich in Berlin.[1] In these novels, for which Plievier is best known among English-speaking readers, he strongly protests against war and sharply indicts those responsible for the suffering. Throughout these novels, the issue of accountability both for the war and for the brutality of the fighting is central to Plievier's analysis of the events. In particular, Plievier bitterly denounces the Hitler and the Stalin regimes for the enormity of wanton destruction their totalitarian systems have caused.[2]

To convey the horror of the war, Plievier uses a film-like technique that enables him to capture the scope of the fighting and the magnitude of the suffering. Instead of choosing individual protagonists, Plievier is concerned with the fate of large groups involved in the fighting. In *Moscow*, his focus shifts constantly between the German and the Red Armies, the civilians caught in the German advance, and Stalin and his regime in Moscow. *Stalingrad*'s collective protagonist is the German Sixth Army writhing in agony (*Stalingrad* 193). In *Berlin*, Plievier depicts the fate of the citizens caught between the Nazis and the approaching Red Army. Plievier's wide camera lens and his careful attention to historical detail recreate for the reader the totality of the events.[3] By carefully blending together documents such as letters and orders, montage, interior monologues and fragmentary scenes, Plievier creates a mosaic of individual fates (Kauf 21; Rühle 248).[4] These individual fates enable the reader to experience the war from many different perspectives and they give the novels their power and immediacy.

The power and immediacy of the protest in the novels against war owes much to Plievier's own experiences during the war. As an unwilling exile in the Soviet Union from 1934 until 1945, Plievier witnessed the German advance on Moscow which caused his evacuation to Tashkent.[5] He saw at first-hand the panic in Moscow, the flood of refugees, the unprotected and starving towns, the snow, the typhus and dysentery and the deaths of countless millions (Wilde 506-507). Although he was not at the Stalingrad front, the Soviet government assigned Plievier the task of analyzing letters and diaries taken from dead or captured German soldiers. Plievier read this material as the battle for Stalingrad was being fought and became so involved in the fate of the trapped soldiers that he felt he had to shout to the German officers to stop this battle that had become mass murder (Wilde 395). Later he was able to interview survivors of Stalingrad.[6] In 1945 at the end of the war, Plievier experienced shock on seeing the destruction of his native city of Berlin when he returned there with other leading German exiles from the Soviet Union. Plievier's strong protest against war, already evident in the Weimar Republic, was thus strengthened further by the profound impact that war made on him during his exile years.

The power of Plievier's protest against war is already evident in *Stalingrad*, the first novel of the trilogy to be written (although *Moscow*, which Plievier wrote later, is first chronologically).[7] Central to the novel is Plievier's depiction of the horror of war and the appalling and senseless loss of life.[8] Plievier describes the area around Stalingrad as an apocalyptic land, a vast graveyard of rubble and corpses where the colors—the grey of lice and dirt; the white of the endless snow, which emphasizes the extreme cold and the isolation of the trapped army; the red of bursting shells and blood, and the black of crows, fat from eating the dead bodies—reinforce the misery and suffering. (The sight of the crows makes Colonel Vilshofen reflect that the crow would have been an appropriate emblem for the Nazi regime.) From the opening pages, Plievier stresses death. Gnotke, who is in a penal battalion for refusing to obey a brutal order, is digging mass graves. By the end of the novel, even such mass burial is impossible. Instead, frozen human flesh fills freight cars, and there are mountains of unburied corpses. Plievier describes soldiers dying from horrible wounds, from minor wounds that become infected for lack of treatment, from starvation, typhus and dysentery. This mass suffering and death are all the more agonizing for the reader, since Plievier does not treat the soldiers as statistics but as suffering human beings, as individuals who have families who love them. Plievier reinforces the horror of war through his depiction of the field hospitals where the doctors work long hours to help the never-ending assembly line of broken bodies. The doctors stand in pools of blood surrounded by amputated limbs and pus.

The pus, blood and stench of decaying wounds not only represent to Plievier the physical agony of the army but also become an image of its moral disintegration caused by the extreme hardships and by Nazi ideology. Although the novel has been compared often to Erich Maria Remarque's novel about World War I, *All Quiet on the Western Front* (Klein 23; Trilling 555), there is a striking difference. The hardships that the men endure do not make them forge the strong bonds of comradeship that helped support the soldiers in Remarque's novel but instead isolate them from one another as they struggle to survive. There are examples of some who do manage to retain their humanity despite brutalizing conditions. Gnotke cares for the soldier Gimpf like a father. Some officers such as Vilshofen treat their men as individuals, with respect and care for their safety, and there are examples of soldiers rescuing their comrades, of doctors despairingly trying to help the wounded and of chaplains comforting the dying. But many increasingly show a moral degeneration. Instead of helping one another, some soldiers trample to death the wounded and each other in their panic to escape. The survivors then use the corpses of their trampled comrades as a ramp to reach the door of the plane. Callous looters rob the wounded and dying, deaf to their pleas for help. Vilshofen has even seen bodies with the skulls broken open and the brains eaten, a result, he says, not only of desperate starvation but also of Nazi ideology that makes the strong literally eat the weak, a bitter comment on the Nazi notion of the master race.

Plievier is not content with merely depicting the suffering of the army and its moral disintegration but explores the reasons for the disaster and the crucial issue of accountability. For Plievier, all those involved are, to some degree, culpable. Plievier assigns most blame to Hitler and the Nazi regime, both for starting the war and for refusing to let the army break through the Soviet lines when it would still have been possible. He criticizes Hitler for not allowing the army to surrender even though the situation was hopeless and Hitler could neither supply nor rescue the army. Plievier also indicts the Hitler regime for its cynical misuse of the army for propaganda purposes. In the cellars of Stalingrad, the wounded hear a radio speech by Göring in which he proclaims the heroic death of the army. The Nazis intend to manipulate Germany to fight more energetically, and the myth of the "heroic" fight to the death of the Sixth Army lends itself to their purposes—purposes for which, Plievier shows, they are willing to sacrifice thousands of lives.

Also responsible to a great extent for the suffering are the German officers at Stalingrad, who have become executioners of their own men. As officers, they are responsible for helping Hitler come to power and for going along without protest on what Vilshofen terms Hitler's marauding expeditions. They are also responsible for their criminal and murderous obedience to the insane orders (79) which have turned healthy young men into wretches on their way to the slaughterhouse (283). By stressing the suffering and death in the last three weeks of battle, Plievier strongly indicts the officers and the Nazi regime for refusing the Soviet terms of surrender and insisting on fighting to the death. For most of the officers, following orders is more important than the safety of their men. Plievier shows how many of the officers care little for their men. While the men are starving at the front and clad in rags that do not protect them from frostbite, the officers and the staff are warm and well-fed in the rear. The officers and their staffs still have warm clothes, canned goods, and even such luxuries as chocolate and cakes at a time when the ordinary soldiers receive a few peas a day.

Although Plievier reserves his sharpest criticism for the Hitler regime and the higher ranking officers, he does not exonerate the ordinary soldiers and the lower ranking officers from guilt. Plievier clearly sympathizes with their suffering and refers to them on occasions as sacrificial victims, but he shows how some are guilty of brutality. Gnotke's friend Gimpf, for example, obeys an order to kill young Russian children, an act which torments him for the rest of his life. Others, like Sergeant Urbas, can drive unmoved past ditches filled with the bodies of executed civilians and prisoners-of-war. Although most are not guilty of such brutality and callousness, Plievier nevertheless holds them accountable. As Captain Steiger realizes while he is trampled to death by those desperate to fly out, he, too, is responsible. Although he did not want to profit from the war, he went along without protest and, by so doing, incurred guilt.

Responsibility for the war lies not only with the Nazi regime and those actually fighting but, in Plievier's view, with the entire German people. He points out the role of the industrialists who supported Hitler as well as the militarism inherent in German culture that has led to a thirty-year nightmare from "a Verdun on the Meuse to the Verdun on the Volga" (91). Like Captain Steiger, the German people are guilty because they went along. Even Germany's impressive achievements in culture have taught the Germans nothing but are used, like the general who reads Goethe, as a narcotic (Sevin 100); they have not prevented the murder of young children. Unlike most exiles in the Soviet Union, Plievier did not therefore divide Germany into a criminal group of Nazis and a large group of innocent, victimized people, but assigned responsibility to all.[9]

Despite this bleak assessment, Plievier still has faith that people will grow to understand the criminality of the Nazi regime and its "vicious contempt of human lives" (169). Two who become more aware and who grow in moral stature as a result of their experiences are Gnotke and Vilshofen. Vilshofen in particular comes to see the criminality of the war and believes that it is his duty to resist. Beyond Stalingrad, for him, means to fight against the Nazi regime, to turn away from German wrongdoing, to rebuild a society in which all can be free and secure and, above all, to struggle against military madness and all future wars.

This strong anti-war position, voiced here by Vilshofen but evident throughout the novel, coupled with Plievier's powerful depiction of the battle for Stalingrad and his discussion of responsibility, made the novel into a best-seller both in Germany and England and the United States.[10] In Germany, in particular, the novel's focus on the responsibility of the German people for World War II led to heated debate in literary, political, moral, philosophical and religious contexts (Müller 450-451). It was reviewed not only in cultural journals and feuilletons but also discussed in editorials and letters to the editor, proof of the large audience it reached. Reviews in the English-speaking world focus more on Plievier's depiction of the war than on the issue of accountability. Although some reviewers objected to the novel's graphic descriptions of war and to what some perceived as a chaotic style, most were overwhelmingly positive in their analysis of how the novel recreates the horror of war. The review of Stalingrad in Time calls it "an enormous chart of case histories in a world of mass horror" (98). In The Nation, Diana Trilling praises it for "the passion of its protest against the whole hideous business of war" and for its depiction of German soldiers "as human beings capable of the full range of human suffering instead of as contrivances, puppets of their political fate" (555). Edmund Fuller writes in The Saturday Review of Literature that the novel has "a massive weight and power" and remarks: "Plievier gives as harrowing an account of the horrors of war as I have ever read" (15). In The New Republic, Alexander Klein calls Stalingrad "the greatest document yet to come out of World War II," and he notes perceptively that Plievier's novel "is far more than a report; it is an imaginative, dramatized recreation" (22). Like other reviewers, Orville Prescott in The New York Times admires the "relentless realism" of the novel; it is "tremendous in scope, shattering in impact" (21). The review in The Times Literary Supplement calls it a "monumental achievement" that is "on a level with anything yet written about war" (413). Plievier's powerful protest against war appealed to a war-weary public and accounts for the novel's success. In Germany, it sold over a million copies; throughout the world, more than two million were sold (Müller 450), and it was one of the most frequently reviewed books of German exile literature (Peitsch 93).

Plievier continues his sharp criticism of war and of the Hitler regime in *Moscow*, the second novel of the trilogy, a novel which he had planned in 1941 but was unable to write until after his move to the West in 1947. In this novel, however, he broadens his scope to include the Red Army, the Soviet regime and the civilians caught in the fighting. Because of his depiction of the Red Army in complete disintegration and his indictment of Stalin and the NKVD (the Soviet secret police) as well as his portrayal of the passive resistance of the Russian people to the Soviet regime, the censor would not have allowed the book to appear in the Soviet Union, and even writing the book would have been extremely dangerous for Plievier.

Like *Stalingrad*, *Moscow* vividly depicts the horror of war, but the horror is intensified because Plievier's scope is broader. In addition to descriptions of agonizing deaths and terrible wounds suffered by the soldiers, Plievier focuses also on the impact of the war on civilians. The novel is filled with descriptions of ruined villages and towns, of families torn apart and of the flood of starving and sick refugees, desperate to escape from the fighting. The impact on civilians is emphasized at the outset. Plievier describes a peaceful village early in the morning where the peasants are letting the cows out to graze. After the German attack, all that is left of the village, which is inhabited only by civilians, is a few dazed survivors, rubble and the smell of burned flesh. This scene, which is representative of many in the novel, underscores the criminality of the war.

Throughout the novel, Plievier gives examples of the brutality with which the Germans conducted the war. Sergeant Riederheim, for example, brutally kills two old people, and Colonel Vilshofen's advancing tank group drives over a bridge crowded with cows, horses, herdsmen and drovers and turns them all into a gory mass (259). Yet Plievier is strangely silent about the greatest atrocities carried out by the Germans. He does not mention the role of the Gestapo and the German army in the mass executions of civilians, although he focuses in detail on the brutality of the Gestapo's Soviet counterpart, the NKVD. This omission gives the novel a lack of balance, despite its otherwise powerful depictions of the war.

As in *Stalingrad*, moral accountability for this immense human misery is essential to Plievier's depiction of the war. On the German side, accountability lies with Hitler and the Nazi regime, with the officers and with the soldiers themselves. Plievier indicts Hitler for beginning the war and for the way he and his officers conduct the campaign. Eager to reach Moscow, Hitler gives orders to advance without consideration of the casualties involved. His officers follow these orders with a similarly callous disregard for human life. As in *Stalingrad*, Plievier holds not only the Hitler regime and the officers but also the soldiers responsible, although his criticism of the soldiers is not as sharp as in the earlier novel, and he stresses less their moral disintegration. Gnotke, who, like Vilshofen also plays a role in *Moscow*, tells his friends that all who went along with Hitler are responsible: "This would never have come about without you, Hans, and you, Emil, and me. It all happened when we joined the Party in '32" (313).

Plievier's indictment of Stalin and his totalitarian regime is, however, much stronger in this novel than his indictment of the Germans. Throughout, he emphasizes the repressiveness of the Soviet system and the brutality and terror by which it rules. In particular, he ascribes the immense loss of life on the Soviet side to Stalin's inept conduct of the war. Like Hitler, Stalin carries on the war with a complete disregard for human life. Despite strong indications that the Germans planned to attack, Plievier shows how completely unprepared Stalin and the Politburo were. Stalin forces the Red Army, whose officers he decimated in the purges and whose men he did not equip to fight (only every third man had a gun), to advance, even though this results in enormous casualties. Stalin's poor planning, his refusal to allow his army to retreat, and his insistence on unrealistic defense lines cause the rout of the Red Army. To hide its own mistakes, the regime then searches for scapegoats and shoots many officers as traitors.

Through his portrayal of Stalin's secret police, Plievier underscores the brutality and the repressiveness of the Soviet system that is at war not only with the Germans but with its own people. Instead of supporting the efforts of the Army, the NKVD officers undermine it by executing soldiers who retreat, officers who refuse to carry out orders that would mean certain death to their men and those who, having escaped from behind German lines, were immediately suspected of being spies. In addition, they shoot civilians, and, before they flee from the German advance, they murder all political prisoners. In his depiction of the vast slave-labor camp run by the NKVD, Plievier describes the harsh conditions under which the political prisoners live and their brutal treatment by the NKVD, who regard them as little more than animals. This slave-labor camp becomes, for Plievier, an image of the Soviet system as a whole and its brutality. He notes that, when the Soviet regime has overcome its panic at the German approach on Moscow, signs that life has returned to "normal" in the capital are not help for the Army or civilians. Instead, mass arrests, executions and the deportation of the Volga Germans are carried out by the NKVD.

Yet, in this novel, Plievier does not hold the Russian people and the Red Army accountable for the brutality of the war or for the atrocities of the Stalin regime. Instead, he emphasizes the gulf between the regime and its citizens. Unlike their counterparts in *Stalingrad*, officers in the Red Army such as General Narishkin and Colonel Semyonov refuse to carry out orders that would result in a senseless sacrifice of their men's lives, and they are shot as traitors. For many in the Red Army, in fact, even for those who were dedicated communists, the war opens their eyes to the criminality of the Stalin regime. Captain Uralov, a courageous officer who is one of the most dedicated to the regime at the beginning of the novel, for example, rejects it at the end. He has seen officers he respected shot by the NKVD and has narrowly escaped being shot himself. In the NKVD holding camp, where he is herded together with thousands of other Red Army officers and soldiers whom the NKVD treats as criminals, he asks: "Who had heaped defeats on the nation and covered its body with wounds and lice? There is a Russian proverb that it is the head of the fish that stinks" (245). Plievier thus treats the Red Army officers and soldiers sympathetically on the whole—as victims of a brutal system.

Plievier similarly views the Russian people, whom he had come to admire during his exile years in the Soviet Union, as victims both of their own regime and later of the Germans. Through the peasant Shulga, Plievier describes Stalin's forced collectivization of the land and its destruction of the rural economy. Shulga tells of the typical fate of his village whose people were deported, starved or shot by the authorities. Their hatred for their own government is so intense that they view the Germans at first as liberators, until they see that their brutality is as great as that of the regime in Moscow. Stalin's destruction of their villages is completed by the Germans who leave rubble and corpses in their wake.

Although Plievier's protest against war is as strong in *Moscow* as it was in *Stalingrad*, he has little hope that society can change for the better in the future. Vilshofen's resolve at the end of Stalingrad to struggle against militarism and all future wars is absent in this novel, a result perhaps of the Cold War tensions when Plievier was writing the novel. Although some grow morally during the course of the novel, they are helpless to effect change in totalitarian systems. Plievier's pessimism is indicated by his use of history in the novel. In the beginning, he includes a document from one of Charles V's campaigns in 1537 which describes the sacking and burning of cities as sport. Like this campaign of the Holy Roman Emperor, Plievier stresses that the campaign against the Soviet Union is also one of plunder, although the term now used is requisitioning. What is most significant for Plievier is that, even four hundred years later, such wars continue, and nobody has learned from history. This inability to learn from history is underscored by Plievier's frequent references to the fate of Napoleon's armies in Russia. History appears here to be a brutal repetition of war and plunder, which offers little hope of progress and in which the individual is helpless. This sense of hopelessness is expressed by Colonel Zecke who comes to think that, for the Germans, the best that can happen is a Napoleonic retreat in order to save at least a few men "so that some witnesses would be left to relate one day a bloody moral about ill-gotten gains" (305). Zecke does not say whether people will listen to this bloody moral.

As in *Stalingrad*, the vivid depiction in *Moscow* of the immense suffering caused by the German attack on the Soviet Union and by the Soviet regime, its historically accurate recreation of the battles of Bialystok and Minsk, and the immediacy with which it shows the chaos and terror of war, contributed to the success of the novel. It was well-received and quickly translated into many languages, although it never became as popular as *Stalingrad*. In Germany, it received positive reviews, but, as one critic noted, the East, especially the GDR and the Soviet Union, never forgave Plievier for his depiction of the Soviet regime (Wilde 507). Like the reviews of *Stalingrad*, those of the novel in England and the United States focused in particular on Plievier's powerful descriptions of war and his anti-war stance. The review of the novel in *Time* notes: "The scope and horror of modern war has been described with a combination of pitiless detail and powerful sweep by the best novelist who has written on World War II." It praises Plievier's talents in depicting mass confusion. *Moscow* is "a stunning documentary of victory, defeat, brutality and horror" (102). In *The Spectator*, R.D. Charques criticizes Plievier for touching too lightly on the atrocities of the Nazi occupation of the Soviet Union, a real weakness in the novel, but nevertheless writes that the novel is "firmly disciplined in narrative power, but shattering in its illustration of the error and irresponsibility which go with the strategic and tactical direction of battle" (492). Writing in *Commonweal*, John A. Lynch calls it "one of the most thoughtful and most successful novels to come out of the last world war" (652). Plievier's goal of recreating "a total war on paper" (652), in which Lynch believes he is successful, and his inclusion of a large variety of individual fates displeased the reviewer in the *Times Literary Supplement*, who criticizes the novel for giving the impression of a "series of rather badly cut news-reels" (813) and for its lack of human development. The review in the *New York Times*, however, praises the novel for its "broad, panoramic aspect" whose plot "is carried along by the historic progress of events rather than by any author-contrived plot" (25).

Plievier continues his depiction of the enormity of suffering caused by the war and his sharp criticism of the Hitler and Stalin regimes in the last novel of the trilogy, *Berlin*, whose first parts focus on the last days of the fighting in Berlin. In this work, Plievier gives a vivid picture of the desolation of Berlin, which he calls "a beaten city; a raped city" (296) where the civilians cower in cellars and bunkers amidst the rubble. He describes the fear, panic and despair of the population subjected to bombing and later to the street fighting that takes a heavy toll on their lives. The terror imposed by the Red Army is also emotionally shown. Although Plievier treats most of the civilians sympathetically and in many cases stresses their courage, he also includes characters such as the writer Wittstock, an opportunist, who quickly changes from supporting the Nazis to supporting the Soviets.

Even though Plievier clearly sympathizes with those suffering in Berlin, where many of the casualties were old people, women, children and refugees, he still holds the German people accountable for the brutality of the war. Colonel Zecke, who appeared in *Moscow*, is shocked by the ruins he sees in Dresden and the shattering reality of near-total destruction in Berlin. Yet he reflects that, after Treblinka and Auschwitz, after "mounds of human skeletons from the furnaces and gas chambers," after "annihilation as a political principle, it hardly befits us to speak of being terrorized" (12).

Most accountable, however, is Hitler, whom Plievier describes in detail for the first time in the trilogy. Plievier portrays Hitler, who is hiding in his bunker surrounded by leading Nazis, as totally divorced from reality and deluded—if not mad. The insane orders that he issued to the armies in *Moscow* and *Stalingrad* become even more insane in *Berlin* and, as in the previous novels, result in enormous casualties. Caring nothing about the human cost of his decision, Hitler refuses to capitulate and puts his faith in non-existent battalions that will defend Berlin, a decision that results in young boys and old men being sent out to be slaughtered and the savage street fighting that could have been avoided. Plievier strongly indicts Hitler: "In his hands, Germany had become a bowl filled to the brim with oppression, corruption, deception, violence and murder" (96). While Hitler raves, his entourage of leading Nazis feast, drink and have orgies, a grotesque dance of death that resembles an insane asylum. Plievier comments: "Their way has led through blood, and now they drink, they jump, they dance. Leaving a mutilated Europe behind them, they murder Germany in cold blood and even now are strangling Berlin" (183). In his scornful treatment of Hitler and the Nazis, Plievier unmasks their cynical ideology and their thirst for power, their willingness to sacrifice senselessly countless lives for their own ends. Theirs is the chief responsibility for the immense human misery, he makes clear.

Yet Plievier also holds the Soviets responsible for the suffering in *Berlin*. In contrast to his positive depiction of the Russian soldiers and officers in *Moscow*, Plievier portrays them in Berlin as "savage and licentious" men who "ransacked, murdered and scorched" (70). Plievier describes in great detail the brutality of the occupation, in particular the rapes and murders the soldiers perpetrate when they are both drunk and sober. In addition to the brutality of the occupation, Plievier focuses on the brutal treatment that the survivors of Stalingrad receive in Soviet captivity. Through Gnotke, who returns to Berlin after being indoctrinated in the Soviet Union, the reader learns how the Soviets have destroyed them physically and morally through hunger, propaganda and slave-labor, until only 3,000 of the 91,000 captives survive. Like the Germans in their campaign, Plievier stresses that for the Soviets war means plunder. The corpses have not even been buried before the Soviets begin dismantling factories and sending them with the German workers they have rounded up as slave-laborers to the Soviet Union. Nazi repression has merely been replaced with Soviet repression, a repression that continues under Walter Ulbricht's control in the later part of the novel.

Despite the strength of its portrayal of the desolation caused by war, *Berlin* was not as well-received as the previous novels in the trilogy. The review in *Time* calls it a "terrible and very nearly brilliant book," a "death dance of minor characters" (100). In *The Spectator*, Ian Fraser writes that the novel "enables the outsider to relive the defeat and humiliation of the German capital" (603). Other reviews were not as positive. In *The Saturday Review*, Richard Plant calls the novel "more a fabulously detailed montage of a ravaged city than a work of fiction" (15). The *New York Times* criticizes it for being a "maniacal montage of lurid newsreels," (5) while *The Times Literary Supplement* calls it a "sprawling mass of fictionalized history" (629).

Although Plievier, in his concern with giving a historically accurate panorama of the events, tends to fragment the novel by his inclusion of too many different fates, the trilogy as a whole, with its powerful protest against the brutality of war and its strong indictment of those responsible, is a deeply moral work which, as the reviewer in *Commonweal* writes, ranks as "one of the major accomplishments of contemporary European fiction" (262). Yet Plievier's hopes for progress towards peace become increasingly bleak during the course of the trilogy. Although some, such as Vilshofen, Gnotke, Zecke and Uralov, learn from their experiences and manage to retain their humanity, most do not, and even those who do learn, are helpless to effect change in totalitarian systems. Governments continue to repeat the mistakes of the past, and, as the opening of *Moscow* suggests, history has progressed little from the time of Charles V in the sixteenth century. Instead of progress, wars have become more destructive and governments more repressive (in Plievier's analysis). The suppression of the workers' rebellion of 1953 in the GDR at the end of *Berlin* reinforces Plievier's belief that such repression will continue. Instead of Vilshofen's hopes at the end of *Stalingrad* for a new society of freedom and security after the war, one totalitarian system has merely replaced the other. For Plievier, the legacies of both are corpses.

Notes

[1]Although the last two parts of *Berlin* focus on the post-war years in the Soviet zone and later in the GDR until the workers' rebellion of June 1953, the focus here will be on those parts of the novel that deal with the last days of the fighting.

[2]Plievier was well-known in the Weimar Republic for his pacifist and anarchist views and for his opposition to the Nazis. Because of these views and because of the sharp criticism of the German navy in his novel *Des Kaisers Kulis* (1930) (*The Kaiser's Coolies*, 1931) which angered the Nazis, Plievier had to flee when Hitler took power in 1933. Together with the works of other anti-Nazi writers, his works were burned on May 10, 1933.

[3]Officers whom he interviewed about Stalingrad recall his careful attention to detail. This careful research is characteristic also of Plievier's earlier novels and gave him the reputation of being one of the pioneers of documentary literature in the Weimar Republic.

[4]Plievier's style owes much to the works of Upton Sinclair and John Dos Passos.

[5]Like most exiles, Plievier faced the problem of adjusting to a new culture and had to contend with the pain caused by the loss of his homeland and friends. These difficulties were made worse for Plievier because of the political situation in the Soviet Union where he feared for his life during Stalin's purges, and he made several unsuccessful attempts to leave.

[6]In September 1943, Plievier became a member of the National Committee for a Free Germany, designed as a broad-based opposition group to Hitler, to which many of the higher ranking captured German officers belonged. Plievier was thus able to interview these officers, including Field-Marshal von Paulus, as well as visit prisoner-of-war camps.

[7]*Stalingrad*, Plievier's major exile work, was first serialized in 1943 and 1944 in *Internationale Literatur*, the most important German exile journal in the Soviet Union.

[8]On November 19, 1942, Plievier writes, there were some 330,000 men in the Sixth Army. By January 1943, only 91,000 were still alive, and 88,000 of these died in Soviet captivity.

[9]Dividing Germany into a criminal group of Nazis and a large group of innocent people was called the Two Germanies theory, a theory supported at first by both the German exiles and the Communist Party in the Soviet Union. Later, this theory changed. See Müller 440-444 for a discussion of the shift in Soviet propaganda at the time.

[10]The novel was quickly translated into many languages. It was also one of the few books by German exile writers that portrayed war directly.

Works Cited

Charques, R.D. Rev. of *Moscow*, by Theodor Plievier. *The Spectator* 30 Oct. 1953: 492.

"Death of a City." Rev. of *Berlin*, by Theodor Plievier. *Time* 29 April 1957: 100.

Fraser, Ian. "The First Rising." Rev. of *Berlin*, by Theodor Plievier. *Spectator* 2 Nov. 1956: 603-604.

Fuller, Edmund. "Plievier's Inferno." Rev. of *Stalingrad*, by Theodor Plievier. *Saturday Review of Literature* 30 Oct. 1948: 15, 27.

Kauf, Robert. "Plieviers *Stalingrad* nach dreissig Jahren." *Welt und Wort* 28 (1973): 21-22.

Klein, Alexander. "The Cold War." Rev. of *Stalingrad*, by Theodor Plievier. *The New Republic* 8 Nov. 1948: 22-23.

"Living with Death." Rev. of *Berlin*, by Theodor Plievier. *The Times Literary Supplement* 26 Oct. 1956: 629.

Lynch, John A. "War on Paper." Rev. of *Moscow*, by Theodor Plievier. *Commonweal* 2 April 1954: 652.

"Men Who Stopped Hitler." Rev. of *Moscow*, by Theodor Plievier. *New York Times* 7 March 1954: 25.

Morton, Frederic. "Little Man Forsaken." Rev. of *Berlin*. *New York Times* 28 April 1957: 5.

Müller, Hans-Harald. "*Stalingrad*: Zur Geschichte und Aktualität von Theodor Plieviers Roman." Afterword. *Stalingrad*, by Theodor Plievier. Cologne: Kiepenheuer and Witsch, 1983: 435-453.

Peitsch, Helmut. "Theodor Plieviers *Stalingrad*." *Faschismuskritik und Deutschlandbild im Exilroman*. Ed. Christian Fritsch and Lutz Winckler. Berlin: Argument-Verlag, 1981: 83-101.

Pfaff, William. "Grim Comedy." Rev. of *Berlin*, by Theodor Plievier. *Commonweal* 7 June 1957: 261-262.

Plant, Richard. Rev. of *Berlin*, by Theodor Plievier. *The Saturday Review* 11 May 1957: 15.

Plievier, Theodor. *Berlin*. Trans. Louis Hagen and Vivian Milroy. Garden City: Doubleday, 1957.

——— *Moscow*. Trans. Stuart Hood. Garden City: Doubleday, 1954.

——— *Stalingrad*. Trans. Richard and Clara Winston. New York: Appleton-Century-Crofts, 1948.

Prescott, Orville. Rev. of *Stalingrad*, by Theodor Plievier. *New York Times* 15 Oct. 1948: 21.

Rühle, Jürgen. *Literatur und Revolution*. Munich: Knauer, 1963.

"Scenes of Conflict." Rev. of *Moscow*, by Theodor Plievier. *The Times Literary Supplement* 18 Dec. 1953: 813.

"Second Epistle to the Germans." Rev. of *Stalingrad*, by Theodor Plievier. *Time* 1 Nov. 1948: 98, 100.

Sevin, Dieter. *Individuum und Staat: Das Bild des Soldaten in der Romantrilogie Theodor Plieviers*. Bonn: Bouvier, 1972.

"Slaughter on the Plains." Rev. of *Moscow*, by Theodor Plievier. *Time* 8 March 1954: 102.

Trilling, Diana. Rev. of *Stalingrad*, by Theodor Plievier. *The Nation* 13 Nov. 1948: 555-556.

"Two Kinds of War." Rev. of *Stalingrad*, by Theodor Plievier. *The Times Literary Supplement* 24 July 1948: 413.

Wilde, Harry. *Theodor Plievier: Nullpunkt der Freiheit*. Munich: Kurt Desch, 1965.

Learning to Fight the Nazis:
The Education of Upton Sinclair's
Lanny Budd

Sally E. Parry

George Bernard Shaw wrote to Upton Sinclair in 1941:

> When people ask me what has happened in my long lifetime, I do not refer them to the newspaper files and to the authorities, but to your novels. They object that the people in your books never existed; that their deeds were never done and their sayings never uttered. I assure them that they were, except that Upton Sinclair individualized and expressed them better than they could have done, and arranged their experiences...in significant and intelligible order.
>
> (Sinclair, *My Lifetime* 66)

Upton Sinclair believed that art ought to serve history. He thought that fiction should exist not just for its own sake, but for educating readers about social and economic injustice. His best known work in this respect is the 1906 novel *The Jungle,* which attacked the poor working conditions in the meat-packing industry in Chicago. He felt it particularly important to explain how the capitalist profit system was to a great extent responsible for much of the poverty and despair in the modern world.[1] As William Bloodworth has noted, Sinclair's "strongly expressed sensitivity to inequities in the political and social life of modern capitalistic society" (150) is a continuing theme throughout his work. In planning his *World's End* series of novels, Sinclair felt that by showing how a young man is educated in the ways of the world, he could also show how the western world changed during the twentieth century. Specifically, he wanted to explain how World War II was caused by the schemings of various business and industrial groups which preferred fascism and dictatorship to democracy. However, as the United States entered the second World War, Sinclair's concept for the series moved from purely political education to an emphasis on propaganda for the war effort. By the time of the final volume, *The Return of Lanny Budd,* Sinclair's virulent anti-Communism had significantly altered the political vision he was trying to show the public. The *World's End* series moves from a political and historical education for the reader to a documentation of the evolving political consciousness of Upton Sinclair.

Sinclair's primary goal in developing the series was to explain the conditions which led to the rise of fascism in Europe and the United States. As he wrote to Otis Peabody Swift of *Life* magazine in 1939,

Monopoly capitalists, those of the steel and armaments industries, find themselves confronted with a choice between socialization and collapse. They employ gangsters to protect them, first in the guise of strike breaking agencies, detective bureaus, private guards, and public relations counsellors; when the danger grows greater they employ political gangsters, such as Hitler and Mussolini. This is the genesis of Fascism, and it is perfectly absurd to imagine that conditions are or can be any different in the United States from those in any other capitalist nation.

Sinclair felt that the seeds of the second World War were set with the signing of the Versailles Treaty after World War I.[2] In order to dramatize those forces which were responsible for starting a new war out of the embers of the old, Sinclair created the character of Lanny Budd, through whose eyes we see the changes in Europe and America which were responsible for the rise of fascism. Lanny is a wealthy American art dealer and playboy who is able to travel relatively easily between the Allied and Axis worlds. Because of his wide variety of friends and acquaintances, he is able to hear about the events in Europe from many different points of view.

Sinclair originally planned only one long novel. However, because of the amount of material he wanted to cover, the series grew to eleven novels, starting with *World's End* in 1940 and ending with *The Return of Lanny Budd* in 1953. Lanny is 13 at the start of the series, which is set in pre-World War I France. He is the illegitimate son of an American munitions manufacturer, Robert Budd, and an American artists' model, Mabel Blackless. Beauty, as her friends call her, lives with her son on the French Riviera near Cannes. Although Robbie, Lanny's father, has been forced by his family to marry someone more socially acceptable, he maintains good relations with Beauty and Lanny, provides them with monetary support, and often seeks their help in his European business dealings.

By showing the way in which Lanny matures and learns about the world, Sinclair wanted his readers to become similarly educated about history and politics. As he wrote to his editor, B.W. Huebsch in 1943, "What I am doing is giving the reader a great load of history and some propaganda, and I try to put in adventures as a sort of icing to the cake" (Yoder 487). Sinclair purposely made Lanny a person who is born with no true alliances outside of his mother and father and so must make conscious choices about his political and moral beliefs. Lanny is an American, but lives in France, and, because of his father's business as a "merchant of death," he has been taught to have allegiances to no one, except business associates. Sinclair wrote to James Henle of the Vanguard Press in 1939 that "Lanny...is something of an outsider to all the different groups and interests and therefore in [a] position to observe them all and be pulled and hauled among them." Lanny must, as he matures, develop a political consciousness, formed from the ideas he has taken from his capitalist father, from his pleasure-loving but apolitical mother, from his communist uncle and from a number of friends who range from supporters of National Socialism to members of the French, Spanish and German resistance.

Sinclair makes us as readers identify early on with Lanny, whom we first see as a naive youth, suspicious of all politics. However, this naivete gives way to a realization that any political system which polarizes classes is, in the end, a destructive one. Lanny feels drawn towards Socialism, since he sees it as the form of government which will accomplish the greatest amount of good for people. His political thinking is, in many ways, modeled after Sinclair's (Mookerjee 120). However, unlike Sinclair, he has trouble making a political commitment. Even after a woman labor leader he admires is killed by fascists, Lanny is unable to take any sort of definite action. "He had made certain that there were forces in the world which he hated with all his heart and wanted to fight; but just what they were, and how he could recognize them—that would take further study" (*Between Two Worlds* 288).

Lanny's first exposure to war is through his father, who, as the top sales agent for Budd Gunmakers, sells his arms to all sides prior to America's entry into the first World War. Robbie hopes that Lanny will one day come into the family business and therefore takes him along on several sales trips to Paris and London. He has developed a rationale for weapon selling which he emphasizes to Lanny. "Men hate each other. . . . They insist upon fighting, and there's nothing you can do about it, except learn to defend yourself" (*World's End* 32). Robbie has no moral qualms about selling munitions. He teaches Lanny to be cynical about the idea of patriotism. "Remember, there never was a war in which the right was all on one side. And remember that in every war both sides lie like hell" (*World's End* 216). Since no side is right, it is best for gun merchants to remain neutral and make whatever profit they can.

Lanny's suspicion of all sorts of national self-interest is further intensified when he becomes a translator/secretary for one of President Wilson's staff during the forging of the Versailles Treaty. He notes the many humiliations forced on the losers by the victors, to the point where German civilians are being starved because the Allies are blockading ports until the peace treaty is signed. In addition, the Allies use their leverage to acquire more territory, more material resources and more subject peoples. Lanny is approached by delegates from many countries who assume he has influence on the way the treaty is written.

Earnest strangers would appeal in the name of President Wilson's doctrine of 'self-determination of all peoples'; and Lanny would take their stories to the experts at the Crillon—and like as not would learn that the same people were busily engaged in oppressing some other people, even perhaps killing them wholesale! (*World's End* 495)

Lanny eventually quits his job as translator in disgust over the needless mess that the peace settlement has become.

Although Lanny attributes much of the seemingly inane treaty problems to the greed of various governments, Robbie has a more plausible and more sinister explanation. He knows that the steel and coal industrialists as well as those in numerous other international cartels don't care who wins as long as they stay in business and make profits. In his description of how the world works and how wars are won, Robbie sounds frighteningly like one of the characters in Thomas Pynchon's *Gravity's Rainbow*. However, for Robbie there is no paranoia, just an acceptance of the way things are. He says,

They have their directors in hundreds of different companies, all tied together in a big net—steel, oil, coal, chemicals, shipping, and, above all, banks.... They're building big industry, and they'll own it and run it. Whatever government comes in will have to have money, and will make terms with them, and business will go on as it's always done. (*World's End* 355-56)

Little wonder that Lanny is cynical about the relationship between government and business.

Lanny's early efforts to become more educated about the political situation are only moderately successful, since he receives conflicting information. His many friends and acquaintances represent major political factions of the time. Among the people with whom he discusses world affairs are Bernhardt Monck and Trudi Schultz, members of the German underground; Raoul Palma, a Spanish Loyalist and director of a Socialist school; his uncle Jesse Blackless, a French Communist; Barbara Pugliese, an anti-fascist Italian labor organizer; Sir Basil Zaharoff, an international munitions dealer; and Denis de Bruyne, a conservative French businessman. Lanny enjoys the intellectual stimulation of the discussions, but hates the fact that the people he likes are often ideologically far apart. "All he wanted was that his friends shouldn't quarrel and make it necessary to choose between them" (*Dragon's Teeth* 508).

As Lanny matures, he realizes that, despite what his father has said, the profit motive is not enough of a creed for living a meaningful life. He gads about the world, associating with various classes and types of people, hoping to find some way in which he can do good. He helps his friends who have fallen on hard times, teaches at Raoul Palma's school and supports several artists. Lanny realizes, however, that, in order to make an impact on world problems, he needs to make money. Having received a legacy of paintings from his stepfather, Lanny becomes an art dealer, using his contacts with European aristocracy to sell the art work of the old world to the wealthy Americans of the new world. He feels that this is not a totally selfish profession, since his deals bring hard currency into parts of Europe that have been depressed since the war.

The strongest influence in his political education is his friend Eric Pomeroy-Nielson, a former British flyer, who is crippled as a result of injuries sustained during World War I. Rick, although heir to a title, is sympathetic to the working class and becomes a left-wing journalist after the war. Since Lanny knows many powerful businessmen and government leaders through his father's business and his mother's position as a social leader in French Riviera society, he is able to introduce Rick to many important people. His growing distaste for his father's profession and the insight he receives from Rick about world affairs move him slowly leftward in his thinking. However, Lanny is not an ideologue "and could see that there was some of it [the truth] on both sides" (*Dragon's Teeth* 269). Sinclair assumes that many readers are as confused as Lanny about some of the political changes in the world, especially in Western Europe, and hopes that through the novels readers will become similarly converted to a socialist ideology.

Lanny's other close boyhood friend, Kurt Meissner, provides a contrast to the influence of Rick and his Socialist ideas. Kurt is a German composer who fought for Germany during World War I. After the war, when Kurt is working as a secret agent for his government, Lanny helps him agitate for lifting the British blockade of German ports. Lanny decides that the welfare of harmless civilians is a greater good than supporting the Allies at that time. In addition, Kurt has an affair with Lanny's mother for nearly eight years. Kurt is made an official composer of the Third Reich in the early 1930s and wholeheartedly accepts the Nazi doctrines. Lanny feigns interest in National Socialism in part to please Kurt and eventually in order to work undercover against the Nazis. But his conversion to action comes slowly. As he explains to Trudi Schultz of the German underground, he has been

torn since boyhood by two sets of ideas, two sets of inclinations, two worlds which are in conflict, and each has a claim upon me and lays hold of me and pulls. It used to be tolerable, in the old days when ideas were not taken too seriously; but now the two worlds have gone to war, and they pull as hard as they can and don't care if they pull me to pieces. (*Wide Is the Gate* 494)

As world affairs become more chaotic in the 1930s, Lanny wants to take a stronger stand politically. After one of his friends dies as a result of being tortured in a Nazi concentration camp, "Lanny was haunted by the idea that it was his duty to give up all pleasures and all other duties to try and awaken the people of Western Europe to a realization of the peril in which they stood" (*Wide Is the Gate* 17). But, despite his good intentions, most of his actions seem to be connected with the problems of his friends. Some find troubling his seeming acceptance of fascism. In reality, he uses this perception in order to assist his friends who are persecuted by the fascists. In his guise as an art broker, he travels to Spain to free Rick's son, Alfy, who has been imprisoned by Franco after fighting for the Loyalists. His success is such that he is able to smuggle out both Alfy and a Goya, which he sells to one of his wealthy clients. He assists Johannes Robin, a Jewish business associate of Robbie's, in leaving Germany and also helps Johannes' son Freddi get released from Dachau. Because of his father's connection with Goering, Lanny is able to help Monck steal an airplane engine so that it can be analyzed by the U.S. military. He is not so successful in helping free his second wife, Trudi, from a concentration camp. Despite great heroics in attempting to find her, he learns that she has been tortured and executed.[3]

It is ironic that, as Lanny develops stronger political convictions, he actually has to take more pains to hide them. He is of more use to fighters against fascism when he pretends to side with the fascists. That way he is able to get information from a number of important people including Goering, Hess and even Hitler. His political commitment to democracy and the Allies solidifies when he agrees to work as a double agent for President Roosevelt, for whom he feels an immense amount of admiration.[4] He moves from acting primarily on impulse and friendship to a conviction that he must work for the American government in order to accomplish the greatest good. He realizes that it is more important to defeat fascism first and afterwards help establish governments based on social and economic justice. Sinclair shared these sentiments. Two days before the Japanese attacked Pearl Harbor, he wrote to Nathan Greenberg, "At the present time I am out of sympathy with the Socialist party because I believe that we have to put down Hitler before we can have Socialism or any other good thing in this world."

By the time Lanny agrees to become a double agent, in the novel *Presidential Agent* (1944), Sinclair's reasons for writing the series seem to have changed. While the earlier novels, such as *Dragon's Teeth* and *Wide Is the Gate* showed how the Nazis gained power and supported fascist movements throughout Europe, the later works such as *Dragon Harvest* (1945), *A World to Win* (1946), and *Presidential Mission* (1947) are primarily Allied propaganda. Lanny turns into an almost incessant globe trotter in order to be in those areas of the world where international attention is focused.[5] He is in Germany for the Beerhall Putsch and the Anschluss and in North Africa when the Allies invade. He has tea with Madame Sun Yat Sen just before the Japanese bomb Hong Kong and escapes through the Soviet Union, where he manages to have a conversation with Stalin. Lanny helps rescue British servicemen at Dunkirk and then arrives at Hitler's field command in time for the German march on Paris. He studies nuclear physics with Albert Einstein at Princeton, has dinner with Franklin and Eleanor Roosevelt at the White House and gets to brief Churchill on the European situation. Hitler uses Lanny's own personal medium to contact the dead and invites him to see the view from Kehlsteinhaus.[6] Lanny even interviews Hess after he has been put in a British prison and is requested by Goering as a character witness at the Nuremberg trials.

By having Lanny work for the government rather than as a private citizen, Sinclair hoped to make more believable the number of places that Lanny travels to and increase his reasons for meeting with top world officials. Lanny works as an official double agent both in the United States and abroad. In America, Roosevelt has Lanny investigate people such as William Randolph Hearst, Father Charles Coughlin, Gerald L.K. Smith and Henry Ford who are supporting various domestic fascist movements. He is able to uncover a ring of powerful men and women who are helping to pay for Nazi propaganda in the United States and another group which wants to assassinate Roosevelt.

In Europe, Lanny is able to capitalize on his status as an art dealer in order to visit many people with a wide variety of political beliefs. Almost everyone finds him charming, from members of the Hitler Youth to Winston Churchill. His clientele even extends to Field Marshall Goering, who wants to sell some of the paintings he plunders from Jews and other enemies of the Nazi regime. The proceeds go to a bank account that Goering has set up in New York in case the Third Reich does not last a thousand years. As a supposed sympathizer to the Nazi movement, Lanny supplies information to Goering. He knows Nazi intelligence can get this material from other sources, but it keeps him in the good graces of the Nazi hierarchy. Because of his access to officials of the Third Reich, Lanny is able to give Roosevelt advance warning about various Nazi activities, including the signing of a treaty with the Soviet Union and invasion plans for Poland and France.

Lanny's usefulness as a double agent lessens in the later half of the war. Goering, who was Lanny's prime contact, falls out of favor and has less information to provide. Lanny has also become involved with some German officers who are plotting to kill Hitler, and he is forced to make a daring escape when his part in the plot is suspected. Although he provides some help to the Allies in North Africa, his main service at the end of the war is interrogating German prisoners of war and cataloging art that was stolen by the Axis powers.

In the final two volumes of the series, *O Shepherd, Speak!* and *The Return of Lanny Budd,* Lanny does not return to working for his Socialist ideals when the war is over. Sinclair again changes the political focus so that Lanny becomes the ideal Cold Warrior.[7] Because of a million dollar inheritance from an old friend of his mother's, Lanny is able to set up a Peace Foundation "for the prevention of future wars" (*O Shepherd, Speak!* 4). However, Lanny cannot condone disarmament when the Soviets refuse to disarm. He flies to Moscow at the behest of President Truman to try and talk sense to Stalin, but he is not successful. Lanny's distrust of the Soviets becomes greater after he is captured and tortured by them. At the end of the final novel, Lanny has even turned in his sister to the FBI because she is a spy for the Communists. Sinclair's idealistic and peace-loving young man has become a jingoistic adult whose desire to defeat Communism overwhelms his concern for creating a just society.

Sinclair seems to have based Lanny's change of political conscience on his own. Because of his Socialist connections, Sinclair was accused fairly often of being a Communist, which he vehemently denied.[8] Sinclair's Socialism was of the pragmatic kind, in that he broke with the Socialist Party, when it suited him, over both the world wars and when he ran for governor of California in 1934. At the end of World War II, Sinclair came to the realization that the Communists provided a serious threat to America and Western Europe rather than the model Socialist type society which he once admired. He went so far as to try and make friends with conservatives including J. Edgar Hoover, to whom he sent *The Return of Lanny Budd* in 1952. He said: "This volume is concerned with the Communists and their whole bag of clever tricks.... This makes it a timely book, and I think it would be helpful to you as to many others" (Yoder 498). The war that Sinclair had been fighting against Nazis had become a war to be fought against Communists rather than for Socialism.

The *World's End* series is a curious combination of history, political propaganda and thriller. Sinclair is at his best when he is describing the rise of various political ideologies, especially that of National Socialism. His writing is in the great tradition of historical fiction in which fictional characters interact with real people. A careful researcher, he relied heavily on a variety of people to check his writing for authenticity (Mookerjee 117). Consequently, well-known people are presented in a very human manner. The Franklin Roosevelt of these books appears as a real person with the cares and sorrows of a man who has been elected to lead the nation in a troubled time. Even the leaders of the Third Reich, while reprehensible, have distinct personalities and are not just evil straw men.

The Lanny Budd series of novels served a variety of purposes for Upton Sinclair and his readers. He wanted to educate people about the rise of fascism and make it reasonable that Americans ought to move away from isolationism to involvement in a battle for democracy. He hoped that the world would never again have to endure the tragedies brought about by fascism. He also made a great contribution to the war effort by showing how the "can-do" Americans could accomplish anything and eventually break the Nazi war machine. Finally, the political education which Lanny receives shows the changing political consciousness of Upton Sinclair and, by extension, a section of American liberals whose energies turned from fighting Nazis to fighting Communists after World War II.

Notes

[1]In some of Sinclair's earlier writings, he frankly stated that he wanted to see an end to the American way of doing business. Sinclair wrote in 1926, "We have to get rid of the capitalist system. It is so close to breaking down, and will soon be unable to run the factories it has built, or to bring food to the people in its giant cities. We have got to stop producing goods for profit, and learn to produce them for the use of those who work" (*Letters to Judd* 250).

[2]Sinclair was very disappointed by the settlement Wilson made after World War I, although he had supported American participation in the war (Harris 157-65). With his periodical *Upton Sinclair's: For a Clean Peace and the Internation*, he hoped to pressure the United States government into supporting a more equitable peace treaty (*Autobiography* 218-19).

[3]At times Lanny's adventures seem to prefigure post-World War II superspies such as James Bond. Like Bond he is incredibly attractive to women. He has several love affairs and is pursued by numerous other women. He marries three times, first to a spoiled American heiress; second to Trudi, the German resistance fighter; and third to an American writer of antifascist fiction. Unlike Bond, Lanny is faithful to one woman at a time, considering himself such a man of honor that he refuses a mock marriage with a Jewish woman in Berlin, a decision that he knows will lead to her death. Lanny rationalizes his dubious actions by assuming this would undermine his undercover work.

[4]In *Presidential Agent* Sinclair describes Roosevelt and Lanny as being very much alike. "Both had grown up in comfort and near-luxury, never knowing deprivation; both were generous by nature and dreamed of a kindlier world; both had met with disappointments and disillusionments, but were stubborn and did not easily give up their dreams; now both were fighting-mad in their hearts, but kept a smile on their lips because that was good form"(30). Sinclair did not know Roosevelt well and only had one lengthy meeting with him, while Sinclair was running for governor of California (*I, Candidate for Governor* 74-79).

[5]Sinclair was aware of some of his stylistic weaknesses. He blamed many of them on his early work as a writer of boys' adventure stories. Critics such as Blinderman and Dembo find the Lanny Budd novels strongly related to dime novels. Putt contends that, although there are many artistic problems with the series, *World's End* holds a fascination for readers because of the recurring characters and the amount of information it offers.

[6]Sinclair shared this interest in parapsychology. Rudolf Hess was also fascinated by the occult (Bracher 81-98), and, in the series, he and Lanny attend seances together.

[7]See Jon Yoder's discussion of Lanny Budd as representative of the weakness of the liberal to deal with "periods of extreme stress in American history" (484). He maintains that American liberals after World War II espoused a brand of pragmatism that accepted the lessening of civil liberties in order to maintain the status quo and fight Communism.

[8]The most serious accusation against Sinclair was made by the Dies Committee in 1938. Sinclair wrote that he had never been a communist. He said he believed that "the change from private competitive or monopoly ownership to public and cooperative ownership can be brought about peaceably and gradually under our present Constitution" (Affidavit 2).

Works Cited

Blinderman, Abraham. "Upton Sinclair at Ninety." *Christian Century* 85 (1968): 1200-03. Rpt. in *Critics on Upton Sinclair: Readings in Literary Criticism*. Coral Gables: U of Miami P, 1975. 81-86.

Bloodworth, William Jr. *Upton Sinclair*. Boston: G.K. Hall, 1977.

Bracher, Karl Dietrich. *The German Dictatorship: The Origins, Structure, and Effects of National Socialism*. Trans. Jean Steinberg. New York: Praeger, 1970.

Dembo, L.S. "The Socialist and Socialite Heroes of Upton Sinclair." *Toward a New American Literary History: Essays in Honor of Arlin Turner*. Ed. Louis J. Budd, Edwin H. Cady, and Carl L. Anderson. Durham: Duke UP, 1980. 164-80.

Harris, Leon. *Upton Sinclair: American Rebel*. New York: Crowell, 1975.

Mookerjee, R.N. "Contemporary History as Novel: The Lanny Budd Series." *Art for Social Justice: The Major Novels of Upton Sinclair*. Metuchen: Scarecrow, 1988. 116-22.

Putt, S. Gorley. "World Without End: Upton Sinclair and Lanny Budd." *Scholars of the Heart: Essays in Criticism*. London: Faber & Faber, 1962. 87-109.

Sinclair, Upton. Affidavit to Dies Committee. December 1938. Upton Sinclair Collection. Lilly Library, Indiana University, Bloomington, Indiana.

——— *The Autobiography of Upton Sinclair*. New York: Harcourt, 1962.

——— *Between Two Worlds*. New York: Viking, 1941.

——— *Dragon's Teeth*. New York: Viking, 1942.

——— *I, Candidate for Governor: And How I Got Licked*. Pasadena: Upton Sinclair, 1934.

——— Letter to Nathan Greenberg. December 5, 1941. Upton Sinclair Collection. Lilly Library, Indiana University, Bloomington, Indiana.

——— Letter to James Henle. January 26, 1939. Upton Sinclair Collection. Lilly Library, Indiana University, Bloomington, Indiana.

——— Letter to Otis Peabody Swift. March 7, 1939. Upton Sinclair Collection. Lilly Library, Indiana University, Bloomington, Indiana.

——— *Letters to Judd*. Pasadena: Upton Sinclair, 1926. Rpt. in *An Upton Sinclair Anthology*. Los Angeles: Upton Sinclair, 1934.

——— *My Lifetime in Letters*. Columbia: U of Missouri P, 1960.

——— *O Shepherd, Speak!* New York: Viking, 1949.

——— *Presidential Agent*. New York: Viking, 1944.

——— *Wide Is the Gate*. New York: Viking, 1943.

——— *World's End*. New York: Viking, 1941.

Yoder, Jon A. "Upton Sinclair, Lanny, and the Liberals." *Modern Fiction Studies* 20 (1974-1975): 483-504.

Telling the Truth:
Women Spy Narratives
of the Second World War

Mary Anne Schofield

Spying is a strange business, the way in which it grips those engaged in it. It is like getting hooked on a drug. The commitment becomes total, the dedication complete.

(Code Name Marianne 150)

In July 1940, with Great Britain the only remaining force standing against Nazi domination, Winston Churchill, almost in desperation, ordered his secret service, the Special Operations Executive,[1] to "set Europe ablaze" (Gleeson 12). Churchill called for a romantic, chivalric, almost religious ethos of self-sacrifice from his people; they responded and, indeed, fires were set throughout the European continent. The French branch of the S.O.E., responsible for so much of the "fire-setting," contained a number of young British women who played an instrumental role in this national conflagration effort. These women found themselves in a proverbial no-man's land: alienated because of their sex, women in a man's war. Many of them, together with their sister spies in other countries, have recorded their own experiences during this period or have had their tales told for them. Partaking in what Richard Slotkin calls "mythogenesis," these narratives explore the heroic myth-making of ordinary females into larger-than-life super women. In doing so, these accounts examine not only the boundaries of espionage but also the limits of spy narratology.

It has only been during the last twenty years that the stories of female spies during World War II have been truthfully told. For more than a generation after the end of the war, most portraits of women agents were highly romanticized, filled with a Churchill-esque language that painted an unreal picture of them and their activities. Authored almost exclusively by men, these biographies too often marginalized their heroines, boxing them into cells of unreality. Lise de Baissac accurately summarizes this imprisoning rhetoric:

Films and novels have made people think of an agent's work as glamorous. But believe me, our job was, above all, sheer hard work. What we needed was cold-blooded efficiency for long weary months rather than any burst of heroism. Looking back I find my strongest emotion was acute loneliness—the loneliness of a secret life.

(Gleeson 91)

Her observation encapsulates the theme of the spy life and highlights the major tropes used in espionage accounts. One never told one's tale; one never scripted one's life. Only in the rarest of moments, and then with careful framing and coding of the narrative in terms of "another self" so as not to disrupt the guise of the "secret" life, could the tale be told.

This multiplicity of selves was not recognized by the early male writers. Women agents were, literally and metaphorically, held behind and before a curtain of espionage. Today, thankfully, that has changed, as many women have begun to look more closely at their own or their fellow women's experiences. The truth is finally being told.

Spy accounts featuring World War II female spies have, through the years, been presented in three different ways: 1) those written by men about women—a framed narrative cast in phallocentric language that casts the female spy in a liminal position, making her into a romance heroine controlled by male heroic rhetoric; 2) those narratives created by other women about the female spies that foreground the female experience of the war and make problematic the position of the female in the men's war through both their own narrative voice and through the subject of the account; and 3) finally, those narrated by the spy herself that script a meta-text of the woman *at* and *in* the war, validating the gylanic vision.[2] The spy and her account is a heuristic text that needs to be reexamined in order to place it and her in the infrastructure of the Second World War.

*   *   *   *   *

Silence. The absence of words. The prime tool and best asset of the female and of the spy. Edita Katona, in her memoir, *Code Name Marianne*, remarks early on: "I had learned enough about espionage to know the value of silence" (41). Spying. Espionage. From the French: to discern. The very trade is concerned with meanings, with words and the value of these words. Words cannot be spoken directly; significance is eschewed; information must be coded to be transmitted. Words are the tools of the war. And women through their silence and skill were intimately involved in this word war. Elizabeth Reynolds, for example, was able to "memorize a message and repeat it verbatim so that she had no need to carry scraps of paper nor, as some couriers did, to write the message on obscure parts of their bodies" (Gleeson 56). For the agent, especially the female agent, the entire body becomes the war text and it is this body, inscribed *with* text and *as* text, breaking the long-imposed silence on women agents that is the subject of this investigation.

At first, the majority of published spy accounts were those of men written by men. Though figures validate the high numbers of women involved in the silent, shadow war,[3] these figures did not until recently translate into a breaking of the silence surrounding the female spy. Their story was, instead, pre-empted by the male war machine. Now with the publication of many new explosive texts written by women about themselves and others, it is, at last, possible to read feminine texts that are, as Helene Cixous writes, "subversive...volcanic-...[that] smash everything...shatter the framework of institutions...blow up the law" (*New French Feminisms* 258).

These spy accounts are meta-texts of women in war. These accounts, considered as a whole, form an important *bildungsroman* for the understanding of the female position in this watershed in women's history.[4] They allow us to examine the patriarchal language and to watch, years later, women finding a voice within this resisting rhetoric. (Much like Eisler's "cultural transformation" theory, we watch a movement from male domination to female actualization.) They reify the gaze and permit a detailed examination of the mirror and who or whom is reflected.[5] These narratives can be seen as "ecstatic espionage" accounts of women writers of the Second World War, texts which expropriate the male language and invent a "terrorist text" (Yaeger 3) of their own telling. These are women who seize words and explore orality, incorporating a *jouissance* in their texts, celebrating themselves, their sexuality and their identity. In contrast to the mythic, stylized, romantic heroine created by the male in his rendition of female spies, the accounts by women disrupt this stereotypic portrayal, unscramble it and present a decoded female view of the war and the world.

The first attempts to tell the story of female spies were, without exception, viewed exclusively through the eyes of men. They created heroines in their own image or not at all. R.J. Minney's account of Violette Bushell Szabo's life, *Carve her Name with Pride*, is, perhaps, the best example. Minney turns Violette Szabo into a romance heroine. In his attempt both to romanticize and mythologize Szabo, Minney's tone is condescending. "Though essentially feminine, there was something gallant, debonair and quite genuine about her" (86), he notes with a subconscious nod of male superiority. Yet, even here, he cannot conceive of her seriously. "Did she dream of venturing into the midst of some imagined enemy, vamping some exalted statesman with her beautiful eyes and hiding important documents in her corsage?" (25) he wonders aloud. Unable to grasp the obvious paradox of the female spy, he can only deal with her if he remains dominant, and she muted.[6]

H. Montgomery Hyde's *Cynthia* is a similar appropriation of the female self. He is unable to understand what he calls the "pacing tiger" inside her (4). Cynthia, "the spy who changed the course of the war," has her heroic exploits camouflaged, and she becomes little more than a sex machine in Hyde's narrative. Corresponding to the view so many male authors shared about female spies, Cynthia is seen, almost simplistically, as a *femme fatale*. She uses sex and liquor (79) to extort any material she wants. "I let him make love to me as often as he wanted, since this guaranteed the smooth flow of the political information I needed" (80). When she becomes a member of British Intelligence, her assignment, again expressed in sexual terms, is "to penetrate the Vichy French Embassy in Washington and to purloin its top secrets" (123). In Hyde's view, she has but one way open to her to accomplish her mission: sex.

The question which faced Cynthia was simple. It was quite plain where this conduct was leading, and she had to decide whether to prolong the wooing with the risk that Charles might lose interest or to succomb quickly and perhaps give the impression that she was a promiscuous woman ready for any casual sexual encounter. Either way she might lose her quarry. In the end, she decided that speed was the better policy. (128-29)

In the penultimate scene and the *coup de grace* of her espionage career (one can almost feel Hyde salivating as he writes), Cynthia uses intercourse as a decoy to break into the Embassy and, totally naked, steal the sought-after secret documents (153-54).

Not all male writers, however, were so masculine-thinking in portrayals of their heroines. In marked contrast to Minney's account of Violette Szabo and Hyde's narrative of Cynthia is Russell Braddon's book, *Nancy Wake*. The condescension evident in Minney's book is not found here. There is also very little attempt at romanticizing and mythologizing the subject. Braddon, in fact, is caught between his dominant voice and her muted, though irrepressible, self. What Braddon writes is a very paradoxical account, for he is unable to reconcile Nancy's multiple selves. Early on, he notes: "She's a rebel, she's always laughing and she's very, very feminine" (11). It is this duality of woman and warrior that he does not know how to handle. Even towards the end of the account, Braddon still finds Nancy a cross between "the guerilla chieftain" and "the houseproud hostess" (189).

Unfortunately for Braddon, but fortunately for readers of his text, his story is not dependent upon his ability to present it. He is only the surface narrator. Nancy's story ultimately takes over, thus making Braddon a mere amanuensis. The book is about Nancy's war, and it a strictly feminine one. Wake, at first, was extremely reticent to tell her story. Marginalized so long that she is unable to talk directly, her account grows "painfully and modestly" (218). Since she had "no notes or diaries" (218), the scenes had to be verbally and vividly recalled. "I'm glad I was there. I'm glad I did what I did. I hate wars and violence but, if they come, then I don't see why we women should just wave our men a proud goodbye and then knit them balaclavas" (220). So knitting needles were discarded in favor of guns, patterns in favor of espionage.

Nancy tells Braddon: "Don't you dare...write me one of those miserable war books full of horror. *My* war was full of laughter and people I loved" (219). It was also

a woman's war.... The most feminine race in the world [these daughters of France] were quick to sense that peculiar quality of loneliness which afflicts all soldiers away from home. The Germans they managed to make feel lonelier than any other Army has ever felt before. Also, being French as well as women, they had the capacity to taunt like navvies, to be even more arrogant than the Nazis themselves and—if the need arose— to kill quite ruthlessly. Theirs was an attitude of magnificent defiance and convinced superiority. They were frivolous, cunning, hostile, courageous and utterly lacking in any discretion. (59)

Wake and her narrative will not be trivialized. Her code name, "Witch" (107), is appropriate. It is this attitude of "magnificent defiance and convinced superiority" (59) that defines her. Though Braddon repeatedly tries to stereotype her femininity, at the end he is unsuccessful. Nancy Wake is, on more than one occasion, suddenly transformed into an avenging Fury:

Nancy sprang to her feet at once, infuriated by this display of cowardice, and bellowed after them. Rage had an extraordinary effect upon her.... [H]er complexion paled whilst her eyes flared with green fury, her features tautened into porcelain smoothness and her body straightened until she achieved a posture of statuesque fury. Anger and danger seemed to stimulate her. There was no fear in her face nor in her mind. Rather her brain worked with the speed and smoothness of skates on ice and her casual acceptance of authority crystallized into a full-blooded instinct to command and to lead.... [S]he stood there, feet apart, hands on hips, head flung back and surveyed her fleeing men. Then, like a whip, lashing them through the forest trees and ringing out savagely even above the sound of machine-gun fire, her voice pursued them. (164)

Other furies are born and cry out to be heard above the din of the men's war and over the rhetoric of the male story teller. Two of the best biographical accounts, both written by women who become intimately involved in their subjects' lives as they write, are those of Elizabeth Nicholas's *Death Be Not Proud* and Madeleine Masson's *Christine*.

Death Be Not Proud is the finest example of how one woman tries to find a female voice in order to vindicate all the women spies who did not have a voice. It is a journal of "angst" for the narrator. In it she records not only the life and times of seven women agents (Diana Rowden, Vera Leigh, Andree Borrell, Madeleine Damerment, Eliane Plewman, Yolande Beekman and Sonia Olschanesky),[7] but also her own descent and ascent to self knowledge. "For better or worse, I wanted the book to stand as it was written to be an honest account of a quest" for truth, Nicholas writes (14). In trying to tell her story, Nicholas notes her frustration at the lack of available evidence about her women subjects:

Every obstacle is now placed in the way of those who wish to write of the unlucky ones— those who lost their lives when serving with French Section, S.O.E.: those whose story, if published, would be painted in more somber colours. The seven women of this book fall into that category. I must also make it clear that it has proved impossible to reconstruct the story of each one of them in a manner that bears any relation to coherence or continuity. In spite of all my efforts, I have been quite unable to collect more than a fragment of the story of each; and I have been determined not to reconstruct in my own imagination the missing elements. I have, therefore, told each bit of the story as I myself uncovered it. (19-20)

Her entire book becomes a quest—for herself and the seven women. This becomes a story that Nicholas herself must tell:

Too much, I thought, was being forgotten too quickly; to forgive was one thing; to forget another. And we in Britain had much less to forgive than some people, for we had never been occupied by the Germans. This immunity we owed to those who had fought for us, above all, to those who had died. (33)

In fulfilling her quest, Nicholas seeks to untangle the threads that made up these seven women's lives, exploring the web that joined them together. Almost immediately, she realizes that it would never do to be single-minded: "Clearly, my orientation was entirely wrong; I did not begin to understand France, or the war, or the Resistance. I was in an element beyond my comprehension"

(128). The various stories, like the complexities of the coded radio messages these women sent during the war, were not as simple as they first appeared. To find the truth in the muted stories of these women spies required working meticulously back through the dominant male accounts of their lives. Doing so, however, was disquieting but rewarding. Soon Nicholas realized

I...had removed once and for all the role of the agent from the realms of cops and robbers and had revealed it for what it was: a sad journey through a territory of fear and darkness and a great loneliness. (39)

She continues:

I was painfully innocent in those days. What I had seen as a clear, uncomplicated story of valour and action suddenly became immensely devious, a cess pit of treachery, confusion and double dealing. (43)

When, for instance, she visits the Juif house where one of her heroines, Diana Rowden, had been arrested, Nicholas is confronted with her own spectre of reality and illusion. She sees the scars left by the bullets; she is handed a cup of coffee by the same Madame Juif "who had seen it done... who had stood, backed against the wall, denying she knew anything" (144). Nicholas confronts this demon:

This was an adjustment not easy to make; not for me, for whom clandestine war was something fought on alien soil. It was a drama one read books about, saw filmed on a screen, played on a stage; it was not easy to accept reality. (144)

Nicholas also found what was clearly a male conspiracy of silence.

I had also discovered, from Mrs. Rowden herself, that she knew nothing whatsoever of Diana's work in the field, or the circumstances of her arrest. I felt then—and this was an emotion I was to feel again many times as my quest proceeded—that it was shocking that I, in a few weeks and without any official backing or approval, had been able to uncover information that had been withheld from the next of kin of those who died. (56)

In other words, Nicholas indulges in her own bit of espionage as she decodes the facts and tells the truth about these agents. They chose silence (102-103); she chooses to speak.

As she recreates Diana's journey, Nicholas remarks:

It is not within my powers to put in words the emotions of that September journey through France.... The desperate adventures set coldly in print became quick, and the words on paper reality.... I had recreated, in imagination, the events I had read about; when faced with reality, the tidy little fantasies were brushed away, and tragedy was no longer words in a book, but real and strong and pricking. (152-53)

The truth means that Nicholas, like the women spies, learns to gaze directly into the glass, her glance not faltering. "It was as though I had looked through a looking glass and seen not a reflected picture but a vision true and undistorted"

(152). Her quest is complete; her truth as reporter and writer has been validated. She can speak out:

> The story as I now knew it was utterly different from the one I had thought to discover; it bore no relation to the chapters of a Good Girls' Book of Golden Deeds. The deeds were, God knows, golden; but the background was too often grey and shoddy and without honour. I could have wished that the shell had remained uncracked, that the glossy picture of success and subtlety had remained untarnished. One thought only comforted me, that no tarnish could ever touch the reflections left by those women who had died.... For them, then, the sacrifice; for us, the promised fruits of a victory they helped to win. (236)

Madeliene Masson also writes a double helix account that not only uncovers the real story of the famous Christine Granville (note subtitle: *A Search for Christine Granville*), but, in the process, discovers her own self and her role as a storyteller of women's tales. The entire account is prefaced by a 38-page introduction in which Masson writes her own story; she adopts Christine as a symbol of her own lost and shining youth (xxv). Ostensibly though, Masson writes, like Nicholas, because nearly all the material previously printed about Granville was wrong. "The most blatant of these inaccuracies is contained in a piece about Christine recently published in an *Encyclopedia of Espionage*. [Though] she, herself, had done a laborious and a thorough job of 'covering her tracks,'" (xxxv) numerous male writers had distorted her life and structured a "Christine myth" around her. The reasons for this, Masson soon discovered, were obvious.

> Those who did not know her well...were irritated by the impact she had on most men; by her antinomian attitude to conventional rules and regulations, and by her disinclination to be pressed into an ordinary mold. Thus they made it their business to distort even the most platonic of her friendships, so that finally a whole area of her life has been shadowed by a question mark. (131)

A sexual myth that viewed Christine as a blatant object of free love was created.[8]

Masson writes, therefore, to invalidate this war text while presenting the real one. And the "real" one is dependent upon the female agent herself. The overt sexuality so strongly stressed in male-written biographies, though obviously present, becomes minor in Masson's compelling portrait. As a woman, Christine was a consummate actress and much of her success could be traced to her skill in that area.

> When necessary, she could get into the skin of the part she was playing. During the time she was in the Italian Alps, she had decided that her role would be that of a naive and trusting peasant girl. Twice she was caught by the Germans, but so convincing was her act that they let her go. (199)

Masson succeeds where others failed because she becomes Christine in this search for herself and for the woman's voice.

Jean Overton Fuller's *Madeleine. The Story of Noor Inayat Khan* is also all too painfully true. "I have felt my only course to be to present the fragments constituted by the evidence of the different witnesses *without any comment on my own and without any attempt to forge links"* (10) (emphasis added). Fuller records her own fragmented, authorial voice while telling of a shattered, misplaced woman who is at home in no country, and yet invaluable to all allied countries during the war. Far from being "a woman who made love to men and [who] drew their secrets out of them," Khan was never, Fuller stresses, "that sort of spy" (182). In the end, however, it did not matter. Madelaine's importance to the Allied side could not save her. Arrested by the Gestapo, she was eventually taken to Dachau and executed. Fuller can say no more—only to hope that her version has countered the stereotypical male, sex-spy version so frequently seen.

Of all the stories of female spies told by women, Roxanne Pitt's account, *The Courage of Fear*, is the closest to the proverbial one that everyone thinks is the "true" spy account. She clearly defines the use and misuse of sex in the field (90-91, 133, 136, 158) as well as "romance"; indeed, her account is dogged by masculine advances that she does not want and does not understand. Ultimately, she uses romance as one of her many covers. And yet, despite the sexual overtones, her entire account is written to expose, rather than glorify, the glamor of spying.

Of those few women who have been able to come to grips with their own lives through insightful autobiographical studies, few are as perceptive as Josephine Butler. Her *Churchill's Secret Agent* presents a different, more affirmative image of a woman who served as a spy throughout the war years. The only feminine member of Churchill's Secret Circle, "Jay Bee," unlike all the other spies previously discussed, was not a part of the S.O.E., an organization whose purpose she considered "subversive" and whose work "involved destruction and possibly killing," (24) all of which she was glad to avoid. Her account of her activities is forthright because, from the beginning, Butler knew who she was. Her self is clearly defined:

My experiences in the war have taught me much. From brutality I learnt mercy; from starvation and want I learnt generosity; from failure and humiliation I learnt leadership and a great faith in God and in my fellow man. Above all I learnt that much as I appreciate the freedom of communication through books and newspapers and the wonders of radio and television, the best communication is between people. (199-200)

Edita Katona's *Code Name Marianne* is another strong, articulate autobiography that forthrightly debunks the romantic heroine myth found in such accounts as Minney or the sexual spy/Mata Hari tradition of Hyde. She sees, instead, the reality of spying.

In every mission I adopted the same attitude of mind. It was a thread running through them all. I just got on with it, and did not allow myself to think. If anybody had stopped me and asked me what I was doing I would have given the first answer that came into my head. Whatever it was it would sound more natural—and therefore more innocent— than anything, however clever, which I had prepared in advance. To think of what might or might not happen would have undermined my confidence and doubts would have nibbled away at me like a cancer. The mental state I deliberately created was like that of a sleepwalker. I did everything in a kind of dream, determined not to wake up until the mission was over. If sleep-walkers are suddenly awakened, they fall down. (59)

Katona does not fall. As spy and as autobiographer, she gladly looks into the mirror that chronicles her life, and she is not afraid to return the gaze and write what she sees.

Helene de Champlain's *The Secret War of Helene de Champlain*, an account similar to Katona's but perhaps even stronger, breaks the silence and reveals the reality of the spy's life, unmasking the supposed romance and glamour. Her account is one of the most explicit. She views her years as a spy as always verging on violation, on rape. Hers is not the supposed sexuality of Mata Hari but, instead, a sex that is detrimental and easily exploitable. As she writes:

I rushed to the nearest shelter, the Jasmin metro station.... In the distance I could hear the thump and rumble of explosions.... I felt a rough hand reach beneath my skirt and move upward between my thighs. Protest was useless. I pushed my way deeper into the crowd. (5)

She actually pushes herself right into the Germans, and she is arrested as she comes out of the shelter (6). She is searched; "he grinned, running his hands over my body in search of weapons. He stopped at my breasts. The man palpated, giving appreciative groans" (9), and then attacked her (10) when she was placed in a cell.

Sexual tropes interlace the entire narrative: rape, faked miscarriages (11), even hiding in the maternity wing of a local hospital to escape detection. When Katona works at the headquarters of the Milice, she rifles the files. Taking cards of suspects, she "would tear them up, put the pieces in my bra, and nonchalantly go to the bathroom" (61).

Such nonchalance was a highly practiced pose. The reality is uncovered as she repeatedly describes rapes, murders. Such visions have their price. "It is strange...how war can make a mercenary of a religious, gentle-mannered girl! Can make her kill, in the hope of eliminating the wickedness of others" (247). Like Nancy Wake, Helene de Champlain has been transformed into a fury; "the thrill and stimulation I experienced from undertaking a mission could be compared to the craving of an addict" (225).

Yet it is an addiction, as all these accounts testify, that produces not dependency but, instead, independent, spirited, self-sufficient young women. Unlike the sexually active, romance heroine of male accounts of female spies, women such as Katona all recount a quest toward maturation. They learn not to be commodified as the object of the gaze but instead to return it.

Once the woman has learned to meet the level glance of men, this gaze is directed inwards. It is this which produces the most honest accounts, anatomies of self exploration. During the height of the war, spies such as those in Muriel Sparks' *Hothouse by the East River* found it necessary to utilize a device known to all as the "scrambler" to mask the frequent radio messages they sent to other agents throughout Europe. The instrument emitted "jangling caterwauls" and a "harrowing noise," (63) which made listening in to the messages virtually impossible. Trained agents, however, soon learned to listen past the noise, to unscramble it and pass on valuable information to the Allied side.

So, too, it can be argued, must authors de-scramble the numerous accounts of women agents during the Second World War. Women who were for so long denied a real voice have finally been given the chance to be seen with honesty and understanding. The silence has been broken, the Churchill-esque rhetoric exposed. The patriarchal language of men such as Minney and Hyde has been undercut, replaced by the portraits of a Masson, a Katona or a Pitt. As the rupture between the two almost diametrically different pictures widens, women agents have been forced to look at themselves honestly. No longer are they marginalized. "The snare of silence," to quote Cixous, has finally been broken (*New French Feminisms* 251). The gaze returns a vision of mature women who can no longer be seduced either before or behind a curtain of espionage.

Notes

[1]Madeleine Masson writes of the S.O.E.: "The task of the S.O.E., its *only* task, was to contribute to the eventual defeat of Hitler's Germany by carrying out para-military operations in enemy-occupied territories by direct intervention and/or support of resistance fighters amongst the nationals of the countries concerned. S.O.E. was wholly non-political" (143).

[2]Riane Eisler (*The Chalice and the Blade*) coins the word *gylany* "to describe the real alternative to a system based on the ranking of half of humanity over the other" (105). It is a world view of partnership rather than domination, of actualization powers rather than force.

[3]See, for example, Gleeson, Cookridge or Michel.

[4]See Joan W. Scott, "Rewriting History," in *Behind the Lines: Gender and the Two World Wars* (New Haven: Yale UP, 1987) 19-31.

[5]See Jean B. Elstain.

[6]A film, directed by Lewis Gilbert starring Virginia McKenna, Paul Scofield and Jack Warner was produced in 1958. Based closely on Minney's account, it perpetuates the overwhelmingly masculine, "stiff upper-lip," gaze at Violette's life.

[7]None of the women studied by Nicholas, indeed, none of the spies examined in this study, appear in Ronald Seth's supposedly definitive *Encyclopedia of Espionage*.

[8]See Selwyn Jepson's comments on 149 as one glaring example.

Works Cited

Braddon, Russell. *Nancy Wake*. London: Pan Books, 1958.

Butler, Josephine. *Churchill's Secret Agent*. London: Blaketon-Hall, 1983.

Champlain, Helene de. *The Secret War of Helene de Champlain*. London: W.H. Allen, 1980.

Cookridge, E.H. *They Came From the Sky*. New York: Thomas Y. Crowell, 1965.

Eisler, Riane. *The Chalice and the Blade*. New York: Harper & Row, 1988.

Elstain, Jean B. "Women as Mirror and Other: Toward a Theory of Women, War, and Feminism," *Humanities in Society* 5 (1982): 29-44.

Fuller, Jean Overton. *Madeleine, the Story of Noor Inayat Khan*. London: Victor Gollancz, 1952.

Gleeson, James. *They Feared No Evil. The Women Agents of Britain's Secret Armies 1939-45*. London: Robert Hale, 1976.

Higonnet, Margaret and Jane Jenson (eds.) *Behind the Lines. Gender and the Two World Wars*. New Haven: Yale UP, 1987.

Hyde, H. Montgomery. *Cynthia, The Spy Who Changed the Course of the War*. London: Hamish Hamilton, 1966.

Katona, Edita. *Code-Name Marianne*. New York: David McKay, 1976.

Marks, Elaine and Isabelle de Courtivron (eds.) *New French Feminisms*. New York: Schocken Books, 1980.

Masson, Madeleine. *Christine*. London: Hamish Hamilton, 1975.

Michel, Henri. *The Shadow War*. New York: Harper & Row, 1972.

Minney, R.J. *Carve Her Name With Pride*. London: Pan Books, 1956.

Nicholas, Elizabeth. *Death Be Not Proud*. London: Cresset, 1958.

Pitt, Roxanne. *The Courage of Fear*. New York: Duell, Sloan and Pearce, 1957.

Seth, Ronald. *Encyclopedia of Espionage*. Garden City, NY: Doubleday, 1972.

Showalter, Elaine (ed.) *The New Feminist Criticism*. New York: Pantheon, 1985.

Yaeger, Patricia. *Honey-Mad Women*. New York: Columbia UP, 1988.

Women's War Stories:
The Legacy of South Pacific Internment

Lynn Z. Bloom

You are going to write 'The Life and Thoughts of an Internee' for me, Colonel Suga ordered Agnes Newton Keith, interned as a civilian prisoner of war in 1943 in Kuching, Borneo, with her three-year-old son. 'You shall write a book for *me*, and I shall censor it.'

I said, 'If you order me to write, I must write. But you cannot order me what to say.'

'All right! All right! All right! All right!'...

So I wrote...a story submitted to Suga at given intervals. I complained persistently of wrongs and mistreatments. I constantly asked for better food and less work. I said that I believed trouble between our races was based on misunderstanding, and that I hoped for tolerance and sympathy in time to come, between our peoples....

But there was another story I wrote in the smallest possible handwriting, on the backs of labels...on the margins of old newspapers.... I stuffed George's toys with these notes...I buried them in tins under the barrack.... In time I lost everything with writing on it...passport, wedding lines...everything except my notes.

From these notes I have reconstructed the true story of my captivity. This is not the story I wrote at Suga's command, it is my story (xiii-xv).

Thus Keith begins *Three Came Home*, the most popular of any woman's account of her internment experiences in World War II, with a storyteller's story that is typical of the women's South Pacific internment narratives to be discussed here. These works share a perspective, values and clandestine method of composition and concealment of the manuscript. In the postwar reconstruction of these autobiographical accounts, their authors, good storytellers all, are transformed from ordinary civilians into wartime heroines, moral or romantic.

War makes storytellers of women whose narrative prowess may have been expended in peacetime on Biblical parables and bedtime stories. The profundity of the cataclysmic, watershed experience of being interned away from their native land during wartime endows their lives with a significance that they are impelled to explain to those who remained, more or less safely, at home. Through writing these stories, they can ensure that they will leave a legacy for their descendants— particularly important for women whose worldly goods were confiscated, destroyed, looted or lost during battle. When not even a prewar photograph, letter or document remains, what is in the human heart and memory must find expression or die.

Like Coleridge's Ancient Mariner, those women who have attained a moral vision tell their stories to witness. Others write to justify unusual actions, expeditious or impulsive, in the alien context of war. In all cases, these narrators speak in a major rather than a minor key, for they have not only survived but have triumphed over adversity. Their stories strive to interpret and preserve the human significance of war rather than its military meaning. Although the women whose stories analyzed here participate in the same wars as men, their stories are very different.

The ensuing analysis will focus on four women's stories of internment throughout World War II in Japanese camps in the Philippines—Keith's *Three Came Home*; Natalie Crouter's *Forbidden Diary*; Margaret Sams's *Forbidden Family*; and Fern Harrington Miles's *Captive Community*. That the first three were commercially published and that Miles's, though self-published, has been made the major selection of a religious book club—is external validation of their vision and their voice, since most private wartime accounts remain unpublished.[1]

The Authors and Their Context

All four of these authors were white, middle-class American women; all except Miles were married to men working in the South Pacific in the 1930s. Keith had lived since 1934 in Sandakan, North Borneo, with her English husband, the Director of Agriculture there. In 1939, she published an award-winning account of her experiences, *Land Below the Wind*. Radical Bostonian Natalie Crouter had resided in Baguio, the Philippines' idyllic mountain-ringed summer capital, since her marriage in 1927 to businessman Jerry Crouter, devoting her considerable energy to rearing their two children and to community and liberal causes. In 1936, Margaret Sams traveled from California to marry her hometown boyfriend, Bob Sherk, who was working as a mining engineer at Nyac, Luzon. Attracted by the lure of romance, adventure and a scale of living that far exceeded their options in Depression-ridden America, they quickly settled in and had a child, David. Miles, then Fern Harrington, a Missourian, was a newly minted Southern Baptist missionary assigned to China shortly before the Japanese invasion necessitated the removal of all Americans. So, after only three days of language study in Beijing, her missionary group was transferred to the Philippines, to be protected by Corregidor's "impregnable fortress."

All the women, as civilians, were captured early in 1942 and remained in internment until the Pacific islands were liberated in the spring of 1945. Miles and the Crouter family spent most of the war in Baguio, a camp of 500 American and British (nearly one-third were missionaries, trapped as Miles was) on the site of former U.S. Army Camp Holmes. For the first few months of the war, the Keiths were held in adjacent, sex-segregated camps of fewer than fifty people in Berhala, Borneo, before Keith and her young son, George, were transferred to another small camp in Kuching. She could be with her husband only on Christmas, for half an hour: "Always there was the feeling that danger, destruction, death would strike before we met again" (229). Margaret Sams saw her husband for the last time on New Year's Eve, 1942, when he left for "a little mopping-up" on Bataan. She learned later that he had survived the Bataan Death March only to be imprisoned in notorious Cabanatuan; he died, skin and bones, of dysentery shortly before the war's end. She and David were interned, first in Manila's 5000-person Santo Tomás (on the campus of Santo Tomás University), and during 1944-45 in Los Banõs, a former agricultural school half that size.

As victims of circumstance, these women had no initiative or control over events external to the camps. As women in camps governed essentially by men, whether Japanese military or American and British civilians, they did not have much control over internal events either; in the Baguio camp, for instance, women were disenfranchised, as a result of male politicking, for the first year of the war. Nevertheless, the authors of these works had to function as their own advocates within the regimented structure of camp life because, except for Crouter's husband, no one else was available to do it for them.[2]

Thus, keeping a diary, though strictly forbidden and punishable by death, became a way for these women to gain some measure of freedom and independence in confinement. By taking the risk to write, they could control not only their self-expression but could regain control of the self otherwise submerged in group identity. The process of writing about their experiences endowed the authors with a personhood, a character they recognized in themselves but that few others saw. Booklovers all, they became almost by accident (except for Keith, the only professional author among them) the authors of books-in-progress. As they wrote, they created themselves the heroines of their own stories, which ultimately became subject to the postwar revision that makes a good war story even better—more focused, more dramatic, more dangerous, and its heroine ever more a woman of courage.

Plot, Point of View, and Character Development

These are good stories, intrinsically interesting tales well-told. Their basic plot structure follows, as Egan observes in *Patterns of Experience in Autobiography*, an age-old narrative pattern that "begins in equilibrium, is disturbed by disequilibrium, and moves into a new equilibrium." This structure, common to myth, folklore, confession and captivity narratives, describes a pattern of "separation, initiation, and return" (41). Thus women's war stories begin briefly, establishing an orderly prewar context. But the onset of war makes chaos of the peaceable kingdom, which is replaced by the daily, occasionally arrhythmic heartbeat of life in internment camp, a tenuous equilibrium. The story's long midsection could be graphed as a fever chart with a sharp escalation just before the American troops arrive to break the fever and bring a return to peace. These stories do not concentrate on the military events of the war itself, for the most part waged out of sight though always throbbing in the background. They focus instead on two sorts of immediate events within the camps—aspects of daily life and the storyteller's own psychological development.

At the outset, the narrators are truly strangers in a strange land, for the camps sprang up overnight, like toadstools. Neither captors nor captives know how to behave, for no one can prepare in advance for an unimaginable experience. Although war is conceived of in terms of men, the camps are bursting with women, children, babies—and more expected. What will they eat? Can they get milk, eggs, vitamins, bread for their children? Where will they sleep, bathe, use the toilet? What will they use for soap (Crouter laments, "Hayakawa says we can have no more soap—only ashes," 109), toilet paper, diapers? Both sides are inventing a new culture as they go along, based on their respective peacetime frames of reference; when the norms of civilian culture don't fit, they have to be modified. As the camps take on a culture of their own, the characters perforce become intimates, symbolized by acquiring a camp vocabulary ("comingling," "cubicilizing," "submarine coffee") that requires translation for external readers. Miles interprets this acculturation:

Camp life which had seemed so abnormal and unbearable at first, had gradually become normal and satisfying in many ways. It had become normal to go to bed before lights out at 9:30; to sleep under a mosquito net on a hard bed in a room full of people...to stand in line three times a day for meals; to drink out of a tin can instead of a glass. Sometimes it was difficult even to imagine what life was like before internment. (76)

Thus these women tell their stories from a new set of multiple split perspectives: American/Japanese, captive/captor, "inside"/"outside," private household/ public camp, prewar/wartime/postwar, and, especially, innocence/experience. From this complex of perspectives, they interpret everything. Crouter maintains that internment has been invaluable for her children, whose newly developed "feeling and imagination for other people's sufferings" will enable them to "understand slums, poverty, malnutrition...more than they ever could by reading it. We have no regrets," she writes, "at keeping them with us even though their teeth, eyes, bones may need a lot of rebuilding. There is no gain without some loss and they have other gains which cannot be taken away from them. So with their parents" (376).

The repetitive, monotonous routine of daily life forms a backdrop for the dramas large and small that make a compelling story more in Jane Austen's intimate social mode than in the transcontinental sweep of *War and Peace*. As will become apparent in the analysis of themes in the next section, these daily dramas consist of the narrator's small but significant triumphs of everyday living— securing extra food, solving problems of housekeeping or childrearing, recovering from illness, feeling appreciated or attractive, besting an intramural antagonist. Throughout most of the war, these positive features balance the negatives— insufficient food, overcrowding, lack of privacy, illness, mud and rain and the rivalries and jealousies exacerbated thereby. In all accounts, the narrative emphasis changes near the war's end as the continual, nagging hunger becomes acute and the internees are on the verge of death by starvation and related diseases. Powerless to save themselves, or, even worse, their children, the narrators must depend for survival on the *deus ex machina*, the U.S. Army, Navy and Marines, which both effect and impose a climax.

The major action in these women's war stories is intimately involved with the changes in and development of their character as a consequence of their wartime experiences. Their stories focus, explicitly and implicitly, on the authors' maturation as women, lovers, mothers, human beings. They are not the same people at the war's end as they were at the beginning, and they will never be the same. The worsening of the war provides the opportunity for these women to grow in moral stature, independence, strength of character, courage and force of will, simply in the course of survival. They do not merely endure, they prevail, through their emotional hardiness, resilience and resourcefulness. In acknowledging her chronic malaria, Keith asserts, with ironic good cheer: "I gained perfect confidence in myself. I knew that if I practised long enough I could live on air, with a pinch of salt. But the time came when I didn't have the salt." She adds: "I learned that it isn't the outward circumstances which determine what one can endure, but something in oneself which either breaks, or stays intact, under strain. It isn't the difference in strain, it's the difference in tensile strength of people" (61-62).

Oddly enough, all of these women find a new freedom in captivity. Their prewar social and economic supports have disappeared—income, servants, male protector, status in an established social structure, house and material possessions, security for the future and assurance of what that future will be like, mobility, options; all are gone with the wind. But, rather than regard this total loss as total devastation, these women rise, phoenix-like, from the ashes of destruction and are, in some critical respects, re-born. Certainly in this testing of their spirit, they experience a renascence. Although this is certainly not true of every war victim, failures do not write their autobiographies. These stories are success stories. Even when Crouter's husband or Sams's lover is present in the same camp, the author's consciousness puts him in his place—subordinate along with all other friends, enemies, children. The writer emphasizes herself as the central character, no matter how powerful her emotional attachment is to anyone else. In fact, in these stories, like many other autobiographies of adversity, the authors often appear to be alone amidst the crowd, political and psychological exiles opposing a hostile external world and resisting an indifferent milieu within the camp.

This is most conspicuous in the case of Margaret Sams. With her husband gone, no friends inside or outside the camp of 5000, and her family ten thousand miles away, Sams felt the exhilaration of isolation. Nine months into the war she realized

that no one in the world cared for David and me, [and] I began to rather enjoy doing as *I* pleased, for the first time in my life. I had no one to account to. As long as I had lived I had had to consider either my family or my husband first. Now, all at once I had nothing in the world to prevent me from coming and going and doing as I pleased, within Japanese bounds, that is.

She had only one primary responsibility instead of many: "As long as I fed and clothed and took care of David to the best of my ability, I was on my own." And Sams liked her new status: "I owed no man allegiance, and I began to enjoy the sensation." She could not count on help from the God she had been taught to trust as a child—"He wasn't going to perform a single miracle for me"—or other people: "I was learning that the world is a hard place, and its people harder." That meant, she concludes, "that my child and I were surviving through the efforts of no one except myself" (102-3).

The unanticipated consequence of this freedom provided the impetus for the writing of *Forbidden Family*, a confession of passion and sexuality unique among women's internment literature of World War II. The plot of Sams's confession and *apologia* is simple, its execution complex. Margaret fell instantly in love with fellow internee Jerry Sams, "one of the most handsome men I have ever seen." She unilaterally decided to bear their baby out of wedlock rather than to have an expeditious abortion, and to rear their daughter by herself, if necessary, for the Japanese had transferred Jerry to another camp the day after she became pregnant. Everything happened in nine month segments: the liaison, pregnancy, living as a "forbidden family" in camp, the postwar wait until Jerry's divorce was final and the couple could marry.

Jerry first invited Margaret to visit his secret "home," a private platform under the high ceiling of a stairwell, equipped with a clandestine refrigerator, a bunsen burner for cooking, a radio, a chess set and two chairs—"something I had not sat on for eight months." He offered her food, "the first time I'd had an invitation to eat someone else's food." And he made her a washboard, "the thing I wanted most in the world right then.... I most likely would have fallen in love with the devil himself if he had offered me help and food" (104-10).

Sams justifies falling in love on the grounds of passion and immediacy: "The circumstances were right for it. No one knew what the next day held; we might be dead, we might be liberated, anything might happen." Her *carpe diem* philosophy, clearly at variance with the moral stance of Crouter, Keith and Miles, is much more characteristic of the public stereotype of men rather than women in wartime. The uncertainty, she says, "made one want to drain the last drop from the minute at hand. Right now, this minute, is the important thing. Live it. Enjoy it if possible." "Probably a poor philosophy," she says, implicitly acknowledging the fact that war does not necessarily ennoble its participants, men or women, but, no excuses, "it is burned into me" (110-11).

Because the authors confess to anger (Crouter calls her diary "a rock through the window," 97), outrage, antagonism and, in Sams's case, transgression of a powerful cultural and religious prohibition, their personae are at times fierce, feisty and always fully human. In telling their stories, they nonetheless seek the validation, vindication and love they did not always find in internment. Confession itself contains the potential for exculpation; Sams, Prodigal Daughter, hoped to write herself back into the community from which she had risked exile. This "fallen woman," as Sams continually calls herself, confesses from, as Weintraub says of Rousseau, "a deep urge for self-justification" (298). She hopes, as Rousseau did, that, by revealing her private experience to the public, not only her immediate family but posterity will come to understand and thus to love her (Sams xi, 298). Telling one's story thus becomes the ultimate act of self-definition and of self-assertion.

Themes

A major theme of women's war stories is the preservation of life, rather than the destruction of it, for which men, as statesmen and soldiers, are largely responsible. The authors' primary task during the war is to preserve their own lives and the lives entrusted to their care, particularly those of their children— or, in Miles's case, others' children. So, naturally, that is what they write about. What middle-class Americans can take for granted during peacetime becomes, during wartime, dramatic to secure, chancy to maintain and necessary to guard to ensure one's very survival: adequate food, clothing, shelter, medical care. The internees, who could bring into camp only a mattress (if that) and a few clothes, have to depend on supplies provided through "the kindness of strangers," even enemies—the Japanese, Filipino friends and former servants living "on the outside," and—too little and nearly too late—the international and American Red Cross. When and if supplies arrive (and they were nearly exhausted during the final nine months of the war), they invent, buy, barter and, in dire circumstances, beg what they need.

Thus repeated endeavors to sustain life become stories within stories; clusters of stories strung like beads along a chronological thread become the overarching narrative pattern. But, unlike accounts of male soldiers or military prisoners of war, women's South Pacific war stories do not focus on terror, torture, horror, violence, military strategy, or even battles, except for the "bombs bursting in air" at the moment of their own liberation.

Sams becomes indignant when people, eager for accounts of rape and torture, and focusing on the male model of war stories, ask, "'Did—uh—anything—uh—terrible—I mean like the stories we've read—happen to you?' And when I say 'No, we were only starved' they seem terribly disappointed, as if to say 'Hell, anyone can be hungry—I thought it was really *rough* over there." "I'm sure," she snaps, "there is nothing as bad as starving and seeing one's children starve" (83). Indeed, of all the accounts I have read of South Pacific internment, no one was raped and only Keith was sexually harassed by a Japanese guard; she was injured not by the guard, but by being kicked and beaten when she would not retract her complaint against him (151-69).

Even in *Three Came Home*, violence is a minor rather than a major theme, for Keith, like her female peers, focuses on food. It is debilitating and demoralizing to be hungry; it is excruciating not to have enough food for one's children, to hear children near starvation, since all internees were, as Sams says, at the war's end "crying, crying, crying for the food which their distracted and hungry parents could not provide for them" (271). Getting even a minimal amount of food, preparing it, hoarding it and rationing it required a continuous expenditure of energy and ingenuity. For instance, when George Keith desperately needed protein, his mother, who "had never before really noticed a hen, except in gravy on a platter," bargained and connived to procure two laying hens through a Japanese guard: "I fed [the hens] with part of my rice ration, with scrapings of bran which I pinched from the cattle shed when I was working outside. I took them out worming in the garden attached to my wrist by strings, as each hen was only permitted to worm its owner's garden"—and the hens laid eggs "like ping-pong balls, with shells like cellophane...and George had protein" (221-22).

Other daily dramas center on surviving, always surviving and never succumbing to medical crises and persistent problems caused—as the war ground slowly on—primarily by malnutrition. Crouter's undernourished teenage daughter, June, hemorrhaged for two weeks when her first menstrual period began, though, with proper Bostonian reticence, Crouter does not identify the cause during her agonized three-week discussion of the problem. (June herself cleared up the mystery several years after the diary was published.) June's dramatic recovery after receiving the gift of life from numerous fellow internees through a spectacular transfusion in her jugular vein is epitomized in Crouter's observation: "We came so near to losing her that I still shake all over when I think of it. I cannot put my mind on anything but June, find it impossible to concentrate on Nippongo"—Natalie was studying Japanese—"Lost possessions have faded entirely" (281).

A major aspect of the preservation of life in women's war stories is maintenance of the *quality of life*, an area of concern too often dismissed as trivial by both male writers and critics. Sams identifies "the luxury items" that transform the state of those who have them from animal to human:

A straight pin, a safety pin, a needle, a piece of thread, a piece of string, a shoe lace, a bobby pin, a bottle, a can, a piece of kleenex, a cup, a spoon, a plate, a washboard, toilet tissue, toothpaste, a toothbrush, a fingernail file, a piece of paper on which to write. (78-79)

Women's war stories lavish detail on the plainest, and most crowded of barracks conditions—everyone in Baguio and Santo Tomás was allotted 33 inches of space, the width of a mattress. They could store what little they had under the bed; hooks and shelves came later. Thus, many of the survival sub-plots detail attempts to secure privacy, personal space, and time to think, write, pray— and play. In their intimate, often cozy, recreations of homelike contexts, these works rival the domestic scenes in Dickens, or in Wilder's "Little House" series. Crouter evokes the snug security of Mole's underground dwelling in *The Wind in the Willows* as she describes warrens of dugouts that families burrowed under the Baguio barracks in 1944 in search of privacy after three years of barracks living, "an excellent spot in which to lie low in case bullets or shrapnel fly":

Various [people] come calling and no two dugouts are alike. Mansells' is huge, has a window with two panes of glass, a door, curtains, couch, chair.... Phil's and Peg's is like the saloon of a ship, with curtains at porthole windows, settees at a table with one leg in the middle of it, a white sheet tacked up on the wall into an effect of white paint, drawings of sailboats on it.... A box is our cupboard and a wooden tray makes a good buffet.... It is compact, casual, a real home.... Scotts came over for coffee and quiet bridge. They purred over the dugout, loved it (342-43).

In women's accounts, parties and holiday celebrations emerge in technicolor against the monochromatic background of daily events. Miles, for instance, describes the illusory warmth of the Thanksgiving fireplace, its fire "simulated by placing a light behind the logs with red tissue paper stuffed between" (113). Even Keith, who hates Christmas because of the disparity between what "one wanted to give—gifts, joy, happiness" and the reality, tells a real-life Christmas fable to illustrate the pan of "material and spiritual paupery" of Christmas behind barbed wire in 1944. The story culminates in her six-year-old's tantrum of disappointment at being unable to have the one gift he really wanted, "a big big big" red wooden boat, "outstanding and stupendous" in comparison with the stuffed horse he stomped to death (228-31).

Women's war stories, like their lives, are also *conservative* of the authors' culture, as it evolves and is modified by the circumstances of captivity. The quality of life often has a moral dimension reflected in the authors' values and ways of living. Miles devoted considerable effort, often when exhausted, to caring for the infants of mothers too sick to do it themselves, including washing mountains of dirty diapers by hand, and concludes: "The joy of seeing a pathetic baby change into a healthy, happy little boy made it all worthwhile. I had discovered the antidote for self-pity: find someone else worse off than you are and do something to help them" (85). Crouter interprets the camp's banana-dispensing machine as the essence of democracy, for it embodies:

cold fact, technical accuracy, with true justice and balance between the large and small banana, the fresh or the bruised, the ripe and the unripe, all of which must be the lot of every one at one time or another.... The Banana Machine does away with favoritism, privilege, graft, politics, personal touch and hurt feelings.

And, just as in a democracy, the Banana Machine offers everyone an equal opportunity to get the perfect banana, which is "bound to come...under the law of averages" (140). What fun.

The authors' values are continually threatened with destruction by two sorts of alien cultures, the culture of their captors, and the new culture that emerges among the crowded internees themselves. A leitmotif of Crouter's diary, for instance, is her condemnation of the privilege and vanity of her fellow internees. Thus she criticizes shirkers who do not perform their assigned tasks, grafters who steal food from the common store, women who curl their eyelashes, people who put their own welfare above the common good:

It is increasingly obvious in here that those who do their share of the community work, no matter how distasteful it is, are the happiest and best adjusted in camp. The unhappiest are the ones who...twist and turn away with all kinds of reasons and excuses, working only for themselves, doing their own washing, their own extra cooking...feeling abused and ill-treated. There must be a balance between personal and community duties. (81)

The narrators of all war stories, men and women alike, are intensely patriotic and unshakably loyal Americans. Yet, despite the privations of camp life, all the women but Sams demonstrate an appreciation of their captors' culture and humanity to a far greater extent than men do—perhaps because civilians were treated better than military prisoners. This rises to a dramatic crescendo at the end of every account, when the Japanese depart in defeat and the internees are liberated. Miles, embedded firmly in the missionary community, remains full of faith, hope and charity from beginning to end of the war, concluding: "Although we had suffered as prisoners of the Japanese, we did not hate [them]. We hated war. We saw the Japanese as individuals created in the image of God with the same potential for good or evil that we had. They, like us, were *victims* of war" (163). Crouter thinks, "We had the time of our lives in here—sorry to leave," and then, disoriented in liberation by the firestorms raging through the streets of Manila, "Where am I? In the past? In the future? In the present? We are where the past and future meet in combat and who will survive?" (475). Keith responds with a global perspective:

I am proud to call myself American; but I do not call America mine. Its goods and plenty, its products, its people, its great ideals, and its freedom belong now to the world. Today we live in a world, not a state.... No matter how good our own conditions now, we cannot ignore starving Europe, a demoralized and fighting Asia. (114)

Conclusion

All tales undergo revision in repeated telling, writing, rewriting, editing and self-censoring. The resulting works of Crouter, Keith, Miles and Sams are triumphs of the storyteller's art. As testaments of survival and growth in adversity they record the progress of these pilgrims, non-military victories which are the ultimate focus and justification of women's war stories.

Notes

[1] See also corroborating published accounts by Herold, Hyland, Moule, Stevens, Tomibe and Vaughan; Crim's self-published memoir, and Herold's extensive manuscript diary.

[2] See Bloom, "Escaping Voices," and Bloom, introductions to Crouter, Sams.

Works Cited

Bloom, Lynn Z. "Escaping Voices: Women's Diaries of Wartime Captivity." *Troops versus Tropes: War and Literature.* Evelyn J. Hinz, ed. Winnipeg: U of Manitoba, 1990, 102-112.

Crim, Bessie. *I Am a Violin: The Story of One Missionary Who Worked as a Nurse for Ten Years (1940-1950) in China and the Philippine Islands.* n.p., self-published, 1984.

Crouter, Natalie. *Forbidden Diary: A Record of Wartime Internment, 1941-45.* Ed. Lynn Z. Bloom. American Women's Diary Series 2. New York: Burt Franklin, 1980.

Egan, Susanna. *Patterns of Experience in American Autobiography.* Chapel Hill: U of North Carolina P, 1984.

Herold, Ethel. "War Memories of Ethel Herold." *Bulletin of the American Historical Collection* 10 (1982): 44-67.

———— Wartime Internment Diary. unpublished typescript, n.d.

Hyland, Judy. *In the Shadow of the Rising Sun.* Minneapolis: Augsburg, 1984.

Keith, Agnes Newton. *Three Came Here.* Boston: Little Brown, 1947.

Miles, Fern Harrington. *Captive Community: Life in a Japanese Internment Camp, 1941-1945.* Jefferson City, TN: Mossy Creek, 1987.

Moule, William R. *God's Arms Around Us.* New York: Vantage, 1960.

Sams, Margaret. *Forbidden Family: A Wartime Memoir of the Philippines, 1941-45.* Ed. Lynn Z. Bloom. Wisconsin Studies in American Autobiography. Madison, WI: U of Wisconsin P, 1989.

Stevens, Frederic H. *Santo Tomás* Internment Camp. n.p.: Stratford, 1964.

Tomibe, Rokuro. "The Secret Story of the War's End." *Bulletin of the American Historical Collection* 7 (1979): 37-45.

Vaughan, Elizabeth. *The Ordeal of Elizabeth Vaughan: A Wartime Diary of the Philippines*. Ed. Carol M. Petillo. Athens, GA: U of Georgia P, 1985.

Weintraub, Karl Joachim. *The Value of the Individual: Self and Circumstances in Autobiography*. Chicago: U of Chicago P, 1978.

Survival! Polish Children
During World War II

Marilyn Fain Apseloff

War novels have fascinated many adult readers, and it is therefore no surprise that children, often imitators of parents and older siblings, are now readers of the genre. The burgeoning number of books set during World War II points to a growing interest; indeed, Lois Lowry's *Number the Stars* (Houghton Mifflin, 1989), about the 1943 Danish resistance to the Nazi attempt to deport the Danish Jews, was the 1990 Newbery Medal Winner for the best written children's book of the year. Obviously, then, the subject has relevance for children as well as for adults, especially now that the Persian Gulf War was televised and brought into numerous homes. The differences between such children's books and those for adults are more a matter of perspective: the former are usually seen through the eyes of a child rather than from an adult point of view.

The child's perspective is crucial, for the effects of the traumas of war influence what kind of adult that child will become if he survives. The lives of an entire generation of children have been changed forever by the circumstances of World War II, and adults must realize this. The past has a bearing on the present. Moreover, like adults, children are unique; they react individually to similar circumstances. Some become self-centered; others think only in terms of family, or a larger group; still others focus solely on revenge. The many war-related books that feature children in them reveal the uniqueness of each protagonist facing a common enemy, yet they also demonstrate how deeply the scars go. Certainly, many of the subjects in the war novels for adults and children are the same: the Holocaust, survival, outwitting the Nazis, sabotage, the underground and more. Both adults and children face a loss of innocence at the behavior of their fellow man and what they are called upon to do, and both assume extraordinary roles during the crises presented by war. Even the larger, most important issues, such as survival—not for personal gain but as a lasting witness to the horrors of war—occur in literature for children as well as that for adults.

Poland has been the World War II setting for a number of such fictional works. Although many fine World War II children's books have been set elsewhere (Denmark, Holland, Germany or Norway, for example), the length of Nazi occupation, the great number of concentration and extermination camps, the ghettos with their uprisings, the destruction and the negative reaction of many citizens towards the Jews in particular, make Poland perhaps the best example of how war so completely altered children's lives. Just as adults confronted by life-threatening crises rarely have only one valid reaction, so, too, Polish children, during the period between 1939 and 1945, responded differently to the Nazi occupation of their land. Some succumbed to starvation; some survived through grim determination and cleverness; some went to their deaths rather than be separated from loved ones; some formed resistance groups to fight back.

Four thoughtful, well-written children's books—*Gideon* by Chester Aaron, *The Island on Bird Street* by Uri Orlev, *Dark Hour of Noon* by Christine Szambelan-Strevinsky, and Ruth Minsky Sender's *The Cage*—all written in the 1980s, show these varying responses very clearly. At least three of these volumes are based on actual occurrences. *The Island on Bird Street* grew out of Orlev's own experiences when he was hiding out from the Nazis in the Warsaw ghetto for two years, although he did change many events and circumstances. Aaron, author of *Gideon*, states that his information, both oral and written, came from survivors of Dachau and other camps. In *The Cage*, Sender recounts her personal experiences of the Holocaust. Only with *Dark Hour of Noon* is there no positive evidence that what occurred in the novel is more than fiction, although that is implied.

The three novels reveal common themes of survival and loss of innocence and three different ways of coping. In the first two, young Jewish boys are asked to deal with situations far beyond their control. In *Gideon* (Lippincott, 1982), the first-person narrator struggles to survive in the Warsaw ghetto by working with a gang to smuggle food and other supplies into the area. To do so, he must sneak out of the ghetto, a deadly game, since the penalty for getting caught is death or deportation to one of the camps. Eventually Gideon is sent to Treblinka. The situation is different in *The Island on Bird Street* (Houghton Mifflin, 1984), another first-person narration. In this novel, Alex has promised to wait for his father at a certain location no matter how long it takes. He, too, must struggle for survival and must make forays out of the ghetto. *Dark Hour of Noon* (Lippincott, 1982), has a different focus because the omniscient narration reveals the emotional changes that Nazi occupation wrought on a Catholic child and her friends as the knowledge of Nazi inhumanity turns them into expert killers. *The Cage*, Sender's personal narrative (Macmillan, 1986), is a contrast to the others because the protagonist, Riva (Ruth), is older than her counterparts and must take care of her siblings. Riva is later separated from them when she is sent to camps, including Auschwitz. All of the protagonists must leave their childhoods quickly behind them.

The author of *Gideon* reveals that he "was with the American troops that opened the gates at Dachau" (vii). His book is a result of conversations with survivors, reading many types of documents on the Holocaust (including diaries and journals), and the imaginary creations of characters who are "combination[s] of fact and fiction" (ix). In the novel, Gideon Malinovsky recounts his experiences of thirty years earlier in the Warsaw ghetto. He comments on his luck to have been fair-haired and blue-eyed so that he was not taken for a Jew. His first recollection is of a time when he was fourteen and ordered to sing with a group and applaud as a group of Nazi soldiers forced Jews to dance naked in the street. More humiliation follows; as the Poles laugh, "I force myself to laugh too. I have long ago learned how essential it is to accept humiliation in order to survive" (5).

Survival is Gideon's main instinct. When he has a chance to escape through the grating of the cattle car taking him and others away, he grabs it, even though Jews left behind will be shot because of his action. "Will they be saved if I surrender? No" (7). The times have made him a pragmatist as he remembers his father's words to him: "By surviving you can not only fight back, you can carry the story of what is happening in this ghetto.... You are no use to our people dead" (8). By the time the short chapter (pages 3-9) ends, references to survival have occurred eleven times. Despite what his father said, for Gideon, survival is a personal rather than a Jewish issue. He feels no loyalty to his people, just anger: "I DON'T WANT TO BE A JEW! I HATE BEING A JEW!" (20).

As is the case in adult novels of the period, ghetto life is described in detail, the depredations, the numerous deaths on the streets from starvation and disease, the attempts to get food. Some information on adult activities is revealed through Gideon's contacts, but he is the focus. Even his parents are secondary; they have chosen a wider perspective than his own of personal survival. Although intent upon self-preservation, he is filled with despair when he learns of the children who have starved to death in an orphanage. "Surviving that night must have fueled my confidence that I could survive forever" (43).

Gideon recalls the days of his innocence with nostalgia: "I felt so old, so estranged, and I longed for my young, innocent self" (51). Such thoughts must be put aside to keep his morale strong. He pretends to be Catholic when he is away from home. Quick-witted, he joins a notorious anti-Jewish gang outside the ghetto after a brazen encounter, during which he successfully dangles the profit motive as bait. He is already in partnership with Yankele, a renegade Jew who lives only for himself and his sister inside the ghetto. He cannot think about the future; when Gideon is asked about his plans one day, he is astonished: "Who could make plans?" (71).

After his father dies resisting the Nazi oppressors in Warsaw, however, Gideon finds himself thinking about others besides himself. When his mother and her charges at the Jewish orphanage in the ghetto are marched off to the extermination camps as Gideon watches from a nearby rooftop, his thoughts turn to obtaining weapons for himself and others around him.

The Nazi attack on the Warsaw ghetto began on April 19, 1943, the first day of the Jewish Passover. At last, the remaining Jews realize that Hitler wants all of them destroyed, and they act accordingly. The Jews, many as young as Gideon, organize for the last stand. Every Jew fights, even a woman in a wheelchair who collects canteens from fallen German bodies.

Brave as they are, however, the Jews fail. Gideon is captured by the Germans and sent to Treblinka, a camp of many miseries. After months of almost unspeakable horror, he is able to escape during a well-organized breakout and eventually returns to Warsaw, where a non-Jewish friend hides him until war's end eighteen months later. Then he is able to obtain both identity papers and a Danish passport. A doctor removes the tattooed number from his arm, and, rejecting his Jewish heritage, he heads for America under an assumed name. Like many adults, he has survived to tell his story in the hope that a similar situation will never happen again.

In the Introduction to *The Island on Bird Street*, Uri Orlev vividly describes the ghetto. Imagine, he asks his readers, a city with a wall built in such a way that it cuts through the middle of a street, house or yard. Like any other metropolitan area, the city will have nightclubs, hospitals and shops, but trolleys and cars no longer run, supplies become short, and only isolated islands of life and activity exist. This was Warsaw from 1941-1943.

In *The Island on Bird Street*, Alex, Orlev's eleven-year-old protagonist, is hiding out in a ruined house that "is really not very different from a desert island" (x-xi). Like Robinson Crusoe, Alex must survive on his own, taking what he needs from other places just as Crusoe did but without his freedom to plant and harvest and walk about openly in search of the things he needs. Instead, Alex can only peer through the air vent at what is going on around him and make forays for food and other necessities while he waits for the return of his father, who had been marched off by a band of Nazi soldiers weeks before.

It is 1942. Alex's mother is missing and presumed sent to a labor camp in Germany. The days pass, and Alex must shift for himself. With his growing independence comes a maturity that he lacked earlier. Each day brings new dangers, and not just from the Germans: there are Polish and Jewish police to fear, and looters who think nothing of killing a real or assumed rival. The normal childhood belief in the goodness of others disintegrates quickly in the face of Nazism and what it breeds. It is not only survival of the fittest, but of the cleverest. Alex soon realizes that he needs a better hiding place, and he selects the ruined upper floors of his building. Using his wits, he constructs a rope ladder and a system for lowering and raising it that will be unnoticed. His ability to work out complex problems grows rapidly.

When Alex hears sounds of the ghetto uprising, he packs a few things and prepares to join the fight, taking with him a gun his father had hidden from the Nazis. In the ruins below his hideout, however, he encounters a German soldier about to kill two partisans. As the soldier raises his rifle, Alex shoots and kills him. The experience reveals to Alex that he is not cut out to be a fighter. "I realized now that wars weren't like the ones in adventure books where children fought like heroes at the grown-ups' sides. One dead German was enough for me" (102). Alex starts shaking, then crying, unable to stop.

When one of the two partisans who has been wounded gets worse, Alex goes to the Polish side of the wall to fetch a doctor who comes, operates to remove the bullet, and leaves bandages and aspirin. Before he can return, however, Germans come for the doctor; someone has turned him in. When his new charge worsens, Alex again goes to the Polish side, hoping to get him out of the ghetto. Other Poles risk their lives to help. Though Alex, like Gideon, is able to pass for a non-Jew, that does not automatically mean safety: he discovers that everyone is liable to suffer from Nazi persecution, especially those trying to help the Jews.

Anti-semitism is a constant factor. The ghetto wall is knocked down to make more housing available for the Poles, for the war has created a housing shortage. Alex hears a variety of people and children coming and going below, among them partisans. He is about to lower his ladder to them when he remembers a warning against trusting all members of the Polish underground: "the right-wingers hated Jews as much as the Germans. If a Jew tried joining the partisans in the forests and fell into their hands, they would kill him without thinking twice" (150). He has learned not to trust others, another loss of innocence.

One day he is down in the cellar area when his father appears. The narration draws to a close after Alex proudly shows how he has managed to survive. He, his father and others set out to join the partisans in the forest. All ends on a pat, upbeat note. Ironically, it was not so easy for Orlev, the author; his mother was killed by the Nazis, "and he and his brother were sent to Bergen-Belsen." He was only eight when his two years of hiding in the ghetto began. No mention is made of whether or not his father, captured by the Russians at the beginning of the war, or his brother survived.

Dark Hour of Noon shows most forcefully the complete loss of innocence that can occur under Nazi occupation. Trina is a timid seven-year-old in a Catholic family when the Germans declare war on Poland. Her mother, Ronka, is a model of strength and resistance. Rather than let the Germans and their sympathizers have her good things, she and Trina throw all the preserves, wine, crystal and china down to the courtyard, where everything smashes. Trina, in contrast, is a frightened child, afraid to go outside once the Nazis take over the town. When they must vacate their apartment and Trina begins to cry, her mother tells her, "Don't you let me see you cry in front of these *Szwabs!*" (21).

When the family is eventually shipped to Warznica to live with a farm family, Trina and her father spend a great deal of time together. On one of their walks, he tells her the legend of the sleeping knights who will rise to help Poland in her hour of need; when Trina takes that literally, he explains, "Each one of us is a knight, and when the time comes, we'll fight" (48).

Some months later, the family moves to Radom, where Tosh, the father, has found work; they share an apartment with the Krols, a friendly Jewish family. Trina finds a best friend in Nina, a girl in a neighboring apartment. Eventually the Krols must move to the ghetto. When Tosh learns that Hannah Krol has given birth to a boy, he makes plans to smuggle the baby out of the ghetto to safety. He is too late: a neighbor relates how the Nazis came, lined people up to left and right (death or the camps), and how a soldier, Hoffman, grabbed the baby, smashed its head against a wall and shot the grieving Hannah.

Trina overhears this story, and it is a turning point for her. She tells Nina about the Krols the next morning and points out Hoffman to her. They decide to recruit three other children they can trust, and together they stalk the German, learning his routines and habits, and making their plans. "Now the time had come for them to fight" (67). After they knock down and subdue Hoffman, each slits the Nazi's throat. Although the experience unnerves all of them, from then on, they are dedicated to avenging the deaths of Polish people. Yet Trina still exhibits child-like tendencies. She and the others mingle their blood in a pact while they plan to blow up a munitions train. The two girls play with dolls, delighting Trina's mother, who does not know that the dolls are pretenses, props to use until they are alone, to disguise their intention to look for ether for their next assassination target. For Christmas 1941, Trina's mother buys her a beautiful doll. "'What am I going to do with a *doll?*' nine-year old Trina thinks. 'I'm not a *child* anymore!'" (87).

When the children blow up a compound, they set wire booby traps for motorcycles. Nina gleefully tells the others, "'Sliced a *Szwab's* head off as clean as a whistle'" (169). The uprising in the Warsaw Ghetto is referred to only briefly as Trina remembers "the stench of burning flesh that had drifted out from behind the charred Ghetto walls the previous spring'" (171). A year has passed since then: it is 1944, and she is twelve. All of the children (the oldest is fourteen) are to deliver messages to Warsaw for the last time; Tosh insists that they leave the city before August. When they discover that there will be an uprising, they elect to stay. Like Gideon, the children retreat to the sewers with no food, ammunition or drinkable water. When one boy is too injured to continue, Trina tearfully takes his boots while another friend mercifully kills him.

When the foursome who are left eventually reach the woods, they separate into two groups. Trina and Nina reach Radom and their families. The other two never return. Although her father is killed by the SS, Trina and her mother live until war's end, returning to Posnan to try to rebuild their lives.

Trina and her friends' loss of innocence turns them into killers, but not in their eyes. When the priest at her first confession chastises her, her reaction is a vehement "'It's *not* a sin! It's *not* murder! Germans are not people!'" (112). That is a misleading message for the reader, one to which other books do not subscribe. It is precisely because the Germans and others like them were people just like those living next door that their deeds were so terrible, that war novels for both adults and children must be written and read; otherwise, there is the possibility of a recurrence.

The last book, *The Cage*, is a departure from the others because the protagonist assumes an adult role, even giving up her child status with extra rations when she insists on being classified as an adult so that her siblings can stay together. This is Riva's personal narrative of her own Holocaust experiences. The book is full of contrast, of spring and Pesach (Passover), of death and renewal, of beauty and horror, of clean, peaceful villages and dirty camp inmates marching in pain. Through her eyes, worsening conditions in the ghetto unfold, and she constantly asks why such things should be happening: "Why are your dreams scattered, destroyed?/Why are you put in this cage?/Why is the world silently watching?/Why can't they hear your rage?"[1] A boy tells her how important it is to survive and write, yet he will appear when his and his sister's names appear on the list for deportation because he knows that his sister is too frail to hide. For him, the family bond is more important than personal survival.

In *The Cage*, a mother still wracked by nightmares from the Holocaust tries to explain to her daughter why she has no living grandparents. She tells her daughter that the horrors of this period could occur again unless people remember and learn from the past. Throughout her narrative, Riva finds herself always asking "why" and not finding answers. For example, the Grubers, friends who have seemed part of the Minsky family, turn on them when the Germans arrive. In chilling fashion, the Grubers show no compassion when the Minskys' possessions are taken from them; in fact, Mrs. Gruber helps herself to her friends' furs. The Poles, individually and as a group, are painted with a black brush.

Riva and her siblings are sent to Auschwitz, where she is separated from her brothers. Seven days later, she is sent to another camp. When Riva contracts blood poisoning and must go to a hospital, the camp overseer shows her some kindness, as does a doctor who finally treats her after hours. In another incident, Riva reads a poem about her mother at an entertainment for the commandant, who gives her a notebook. There is some compassion here, too. Yet, when it is obvious that the Russians are closing in on the camp, the Germans herd the prisoners toward the woods, obviously intending to kill them. Then word comes of the Russian advance, and the Germans flee. When the local Poles refuse to respond to the prisoners' knocking on doors and cries for help, the women return to the camp, where the Russians discover them; they are the first Jews the officer finds alive in any of the camps.

Each of the four volumes shows contemporary children how other youngsters acted during the Nazi occupation fifty years ago. In desperate circumstances, Polish youth, regardless of their religious backgrounds, triumph spiritually if not physically.

Gone is the stereotype of children being led meekly to slaughter. Children were victims of the Holocaust, but they also were fighters. Jews saw friends and countrymen turn against them; others matured far beyond their years. The children pictured in these books, and others like them throughout the occupied countries, are among the many heroes of World War II.

Note

[1]Ruth Minsky Sender, *The Cage* (New York: Macmillan, 1986), n.p. The lines are from a poem preceding the narrative.

Works Cited

Aaron, Chester. *Gideon*. New York: Lippincott, 1982.

Orlev, Uri. *The Island on Bird Street*. Trans. Hillel Halkin. Boston: Houghton Mifflin, 1984.

Sender, Ruth Minsky. *The Cage*. New York: Macmillan, 1986.

Szambelin-Strevinsky, Christine. *Dark Hour of Noon*. New York: Lippincott, 1982.

IG Farben's Synthetic War Crimes and Thomas Pynchon's *Gravity's Rainbow*

Robert L. McLaughlin

In 1989, to mark the fiftieth anniversary of the beginning of World War II, Ian Hogg and Bryan Perrett published an *Encyclopedia of the Second World War*, covering the war from "A-4," the original designation for the V-2 Rocket, to "Zyklon B," the gas used to murder thousands of Jews. Interestingly, both these products were put into use thanks, at least in part, to IG Farbenindustrie A.G., the giant German manufacturer of dyes and chemicals. To find IG Farben's fingers in the alphabetical beginning and end of the war is not surprising to readers of Thomas Pynchon's *Gravity's Rainbow*. *Gravity's Rainbow* is not an encyclopedia, but it has been called an encyclopedic narrative;[1] that is, it contains and expresses the strands of thought and flow of ideas that define the character of its time.

One of the ways Pynchon achieves this is through his use of history. Historical figures interact with fictional characters, and historical incidents are sprinkled through a fictional plot. This use of history forces readers to reconsider their expectations for both fiction and history.[2] IG Farben provides some of the most important historical contexts for the novel. Pynchon sees the IG's influence everywhere; in fact, for Pynchon IG Farben (and, more importantly, the mindset it represents) is, even more than Hitler, the villain of World War II. Pynchon, incorporating the actual history of the firm, uses IG Farben as an important structuring and thematic device to represent Western civilization's tendency to control and corrupt the natural and transform it from the purposes of life to the purposes of death.

IG Farben's power and wealth were based on the ability to manipulate the chemical make-up of molecules. As Pynchon puts it, "chemists were no longer to be at the mercy of Nature. They could decide now what properties they wanted a molecule to have, and then go ahead and build it" (249). In 1856, William Henry Perkin, an Englishman, was able to take aniline from coal tar, the waste material from iron-producing blast furnaces, and, by treating it with other substances, create the first synthetic dye. In Great Britain, this discovery was interesting but not very useful. Britain could more cheaply and easily import from its many colonies the natural materials it needed to make dyes. But Germany, with few colonies and trade routes that were easily cut off, had less access to such natural materials and so was very interested in the creation of synthetic dyes. By 1900, German dye companies dominated the dye field as well as the burgeoning chemical industry in Europe and America. By the end of World

War I, the most important of these firms (BASF, Bayer, Hoechst, Agfa, Cassella, and Kalle [Borkin 4-5]) had joined in a single *interessen gemeinschaft* or "fellowship of interest:" IG Farben. Instead of competing, the firms now cooperated. In 1925, this cartel arrangement was formalized into a merger and one giant chemical company was created.[3]

Germany's defeat in World War I had, to a large extent, been due to its inability to get raw materials through the British blockade. If Germany were to fight in another war and win, it would need to solve this problem. Enter IG Farben and its chemical expertise. In 1915, using chemist Fritz Haber's laboratory experiments, Carl Bosch (the first engineer to win the Nobel Prize and the eventual Chairman of the Board of IG Farben) constructed the first plant for the mass production of synthetic nitrates, for use in gunpowder. The Haber-Bosch process used high pressure to convert nitrogen from the air to nitrates (Borkin 19-20). In 1927 at its Leuna plant, the IG applied a similar process to coal (one natural resource of which Germany had an abundance) for the large-scale production of synthetic oil (Borkin 44-50). In 1930, the IG laid the groundwork for the process by which oil could be converted to synthetic Buna rubber (Borkin 51-52). By the time Hitler became Chancellor in 1933, the IG had perfected, or had the potential to perfect, the industrial mass production of synthetic nitrates, fuel oil and rubber. Thanks to IG Farben, the new Chancellor had at his command the materials needed to begin a new war.[4]

For Pynchon, this kind of control and manipulation of the natural is a perversion and a distortion of the almost spiritual energy of nature. Near the end of *Gravity's Rainbow*, Geli Tripping, an apprentice witch, has a vision of "the World just before men. Too violently pitched alive in constant flow ever to be seen by men directly. They are meant only to look at it dead, in still strata, transputrefied to oil or coal. Alive, it was a threat: it was Titans, was an overpeaking of life so clangorous and mad, such a green corona about Earth's body that some spoiler *had* to be brought in before it blew the Creation apart" (720). There are moments in the novel when the characters are able to participate in this creative energy. An example is the rooftop garden originally planted by

Corydon Throsp [. . .] who [. . .] liked to cultivate pharmaceutical plants up on the roof [. . .], a few of them hardy enough to survive fogs and frosts, but most returning, as fragments of peculiar alkaloids, to rooftop earth, along with manure from a trio of prize Wessex Saddleback sows quartered there by Throsp's successor, and dead leaves off many decorative trees transplanted to the roof by later tenants, and the odd unstomachable meal thrown or vomited there by this or that sensitive epicurean—all got scumbled together, eventually, by the knives of the seasons, to an impasto, feet thick, of unbelievable black topsoil in which anything could grow, not the least being bananas. (5)

These bananas, gathered and cooked into a sumptuous banana breakfast, offer a temporary respite from the war and London under the threat of V-2 Rockets.

Now there grows among all the rooms, replacing the night's old smoke, alcohol and sweat, the fragile, musaceous odor of Breakfast: flowery, permeating, surprising, more than the color of winter sunlight, taking over not so much through any brute pungency or volume as by the high intricacy to the weaving of its molecules, sharing the conjuror's secret by which—though it is not often Death is told so clearly to fuck off—the living genetic chains prove even labyrinthine enough to preserve some human face down ten or twenty generations...so the same assertion-through-structure allows this war morning's banana fragrance to meander, repossess, prevail. (10)

Here, the creative energy of nature, stored and compounded over the years until it bursts out, is a celebration of life and a clear alternative to death.

Historically, however, people have reacted to nature as, in Pynchon's term, "God's spoilers." In their desire to control and dominate nature, people have framed and compartmentalized the natural, cutting it off from its flowing vitality and neutralizing its creative energy. In modern times, this domination has taken the form of molecular manipulation, the chemical synthesis that was the foundation for the success of IG Farben. Pynchon recounts the history of chemical synthesis and marks as a key moment Friedrich August Kekulé's dream of a serpent with its tale in its mouth, by which the chemist was able to visualize the benzene atom, "so that others might be seduced by its physical beauty, and begin to think of it as a blueprint, a basis for new compounds, new arrangements, so that there would be a field of aromatic chemistry to ally itself with secular power, and find new methods of synthesis, so there would be a German dye industry to become the IG...." (412). Pynchon goes on,

Kekulé dreams the Great Serpent holding its own tail in its mouth, the dreaming Serpent which surrounds the World. But the meanness, the cynicism with which this dream is to be used. The Serpent that announces, "The World is a closed thing, cyclical, resonant, eternally-returning," is to be delivered into a system whose only aim is to *violate* the Cycle. Taking and not giving back, demanding that "productivity" and "earnings" keep on increasing with time, the System removing from the rest of the World these vast quantities of energy to keep its own tiny desperate faction showing a profit: and not only most of humanity—most of the World, animal, vegetable and mineral, is laid waste in the process. (412)

In the IG Farben world view, Geli Tripping's vision of nature as overwhelmingly alive is completely reversed: now nature is seen as dead matter, existing only for the use and profit of the human race. Pynchon presents a séance at which top IG Farben executives, in order to get business advice from beyond, summon the spirit of Walter Rathenau, coordinator of German industry during World War I and promoter of industry-wide cartels in service of the state. He shares with them his vision of "coal, down in the earth, dead black, no light, the very substance of death" (166). From coal the IG has created new, artificial substances and products. But, Rathenau reminds his listeners, "this is all the impersonation of life. The real movement is not from death to any rebirth. It is from death to death-transfigured. The best you can do is to polymerize a few dead molecules [....] The persistence, then, of structures favoring death. Death converted into more death. Perfecting its reign, just as the buried coal grows denser, and overlaid with more strata—epoch on top of epoch, city on top of ruined city" (167). Pynchon seems to be presenting either end of a centuries-long process in which the human race's attitude toward nature was totally transformed. As Ecofeminist Carolyn Merchant points out, "Between the sixteenth and seventeenth centuries the image of an organic cosmos with a living female earth at its center gave way to a mechanistic world view in which nature was reconstructed as dead and passive, to be controlled by humans" (xvi).[5] Like Merchant, Pynchon equates the objectification, manipulation and control of nature with the death of nature.[6]

Merchant goes on to argue that "theories about nature have historically been interpreted as containing implications about the way individuals or social groups behave or ought to behave" (69). It follows that along with IG Farben's objectification, control and use of nature comes the objectification, control and use of people. In both World Wars, the IG made use of foreign workers forcibly transported from Germany's conquered territories to keep German factories running (Borkin 22; Sasuly 124-25). Even more reprehensibly, in 1941 the IG began construction of its largest synthetic fuel and rubber plants at Auschwitz, using the inmates there as slave labor.[7] But construction was hindered by the long distance the inmates had to walk to and from the work site while being closely guarded by the SS. The disciplinary shootings and floggings had a demoralizing effect on the regular employees. And too many arriving inmates were being sent straight to the gas chambers, leaving too few to do the work. With the plant falling behind schedule and over budget, the IG decided in mid-1942 to open its own concentration camp, Monowitz, closer to the construction site. As Joseph Borkin says,

Although it belonged to I.G., Monowitz had all the equipment of the typical Nazi concentration camp.... The entire camp was encircled with electrically charged barbed wire. There was a "standing cell" in which the victim could neither stand upright, kneel, nor lie down. There was also a gallows, often with a body or two hanging from it as a grim example to the rest of the inmates. Across the arched entrance was the Auschwitz motto, "Freedom through Work." (121)

Transports containing new inmates stopped first at the IG works, where the strongest and the skilled were chosen for work; the rest were taken to the main camp at Auschwitz or "selected" for extermination at Birkenau. Denied a decent diet, humane living conditions and adequate health care (even the SS complained about the lack of hospital space at Monowitz [Borkin 124]), the inmates worked as long as they could and were then shipped to Birkenau. Borkin's summation shows that the IG's attitude toward natural resources had been extended to human resources:

By adopting the theory and practice of Nazi morality, [IG] was able to depart from the conventional economics of slavery in which slaves are traditionally treated as capital equipment to be maintained and serviced for optimum use and depreciated over a normal life span. Instead, I.G. reduced slave labor to a consumable raw material, a human ore from which the mineral of life was systematically extracted. When no usable energy remained, the living dross was shipped to the gassing chambers and cremation furnaces of the extermination center at Birkenau, where the S.S. recycled it into the German war economy—gold teeth for the Reichsbank, hair for mattresses, and fat for soap. (126)

Gravity's Rainbow offers many examples of the tendency to treat people as objects, the most obvious being the mass murder of whole groups of people, the Jews of Europe, the Hereros of Southwest Africa and the Kirghiz of Central

Asia. But the IG's use of people as objects is most specifically seen in Prof.-Dr. Laszlo Jamf's conditioning of Tyrone Slothrop. Jamf is a teacher, Pavlovian behavioralist and chemist who works for IG Farben, its subsidiaries and its cartel partners. He manifests the IG's attitude toward the natural: molecules can be manipulated and controlled to create new molecules, improving on the natural. In fact, Jamf propounds a kind of fascist chemistry marked by domination and control. One of his students remembers, "That something so mutable, so *soft*, as a sharing of electrons by atoms of carbon should lie at the core of life, *his* life, struck Jamf as a cosmic humiliation. *Sharing?* How much stronger, how everlasting was the *ionic* bond—where electrons are not shared, but *captured. Seized!* and held!" (577). Among Jamf's achievements is the creation of an unusual plastic: Imipolex G, an "aromatic Heterocyclic polymer," which is, in a strange synthetic imitation of life, erectile; that is, when stimulated, it transforms "from limp rubbery amorphous to amazing perfect tessellation, hardness, brilliant transparency, high resistance to temperature, weather, vacuum, shock of any kind [...]" (699). Yet this manufactured imitation of life becomes associated with inanimation and death, especially when Gottfried, encased in an Imipolex shroud, is sacrificed.

Imipolex G plays an important role in Jamf's Pavlovian experiments as well. And it is in these conditioning experiments that Jamf applies the methods from his chemical work, manipulation and control, to people, specifically, to the novel's main character, Tyrone Slothrop. Apparently, the Slothrop family received certain monies, including Tyrone's Harvard tuition, for allowing Baby Tyrone to be used in Jamf's conditioning experiments. Jamf conditioned Baby Tyrone to have an erection whenever in the presence of a certain stimulus. Although there are some chronological ambiguities, the stimulus was probably Imipolex G. Years later, wandering through post-War Europe, realizing with increasingly justified paranoia that he is the center of several plots, all seemingly related to the IG, Slothrop will put together some of the pieces of his past. He realizes that his father betrayed him, selling him to the IG.[8] He will not quite reach the revelation that Jamf's experiments on him are representative of his cultural conditioning, the socialization by which he was initiated into the IG world view. His erections, which contain the potential for passing on the energy of life, have been conditioned with the stuff of death to serve the world view of death. As Slothrop reads about Jamf and his own past, "His erection hums from a certain distance, like an instrument installed, wired by Them into his body as a colonial outpost here in our raw and clamorous world, another office representing Their white Metropolis far away...." (285).[9]

As both a victim and a product of the IG, Slothrop perpetuates and applies to others the mindset that has victimized him. His conditioning is particularly evident in his attitude toward women. Just as Baby Tyrone's erections were associated with the stuff of death, adult Slothrop's erections are associated with the V-2 Rocket blast sites. Slothrop keeps a map of his sexual encounters (names, places and dates) that matches exactly the maps marking the places of the V-2 explosions, except that Slothrop's encounters *precede* the explosions by a day or two. This coincidence sends army and corporate investigators scurrying, but we later discover that Slothrop has fictionalized his map, rearranging the facts of his encounters for the sake of discretion.[10] Nevertheless, Slothrop's map-making shows his impulse to objectify women, taking living people and reducing them to dead categories (names, stars, colors, numbers), records of his use of others for his own pleasure. On his quest to discover the mystery of his conditioning and to answer fundamental questions about his identity, Slothrop learns many things about America and the nature of power, things that expose as false the view of the world he has always accepted. But, despite some emotional encounters that shake his confidence in his view of women, Slothrop continues to see his lovers as objects. His best chance to break this chain of objectification and control and thus his worst failure is in his encounter with Bianca. Slothrop has the chance to save her, and, after they have sex, a part of him is tempted by her love: "Right here, right now, under the make-up and the fancy underwear, she *exists*, love, invisibility.... For Slothrop this is some discovery" (470). But he rejects the chance, and his refusal to treat Bianca as a person leads to her death. She becomes, like Baby Tyrone, one more betrayed child.[11] This cycle of victims and victimizers guarantees the continued rule of the world view of objectification and death.

On a wider scale, Pynchon sees the institutionalization of this world view in cartel building. The historic IG Farben was extensively involved in the creation of cartels, agreements among various companies with similar interests to limit competition, assign geographic exclusivity and set prices. The IG itself began as a cartel, the German dye industries joining together to protect their interests. As it grew in power, the IG instigated cartel arrangements with many non-German firms. Losing money in the short run, the IG gained important areas of influence in Germany's potential enemies and kept exclusive control of many of the processes that would give Germany an advantage in wartime. By 1939, the IG had ownership interest in or working agreements with hundreds of companies in dozens of countries. Richard Sasuly says, "Through the system of cartels..., a main center in Germany could virtually dictate the amount of chemical production in almost any country on the continent of Europe.... While relying on their own scientists to maintain technical leadership, IG could nevertheless keep constant watch on all new discoveries in other countries through patent pooling agreements" (90). Despite these pooling agreements, the IG zealously guarded its own patents in order to maintain exclusive control over its technology. Borkin and Welsh report, "Patents were applied for and obtained 'en masse,' in every country having a patent system, but largely in Germany, England, and the United States.... [They became] tourniquets on the economic vigor of Germany's likely antagonists" (43).

Among Germany's eventual enemies, the IG had cartel agreements in the Netherlands with Dutch Shell, in Britain with Imperial Chemicals, and in the United States with Ford Motor Company, Sterling Drug and Standard Oil of New Jersey. This last agreement was especially significant. In 1926, Standard Oil executives Frank Howard and Walter Teagle toured one of the IG's synthetic fuel oil plants; they were amazed at the sophistication of the technology, concerned about its potential effect on world oil prices, and aghast that Standard was not a part of it. In 1928, the two giant companies came to an agreement: for $35 million, the IG turned over to Standard all non-German rights to the synthetic oil process. The immediate results of the agreement were that IG obtained the lump sum it needed to finish perfecting large-scale production of the process, and the two companies created a joint company, Standard-IG Co., to oversee the working out of the deal (Borkin 47-51). In 1930, IG and Standard Oil reached a second agreement. This time, Standard was interested in IG's synthetic rubber process, and another company was formed, the Joint American Study Company (Jasco), "to test and license new processes developed by either party in the 'oil-chemical' field" (Borkin 51). However, the IG kept exclusive rights to the patents it developed, Buna rubber especially (Sasuly 148). This allowed the IG to keep a certain amount of control over United States research into synthetic rubber, and, despite the patent-sharing agreement, the IG continually stalled revealing its Buna rubber technology. (Of course, when the U.S. finally entered the war and its sources of natural rubber were occupied by Japan, the resulting rubber shortage severely curtailed the war effort.) As a further token of friendship, Standard President Teagle joined the Board of Directors of the American IG Corp. In addition to the tangible returns of this cartel agreement, the IG gained a great deal of influence and an important ally. As Sasuly sums up, "The biggest part of the payoff for IG Farben was support by Standard Oil of IG's chemical position all over the world, *including the United States*" (147). Further, just after the war began in Europe and the possibility of war between the United States and Germany became stronger, Standard Oil's Howard met at The Hague with IG representatives to discuss protecting their joint holdings in wartime. Standard purchased the IG's shares of Standard-IG Co. and Jasco for nominal amounts, and the IG assigned United States and Allied rights to all jointly held patents to Standard. Off the record, Standard agreed to hold 20% of all fees derived from these patents for IG, to be delivered after the War (Sasuly 149-50; Borkin 83-88). Standard was convinced (incorrectly as it turned out) that its dealings with the IG were sufficiently camouflaged to prevent the United States government seizure of enemy property and that its mutually profitable relation with the IG would be ready to resume, no matter which side won the war.

IG Farben also had a different sort of cartel arrangement with its own government. One of the influences behind the original formation of the IG was Walter Rathenau's insistence that all German industries cooperate to support the government's effort in World War I. After the war, Rathenau continued to encourage economic cooperation in service to the state. For the IG in particular, corporate goals and profits were tied up with government policy and programs. The line between government and business became even less clear during the years of the Weimar republic as business executives, including many employed by the IG, simultaneously held important policy-making cabinet posts (Borkin and Welsh 53). The IG and German business did not support Hitler immediately; his humble origins and lower class supporters offended those from traditionally aristocratic backgrounds (Sasuly 64-65). For his part, Hitler used the IG as a symbol of all that was wrong with big business, an "'instrument of international finance capital' dominated by...Jews..." (Borkin 54). Yet, at a secret meeting with IG representatives in November 1932, Hitler enthusiastically promised to support the synthetic fuel program. In February 1933, a month after Hitler had been named Chancellor, German business leaders met with Hermann Goering and agreed to support Hitler publicly and financially. The largest contribution, 400,000 marks, came from IG Farben (Borkin 55-56). The common sense of the IG's and Hitler's mutual support is clear. Germany's ability to wage war was dependent, to a great extent, on the synthetic processes the IG had developed. In turn, the IG had invested billions in these processes, and, because natural oil, rubber, etc. would always be cheaper than the synthetic forms, IG needed a war to make a profit on its investment (Sasuly 138). Thus, an important cooperative relationship between Hitler's government and the IG took shape, and the spheres of business and government overlapped even more. Shortly before he was named the chairman of the IG's board of directors, Hermann Schmitz was named an honorary Nazi deputy in the Reichstag (Borkin 58). In 1937, the entire IG board of directors joined the Nazi Party, and all Jewish directors and managers were replaced (Borkin 72). Many top IG executives served as well in important government posts, often involved with industrial policy (Sasuly 108-09). Corporate and government concerns further overlapped in the IG's international dealings. IG salesmen in other countries served as industrial spies, reporting back to the IG's intelligence headquarters, "Berlin NW7," run by Chairman Schmitz's nephew, Max Ilgner. Sasuly reports, "The Army thought so highly of NW7's general intelligence work...that one of Ilgner's serious problems was to prevent [Army Intelligence] from bodily taking over whole sections of NW7. The problem was solved by putting some of the younger men in uniform and letting them stay on their old jobs in the IG Farben intelligence service" (98-99).

Once the War began, the IG became a conquering army in its own right. IG representatives followed Hitler's invading forces, quickly taking over rival chemical companies in Austria, Czechoslovakia, Poland, Belgium and France. The IG's aggressiveness was marked by two guiding characteristics. First, IG executives wanted to absorb or control all competitors in the dyestuffs industry. Sasuly explains, "Dyestuffs were the oldest and most basic of IG's lines of production. Year after year they continued to yield rich profits. Emergency war production might prove uneconomic and slacken off but IG expected its dye trade to go on forever" (119). By the time Germany had conquered France, the IG had drawn up "new order" plans for the absorption of not only the chemical industries of the countries with which Germany was already at war but also those of the Soviet Union, Switzerland, the United States and Germany's ally Italy (Borkin 99-100). Second, the IG wanted its takeovers to have the appearance of legality. Although takeover deals were made in the context of threats, expulsion of Jewish owners, or calling in of loans by newly Nazi-controlled banks, the agreements were meant to stand up to any postwar scrutiny (Sasuly 118). Through the overlapping of corporate and governmental spheres, Walter Rathenau's credo of industry in service of the state had been turned upside down: IG Farben had been able to make government policy and actions serve its own interests.

Pynchon uses IG Farben's historical interindustrial and intergovernmental cartel arrangements on both a literal and symbolic level. They appear in many specific ways in the novel. Slothrop discovers that the IG-Dutch Shell-Imperial Chemicals cartel has a hand in the development of the V-2. The merger of government and industrial interests is seen in the mixture of Nazi and IG officials attending the Rathenau séance and, on a more comic level, in the black market collaboration of Major Marvy and Bloody Chiclitz. In addition, the V-man Wimpe, Tchitcherine's devil's advocate, is one of NW7's *Verbindungsmaenner*, or spy-salesmen. He eventually goes to work at Chemnyco, the IG's actual cover for its spy operations in the United States.

On a broader level, these cartel arrangements add to the sense of ominous paranoia many of the characters feel. These characters, like Slothrop, suspect that their lives are controlled by forces they can not understand, forces that transcend and are masked by the more easily perceived systems of government, business and religion. They live in a War world of sacrificed comforts, necessities and lives but suspect that the sacrifices, the life under the Rocket blitz, the news from the front, and the governmental posturings are all clever distractions designed to keep the public's attention away from the real stories and the real conflicts over power and profits. That military success takes a back seat to corporate profit seems clear. Pynchon presents a fictional subsidiary of IG Farben, Spottbilligfilm AG, whose unfortunate management is sacked because they developed "a new airborne ray which could turn whole populations, inside a ten-kilometer radius, stone blind. An IG review board caught the scheme in time. Poor Spottbilligfilm. It had slipped their collective mind what such a weapon would do to the dye market after the next war" (163). Confronted with the primacy of profit over national loyalties, one character wonders as he looks at the ruins of an IG synthetic oil plant that perhaps the plant

is *not a ruin at all. It is in perfect working order.* Only waiting for the right connections to be set up, to be switched on...modified, precisely, *deliberately* by bombing that was never hostile, but part of a plan both sides—*"sides?"*—had always agreed on [....] It means this War was never political at all, the politics was all theatre, all just to keep the people distracted...secretly, it was being dictated instead by the needs of technology...(520-21)

The IG represents the possibility that the defining structures of our world serve the financial and ideological needs of a controlling elite. This elite's presence, overt and covert in these defining structures, suggests to the characters sensitized in their paranoia that the world they accept as real is, instead, arbitrary and factitious and that the mindset that defines and makes acceptable that world is also arbitrary.

These factitious defining structures that mask the controlling elite contribute to the cultural conditioning of entire populations. They are used to institute on a cultural level the death-oriented IG world view. People are conditioned to replicate in their own actions the objectification and control of the elite, to be dissatisfied with the earth and long for transcendence, to dominate others while being only marginally aware of their own domination, and to direct their frustrations at the wrong targets. All of these actions legitimize the IG world view and maintain IG and its associated controlling elites in power. Through manipulation of public perceptions, the world view represented by the IG and the interests it serves has been instituted, not as one among many possible realities, but as the only reality.

IG Farben, then, plays an important role as symbolic villain in *Gravity's Rainbow*. On one level, Pynchon criticizes the company for involvement in Nazi Germany's many crimes against humanity. But he also shows us that responsibility for this involvement spreads to many other companies and across national boundaries. On a more important level, Pynchon criticizes IG Farben for its acceptance and promotion of a world view and a process by which nature is destroyed and people are dehumanized. He also shows us that this world view is not exclusive to Nazi Germany but defines all of Western culture and civilization. Finally, even more disturbingly, Pynchon refuses to let us distance ourselves from IG Farben's world view. He shows us how it has shaped our understanding of our world, how it affects us as individuals, and how we are its product, passing on to future generations its deadly effects.

Notes

[1]See Mendelson for the case for the novel's being an "encyclopedic narrative."

[2]For various approaches to understanding Pynchon's use of history, see Sanders; Stark (Ch. 4); Martin; Marquez; Smith; Hite (Ch. 4); and Swartzlander.

[3]See Borkin and Welsh (20-32), Sasuly (18-37), and Borkin (4-37) for historical background on chemical synthesis and IG Farben. Borkin and Welsh and Sasuly seem to have been sources for Pynchon (see Qazi 10, 16).

[4]See Tölölyan's analysis of Pynchon's use of the history of IG Farben (53-58) and Moore's discussion of its thematic implications (137-46).

[5]Merchant analyzes how this reversal of attitudes about nature evolved.

[6]Other critics have cast this conflict in similar terms. Black sees the living earth vs. dead earth paradigm as a manifestation of the conflict between Romantic and nineteenth-century scientific world views. Eddins argues that the conflict is one between two religious perspectives, Orphism, which reveres the earth as a living thing, and Gnosticism, which wants to control the earth into perfect stillness and death. LeClair (38-66) identifies Geli Tripping's vitally alive earth with Lovelock's Gaia.

[7]See Borkin (116-26) for the story of IG Auschwitz.

[8]See Wolfley (882-83) and Slade (32) for arguments that, in the context of the novel, a child's social conditioning is equivalent to parental betrayal.

[9]Wolfley (883) and Schaub (48) both argue that Imipolex G represents an outside force controlling Slothrop's sexual actions. Earl (229-30) shows that the penis has traditionally been seen as a part of a man that is beyond the control of his will.

[10]Duyfhuizen points out that the map is a fiction; thus, the investigation of the relation between Slothrop's erections and the Rocket begins with a false assumption.

[11]Kappel argues, "Bianca's corpse shows Slothrop the sobering moral limits and the destructive capability of his compulsive sexuality and amorality..." (247).

Works Cited

Black, Joel. "Probing a Post-Romantic Paleontology: Thomas Pynchon's *Gravity's Rainbow*." *boundary 2* 8.2 (1980): 229-54.

Borkin, Joseph. *The Crime and Punishment of I.G. Farben.* New York: Free P, 1978.

Borkin, Joseph, and Charles A. Welsh. *Germany's Master Plan: The Story of Industrial Offensive.* New York: Duell, Sloan and Pearce, 1943.

Duyfhuizen, Bernard. "Starry-Eyed Semiotics: Learning to Read Slothrop's Map and *Gravity's Rainbow*." *Pynchon Notes* 6 (1981): 5-33.

Earl, James W. "Freedom and Knowledge in the Zone." *Approaches to* Gravity's Rainbow. Ed. Charles Clerc. Columbus: Ohio State UP, 1983. 229-50.

Eddins, Dwight. "Orphic Contra Gnostic: Religious Conflict in *Gravity's Rainbow.*" *Modern Language Quarterly* 45 (1984): 163-90.

Hite, Molly. *Ideas of Order in the Novels of Thomas Pynchon.* Columbus: Ohio State UP, 1983.

Hogg, Ian, and Bryan Perrett. *Encyclopedia of the Second World War.* Novato: Presidio, 1989.

Kappel, Lawrence. "Psychic Geography in *Gravity's Rainbow.*" *Contemporary Literature* 21 (1980): 225-51.

LeClair, Tom. *The Art of Excess: Mastery in Contemporary American Fiction.* Urbana: U of Illinois P, 1989.

Marquez, Antonio. "The Nightmare of History and Thomas Pynchon's *Gravity's Rainbow.*" *Essays in Literature* 8 (1981): 53-62.

Martin, Richard. "Clio Bemused: The Uses of History in Contemporary American Fiction." *Sub-Stance* 27 (1980): 13-24.

Mendelson, Edward. "Gravity's Encyclopedia." *Mindful Pleasures: Essays on Thomas Pynchon.* Ed. George Levine and David Leverenz. Boston: Little, Brown, 1976. 161-95.

Merchant, Carolyn. *The Death of Nature: Women, Ecology and the Scientific Revolution.* 1980. San Francisco: Harper and Row, 1989.

Moore, Thomas. *The Style of Connectedness:* Gravity's Rainbow *and Thomas Pynchon.* Columbia: U of Missouri P, 1987.

Pynchon, Thomas. *Gravity's Rainbow.* New York: Viking, 1973.

Qazi, Javaid. "Source Materials for Thomas Pynchon's Fiction: An Annotated Bibliography." *Pynchon Notes* 2 (1980): 7-19.

Sanders, Scott. "Pynchon's Paranoid History." *Mindful Pleasures: Essays on Thomas Pynchon.* Ed. George Levine and David Leverenz. Boston: Little, Brown, 1976. 139-59.

Sasuly, Richard. *I.G. Farben.* New York: Boni and Gaer, 1947.

Schaub, Thomas H. *Pynchon: The Voice of Ambiguity.* Urbana: U of Illinois P, 1981.

Slade, Joseph W. "Escaping Rationalization: Options for the Self in *Gravity's Rainbow.*" *Critique* 18.3 (1977): 27-38.

Smith, Thomas S. "Performing in the Zone: The Presentation of Historical Crisis in *Gravity's Rainbow.*" *CLIO* 12 (1982-1983): 245-60.

Stark, John O. *Pynchon's Fictions: Thomas Pynchon and the Literature of Information.* Athens, Ohio UP, 1980.

Swartzlander, Susan. "The Tests of Reality: The Use of History in *Ulysses* and *Gravity's Rainbow.*" *Critique* 29 (1988): 133-43.

Tölölyan, Khachig. "War as Background in *Gravity's Rainbow.*" *Approaches to* Gravity's Rainbow. Ed. Charles Clerc. Columbus: Ohio State UP, 1983. 31-67.

Wolfley, Lawrence C. "Repression's Rainbow: The Presence of Norman O. Brown in Pynchon's Big Novel." *PMLA* 92 (1977): 873-89.

The Art of Making War:
The Political Poster in
Global Conflict

James Rodger Alexander

The visual imagery remains haunting although nearly fifty years have passed since an artist named Wesley set it in ink. Drawn in the center of a vertical rectangle is the head of a cocker spaniel with its chin resting solemnly upon the apron of an enlisted man's naval jumper thrown casually over the back of a stuffed chair. Directly above the dog's head, hanging on a wall in the background, a gold braided rope holds a banner with a gold star in the center of a white field that is bordered in red. At the very bottom of the image, in white letters against the blue chair, three words state simply "...Because Somebody Talked."

Even to someone unfamiliar with the symbolism, the cause and effect relationship between the imagery and the words is distinct, resulting in an emotional response of loss. In 1943, when this World War II poster was first issued, the effect was even more powerful. The cocker spaniel, the most popular breed of dog in the country, served as a symbol for America.[1] The gold star, sign of a serviceman's death, was unfortunately appearing in more and more American homes as a symbol of enduring the ultimate sacrifice for maintaining freedom. The simple message was a reminder of the civilian responsibilities on the home front. [Figure 1]

Only four years earlier, as the decade of the 1930s drew to a close, the role the United States was to play in the drama of escalating world tensions, and the resultant consequences described above, had not yet been defined. In Europe, however, the lines had clearly been drawn. The armistice signed at the eleventh hour of the eleventh day of the eleventh month of 1918, to conclude "the war to end all wars," was less than fifteen years old when, on January 31, 1933, Adolf Hitler ascended to the position of Chancellor of Germany. The Treaty of Versailles, still not ratified by the United States Senate, had left the vanquished German people humiliated, and their country saddled with debts which destabilized the political structure. The emergence of National Socialism offered the German people a focus, an identity and a solution. The costs were, for the moment, of little consequence. Even the rest of Europe voiced little alarm at the transformations occurring within their neighbor's borders. The struggle against a world-wide depression presented a more immediate danger, and international trade required stability more than democracy.

Fig. 1. "...because somebody talked!" Poster Art by Wesley. Distributed by the Office of War Information, 1943. Collection of James Rodger Alexander.

With scant resistance, the Nazi party solidified control within Germany between 1933 and 1938 with the assistance of the Minister of Propaganda and Public Enlightenment, Joseph Goebbels. As part of his campaign to consolidate power, the party heavily subsidized the production of one of the cheapest wireless sets in Europe known as the V.E.—Volksemfanger. During this five year period, the number of radios in German homes quadrupled and the stirring speeches of the Fuhrer became a fixture in many households.[2] While taking full advantage of this contemporary vehicle of mass communication, Goebbels also recognized the power of visual persuasion and utilized the strengths of the political poster to promote the message of the Nazi party, to rally support for the emerging Third Reich, and to establish Hitler's persona as the symbol of the Fatherland. While radio was an effective medium for bringing Hitler's speeches directly into the homes of the German people, the radio could always be turned off. The political poster, however, invaded the fabric of daily German life, helping to set levels of expectation and to establish rules of conduct within the new order. These posters were designed to be visually direct, verbally simple and charged with emotional impact. This simple, yet insidious, form of advertisement was an integral aspect of Goebbels' overall strategy at the time.[3]

In the early work of artist Hubert Lanzinger, for example, Hitler appears as a knight in shining armor mounted upon a dark stallion and bearing the Nazi flag. The historical symbolism is obvious. Another poster of that same period by an artist named Stauber depicts a vibrant and forceful Fuhrer carrying the party standard and leading a mass of uniformed faithful forward from the storms of economic chaos into a newer and brighter tomorrow. The optimistic message contained within the oakleaf border is simple and direct—"Germany Lives." As the Nazi hold on Germany strengthens, Hitler is portrayed as a diplomatic figure in a princely pose with, in one case, a clear proclamation at the bottom to support "Ein Volk, Ein Reich, Ein Fuhrer."[4] A later version of this same portrait presents the Fuhrer with a simple inscription beneath, "Ja," both suggesting and demanding an affirmative response. This series of posters predicts and reflects the change in Hitler's status from a chancellor to be followed into the Fuhrer to be obeyed.

By the fall of 1939, Europe stood precariously balanced on the precipice of war. While the American people strongly preferred a successful European resistance to Nazi expansionism, a clear majority opposed committing the lives of young American men to the conflict.[5] The argument between the forces of isolationism and the proponents of interventionism was waged from the lecture podiums and was broadcast across the airwaves into the homes of the American people. Both sides were well armed with articulate spokesmen who unleashed an impressive salvo of verbal artillery in this war of words. By December 30, 1940, six months after the fall of France to Nazi forces, President Franklin Delano Roosevelt was calling for a war-basis aid package to Britain. However, as late as September, 1941, an American hero of equal stature, Charles Lindbergh, warned in a radio address that "the greatest advocates of bringing us into war are the British, the Jews, and President Roosevelt."[6] Similar isolationist sentiments were repeated to over three and one-half million Americans by Father Charles E. Coughlin who, in his weekly radio broadcasts, called Roosevelt "a war monger whose real name should be 'Rosenfeld'."[7] While the radio was an effective forum to discuss issues, each side also utilized the visual power and emotional impact of the political poster to appeal to the hearts of the American people while attempting to build a majority consensus.

Although the United States government had no official propaganda apparatus in place at that time, private organizations such as the Committee to Save America By Aiding the Allies worked to encourage American intervention by portraying Great Britain as America's first line of defense. In an early 1941 poster by Henri Guignon, the head of Winston Churchill appears superimposed upon the body of a stubborn bulldog firmly defending the Union Jack and defiantly confronting the viewer. The message at the dog's feet assures that Britain is "Holding the Line." But, an unspoken question was raised in the daily newspaper headlines during the seventy-six straight nights of the bombardment of London: "How Much Longer?" The powerful isolationist America First Committee responded with its own campaign of visual persuasion. A 1941 poster design for this Chicago organization depicts the Statue of Liberty against a turbulent red sky, with its torch of freedom being blown away by a passing artillery shell. In bold black letters across the bottom of the page on an angle which parallels the path of the shell, the message reads "War's First Casualty." The warning about the cost of war is clear. The verbal and visual rhetoric from both sides of this debate continued to escalate until the struggle for the direction of the American commitment came to an abrupt conclusion on the morning of December 7, 1941. Within hours after the Japanese attack on Pearl Harbor, nearly all the isolationist voices were silenced. Four days later Germany declared war on the United States, and the American people responded with a single voice.

The Nazis had prepared for the war by approaching the conflict on four fronts simultaneously: military, economic, political and propaganda. The German army was well-trained and equipped. In addition, the party's propaganda campaign had been successful in establishing national pride and personal commitment to the cause of the German people as outlined within Nazi doctrine. By comparison, at the end of 1941, America was neither economically nor militarily prepared to engage in global warfare. However, the surprise attack on Pearl Harbor, while crippling the United States Pacific Fleet, coalesced American opinion behind a commitment to total victory. This single event provided the political advantage of having been the victim of an unwarranted attack. With established popular support and a clear political objective, the United States entered the conflict with a determination and a propaganda momentum which could be visually exploited.

Electronic methods of mass communication had evolved since the end of the First World War and were to play an important informational role in this conflict. However, the political poster, with its power of visual persuasion and emotional content, remained an effective means of reiterating themes to the general public with clarity and simplicity. In addition, there existed the knowledge, proven by valuable experience, of the important role the political poster had played in bringing World War I to a successful conclusion. Many of those visual images were still alive in the minds and hearts of the nation. Some posters were reissued without change to summon the next generation to answer their country's call.

When the United States had entered into the first global conflict in 1917, the poster had already been an integral part of the social and commercial culture of the country for over twenty years. The popular success of the commercial poster in Europe had not gone unnoticed in this country. In 1889, Harper and Brothers commissioned the French decorative artist, Eugene Grasset, to design a cover for *Harper's Bazaar* and two holiday posters for *Harper's* magazine. Many other popular "slick" publications of the time followed suit with their own talented artists. Sales increased dramatically, and the art poster became an instant success on this side of the Atlantic. By 1893, *Harper's* magazine had committed to producing a monthly cover as well as a poster placard to be displayed in store windows to encourage sales. Soon, demand for these posters exceeded the demand for the product they promoted.[8] By the turn of the century, the art of visual persuasion had become firmly woven into the fabric of American culture. By the time of its entry into the Great War[9] in 1917, the United States had a company of accessible artists whose ammunition of visual imagery could be utilized to inform the public about the conflict and to solicit its support to ensure a victory.

On April 17, 1917, artist Charles Dana Gibson hosted a dinner for some of the country's most gifted illustrators and poster artists including James Montgomery Flagg, Howard Chandler Christy and J.C. Leyendecker. What emerged from that gathering was an organization of artists called the Division of Pictorial Publicity. This patriotic group offered its services, free of charge, to the government and met weekly to divide up the work to be produced. In early 1917, one of the most immediate needs was to issue a call for recruitment into the armed services. In response to that demand came three of the most memorable poster images to emerge from that war, although each of them approached the concept of recruitment from a distinctly different point of view.

Perhaps no poster in American history, either commercial or political, is more ingrained in the culture than James Montgomery Flagg's image of Uncle Sam pointing directly at the viewer and demanding, "I Want You For The U.S. Army." Using himself as the model, Flagg created a visual symbol for the country. The image was simple. The message direct. The impact imperative. It remains so today when linked to a national emergency. The power of this direct appeal can be found in the recruiting efforts of nearly all the belligerents of the time. In fact, Flagg's 1917 effort is almost identical to Alfred Leete's 1914 depiction of Lord Kitchener pointing out to the British public with the proclamation "Your Country Needs You."

In contrast to Flagg's direct approach was the seductive call for enlistments created by Howard Chandler Christy, who had been successful in persuading the public in the commercial arena by the use of his signature image, "The Christy Girl." In one 1917 version of his recruitment posters, this young woman, dressed in an oversized naval jumper with her hands proudly gripping the garment near her breasts, looks at the viewer out of the corner of her eye as the text issues a challenge: "*Gee!*! I wish I Were A *Man*. I'd Join the Navy, Naval Reserve, or Coast Guard." What man could resist such an invitation or reject such an obvious challenge to his manhood? A similar challenge was issued two years earlier in a poignant poster designed by the British artist Saville Lamley. A small girl sits on her father's lap while her brother plays with toy soldiers at his feet on the living room floor. The man, in his business suit with his hand drawn to his chin, appears to have difficulty responding to his daughter's simple question: "Daddy, What Did *You* Do During The Great War?" Both examples attempt to persuade the viewer to assume responsibility in a national crisis. The British poster suggests a future price for inaction, while the Christy poster uses the successful commercial style of a known artist to persuade the viewer to buy a new product: WAR.

A third recruiting method linked the need for action to a specific event. Perhaps no poster was more effective in this area than the Fred Spear poster of 1915. While the issuance of this poster preceded the American entry into the war by nearly two years, it was a direct response to the German sinking of the *Lusitania* on May 7, 1915, in which 128 Americans, including 63 children, were lost. The poster depicts a baby clutched closely to its mother's breast as the two of them sink into the green depths of the ocean. Bubbles float from their drowning faces towards the surface above the top of the poster. One simple word accompanies this powerful image: "Enlist." Nothing else was necessary. This persuasive effort was able to blend visual imagery together with minimal text to portray the helpless as innocent victims while soliciting recruits for a potential response.

While many variations were used to encourage recruitment for the war effort, most of them employed one of these three basic concepts: utilization of national imagery, variation of an artist's established commercial style, or pictorial response to a specific event. The accompanying slogans were intended to convey the message that victory was each individual's responsibility, whether on the battlefield or on the home front. In this latter respect, James Montgomery Flagg created a distinctly clear poster for The United States Shipping Board of three vibrant young men walking proudly ahead in perfect unison toward victory. In the center is a worker dressed in overalls and carrying a hammer in his right hand. He walks arm in arm with a Marine on his left and a sailor on his right. They march briskly across the picture plane from left to right. Beneath their feet the words "Together We Win" equates the worker with the combatants and equates hard work on the home front to duty on the frontlines. All are necessary components working together for victory.

The poster proved to be an effective vehicle of communication and was applied to a variety of wartime necessities. The war proved to be very expensive, and all belligerent nations found it necessary to solicit funds from the public by issuing war bonds. Each country pursued this common need in ways that utilized imagery most directly related to the hearts of its citizens. In the United States, perhaps no call for financial assistance was more compelling than the 1918 poster by J.C. Leyendecker for support of the Third Liberty Loan Campaign. A Boy Scout in uniform, down on one knee, passes a sword engraved with the words "Be prepared" to a stoic female figure behind him, draped in the American flag and carrying a shield with the seal of the United States of America engraved on it. The words at the top of the poster say "U.S.A. Bonds," while carved in the stone platform upon which the boy kneels are the words "Weapons For Victory." Once again the image and the words merge to suggest a cause and effect relationship while projecting an emotional impact that solicits support.

Referring to childhood imageries, the Boy Scout motto used in this context suggests that proper preparation has a monetary cost.

Within the short nineteen-month span of the United States' active participation in the World War I, the Division of Pictorial Publicity designed nearly 1500 posters, of which 700 were produced.[10] In addition to recruiting men and soliciting funds, posters were employed to explain national policy, to spur industrial production, to encourage the conservation of war material, to inspire charity for the participants and refugees, and to warn people on the home front of the consequences of their actions.

The United States emerged from the Great War physically intact and as the greatest economic power in the world.[11] In the decade following the war, advertising agencies used enormous budgets to persuade the public to purchase a variety of new products on the market.[12] With radio still in its infancy, a majority of this effort was devoted to visual persuasion both as posters and as smaller versions which appeared in the various print media. However, following the economic collapse in 1929 and the subsequent depression, the poster found a new voice and new causes.

During the economic despair of the 1930s, the poster increasingly was used to address issues of social concern. In the United States, after the election of Franklin Delano Roosevelt in 1932, the government began to play a more active role in cultural activities. It evolved into an important client and employer of artists through the creation of the Federal Arts Projects (FAP) Division of the Works Progress Administration (WPA) in 1935. Poster art flourished under government sponsorship. The WPA/FAP directed its energies and powers of visual persuasion toward winning the domestic war against fear, poverty and unemployment. Additionally, posters were designed to educate the population on issues of health and safety such as venereal disease and cancer, as well as on the proper care of children, the value of a good diet and the importance of personal hygiene. Many assumptions held today regarding health and hygiene are a result of the creative and persuasive posters created by the WPA/FAP. These posters were a democratic, demystified form of art which used visual imagery to inform the public about issues of social concern. They were a simple, inexpensive and practical means of maintaining public morale through the dark days of the depression.

Under continual public scrutiny by conservatives, in 1937 the government created restrictions requiring American citizenship for participation in these programs. Additional programmatic restrictions and budgetary cuts in 1939 caused a loss of nearly 70% of the experienced poster artists from government service.[13] By the early months of 1942, just as the country entered into the conflict, most of the remaining artists had been reassigned to the Graphic Section of the War Service Division and were relegated to designing aircraft charts, uniform identifications and menus for Officers' Clubs. The need to transfer ever increasing resources to the war effort, coupled with conservative opposition to the "boondoggling" support of artists, resulted in the elimination of funding for the WPA/FAP in 1943. The agency received "its honorable discharge" from President Roosevelt.[14] The government's eight-year experiment in the use of visual imagery to affect domestic social policy came to a close. A series of political decisions caused many of the finest government-trained poster artists to be dismissed from service at the precise moment that their talents could have been best utilized.

For the citizens of the United States, barely a generation, 23 years and 26 days—separated the end of the "war to end all wars" from their entry into its sequel. During that time, dramatic improvements had advanced the art of mass communications. The first radio station in the country, KDKA, had not gone on the air until November 2, 1920, yet, throughout the decade of the thirties, political leaders from Fiorello La Guardia and Franklin Delano Roosevelt to Adolf Hitler quickly grasped its power of immediacy and its impact on people's lives. Even as the world slipped slowly and inevitably into a second World War within three decades, television made its public debut at the 1939 World's Fair in New York City. Despite these new electronic wonders, the persuasive power of the poster would again play a pivotal role in the successful conduct of a war. Soon the 1917 image of Uncle Sam created by James Montgomery Flagg was resurrected and was pointing out from the windows of recruitment offices and off the walls of buildings reminding able-bodied men of their patriotic responsibilities. The government had been reluctant to maintain any propaganda apparatus intact between the two wars but quickly established the Office of War Information (OWI) for overt public information. A plethora of organizations—from the governmental War Production Board and the United States Treasury Department to such private groups as the C.I.O. Political Action Committee—designed, printed and distributed posters which educated the public, recruited men to serve, implored women to join the work force, encouraged greater productivity, discouraged waste and warned citizens about dangers on the home front.

No artist-generated organization equivalent to the Division of Pictorial Publicity emerged. Rather, individual artists were absorbed into various existing organizations. Even though Flagg returned to add a series of new works to his classic recruitment poster, a younger generation of artists emerged to develop contemporary images to rally the public. Similar to their First World War predecessors, these artists' works would help galvanize patriotic support for what promised to be a long and difficult uphill battle against formidable opposition in two different theaters of war. Notable among these new artists who articulately blended patriotic images and words together to help build a united home front were Ben Shahn, Thomas Hart Benton, Norman Rockwell and the recent emigrant from occupied France, Jean Carlu. Together with numerous other artists, they produced visual images and political slogans which influenced the American people for half a decade and shaped American culture for a generation.

James Montgomery Flagg, in his role as Uncle Sam, still insisted that "I Want You For The U.S. Army." He also produced an updated recruitment poster for the Marines. This later effort displays a confidence gained through victory and depicts a soldier, gun in hand, reaching out with self assurance to the viewer and offering "Want Action?" At the bottom of the poster comes the invitational response to "Join The U.S. Marine Corps." With a similar air of confidence, Tom Woodburn created a recruitment poster in which the upper two thirds of the picture plane is occupied by an angelic liberty figure wrapped in a flag and holding a laurel wreath in her outstretched right hand near the text "The United States Army." Below this figure, standing side by side in profile, with weapons on their shoulders, are seven images of soldiers, from the present back through the nation's historic conflicts to the Revolutionary War. The banner beneath them reads "Then...Now...Forever." The clear reminder is that the cost of freedom is to serve proudly when your country calls, and your country is calling now. [Figure 2]

These new recruitment posters are similar to their predecessors in the First World War in their successful blending of visual imagery with minimal text to convey a strong message. Stylistically, however, they avoid the turn-of-the-century romanticism of the earlier works and are more direct, even confident, in their solicitation. The role of the poster in this conflict was, conceptually, different. With the print and electronic media providing primary information about the war, the poster was used graphically to reiterate policy. In attempting to integrate wartime policies into the structure of daily life, the United States and its allies carried a distinct advantage into the conflict against their enemies. For propaganda to be persuasive over a period of time, it must, at its core, have a credible basis. This is not to suggest that propaganda is completely truthful, but rather that the basis for a persuasive argument must have its foundations constructed in truth. The Nazis believed in a German master race and planned to rule over an occupied Europe. Their propaganda, however, projected the need to develop a unified Europe to confront the threat of Bolshevik expansionism. To justify their anti-semitic beliefs, they linked Jewish people to that perceived threat. The exposure of these distortions did not lose the war, it merely uncovered the deceit used to rationalize Nazi military aggression and led to a deterioration of support on the home front when the military tide turned.

On the Allied front, by contrast, the policy was clear, and it was accurately reflected within the verbal and visual propaganda. The Allies believed that the Nazi movement was evil, and they intended to destroy it completely. As a loose confederation of 33 different entities, the Allied movement necessarily based its success upon the clear single objective of unconditional surrender of the German Army and the total destruction of the Nazi movement and German militarism.

Unlike the brief American experience in the First World War, the United States' involvement in this conflict lasted for nearly four years, requiring a more extended commitment and sacrifice. Propaganda concerns were not only directed at seeking recruits and soliciting funds through the sale of war bonds, but also at affecting the daily conduct of citizens on the home front. Rationing of certain resources such as rubber, sugar and gasoline was necessary. People were encouraged to accept the sacrifices and to avoid the black market in these goods. Much of the dramatic visual imagery created, and many of the most memorable slogans invented, evolved around the issues of conduct on the home front and guarding against possible enemy agents who might gather information that could effect the outcome of a battle: "Loose Lips Sink Ships;" "He's Watching You;" "The Walls Have Ears." Three of the most visually successful American posters in the genre involved an articulate blending of word and image into a haunting reminder of personal responsibility. On a red background, artist John Atherton planted a simple white cross with a soldier's helmet and ammunition belt hanging on either side. The message was clear and precise. At the top of the poster in white letters was a statement of the cause: "A Careless Word." At the bottom,

Fig. 2. United States Army recruitment poster. Poster art by Tom Woodburn. Distributed 1942. Collection of James Rodger Alexander.

in the same color letters, came a reminder of the effect: "...Another Cross." [Figure 3]

In a similar fashion, but using more subtle imagery, the 1943 poster by Stevan Dohanos shows a single right hand wearing a Nazi ring and holding a German Iron Cross medal against a plain white background. The text at the top simply announces "Award" and attracts immediate attention. Just below the medal, in a quieter tone, it reads "For Careless Talk." The message is troubling and not immediately clear. The smaller text at the very bottom, however, clarifies the ambiguity and addresses the viewer directly: "Don't Discuss Troop Movements—Ship Sailings—War Equipment." A second poster by Dohanos produced in the same year is similar in its impact. This time a hand wearing a swastika signet ring fits the last piece of a jig-saw puzzle together completing the message "Convoy Sails For England Tonight." The warning at the top of the poster, "Bits of Careless Talk Are Pieced Together By the Enemy," relates to the metaphoric imagery and reminds the viewer that even the slightest indiscretion can be pieced with others to produce tragic results. The common theme in all three posters is that, even on the home front, one must guard against aiding the cause of the enemy.

Equal to these three American works in addressing the issue of citizen responsibility are a pair of powerful and direct posters by one of Britain's finest illustrators—the Official Poster Artist of the British War Office, Abram Games. In one example, a soldier's head appears in the background. A spiral generates from his mouth and increases in scale until it penetrates, from behind, three soldiers in the foreground. The image is clear and the meaning precise. The text reinforces the graphic illustration with a pair of subtly interwoven messages. The first reads simply "Your Talk May Kill Your Comrades." But by varying the color of the typography from red on the first word, to white for the next three, and finally orange for the last two, a second and more immediate message is imparted with just the white letters; "Talk May Kill." In the top half of a second poster, Games depicts a soldier's head in profile with his mouth open in conversation. The bottom half shows a sailor struggling to keep above the waves of the dark green ocean waters. Two words, "Talk Kills," separate the soldier as cause from the sailor as effect, and the clear warning is to keep your own confidence or risk someone's life.

The war waged on the battlefield could only be as successful as the battle waged on the home front to keep the soldiers supplied. This battle was also waged on two levels. The first was a campaign to equate the value of factory production at home to the valor of fighting on the front lines. Slogans with this goal in mind attempted to portray the worker and the soldier as teammates and included: "It All Depends On Me" or "Give 'Em Both Barrels." The latter slogan merged with the sophisticated European imagery of artist Jean Carlu. In the foreground is the profile of a soldier with a machine gun. In the background is a worker holding a rivet gun in the same posture, almost like a shadow. While visually dramatic, this particular poster was ineffective because of a failure of cultural translation. The worker is wearing a hat which, while perfectly appropriate for a European laborer, appears to be the hat of a prohibition gangster in the American context. Factory workers took offense at this depiction, and the poster was soon withdrawn. However, a second poster by Carlu in this genre

Fig. 3. "A Careless Word...Another Cross." Poster Art by John Atherton. Distributed 1943. Collection of James Rodger Alexander.

proved to be much more successful. In the same simple and direct profile style, a work glove holds a wrench, which is prepared to torque a bolt. The text reads "America's Answer!" The response is stated "Production!" in which the first "O" in the word is the aforementioned bolt. [Figure 4] Using the more illustrative style of presentation that made his work synonymous with American culture in the post-war era, Norman Rockwell also addressed the issue of factory production. A battle-worn soldier sits attentively firing his machine gun as both empty shell casings and the long ribbon of the expired ammunition belt fall from his gun to rest at his feet. While the laborer is no longer visible, the message is clearly directed toward his responsibility: "Let's Give Him Enough, And On Time."

The second level of the production battleground was the need to enlist women into the labor force to replace the men who had joined the Armed Forces. In this campaign, the Ordinance Department of the U.S. Army was just one organization which produced a series of successful posters displaying women in the work place, while depicting the pride of their beloved soldiers overseas in their transformations. A typical example shows a soldier from the shoulders up, holding a snapshot of his girl back home. The profile picture shows her wearing a head scarf with her factory I.D. badge pinned on her work blouse. There are rows of shell casings in the background. The soldier's broad smile indicates his obvious pride as he announces "My Girl's A WOW!" The double entendre is intended to be descriptive of both her beauty in work clothes and his pride in her role as a *W*omen *O*rdinance *W*orker. The poster serves not only to invite female workers into the labor force but also, in the culture of the 1940s, to equate working women with beauty. [Figure 5]

With the surrender of the German Army at 2:41 a.m., Monday, May 7, 1945,[15] the war in Europe came to a close, but in the Pacific the American soldier fought on. One more time James Montgomery Flagg reinterpreted his image of Uncle Sam to fit the occasion with a poster meant to rally support for the final assault on Japan. In red and white striped pants and a blue vest with white stars worn over a white shirt, his hair blowing in the winds of war, Uncle Sam is pictured rolling up his sleeves (in itself a metaphor) with a wrench in his hand. The text reinforces the aggressive posture with bold red letters. "Jap...You're Next!" At the bottom of the poster, in more traditional typography, is a message making specific use of the first person plural noun as it announces with a confidence reinforced by European victory, "We'll Finish The Job!" [Figure 6]

The job was finished on August 14, 1945, five days after the second Atomic bomb was dropped—this time on the industrial town of Nagasaki, Japan. As the American people began to adjust slowly to peace time, the poster continued to play an important role in helping to control postwar inflation, encouraging the continued planting of victory gardens, and redefining the role of women in the postwar American cultural fabric. In the first of a pair of companion peacetime posters, Flagg's Uncle Sam still sternly implores all citizens: "You Can Lick Runaway Prices." It lists seven steps to follow to achieve an economic victory. The second poster uses the same format, replacing Uncle Sam with a woman, now attired as a housewife in an apron, who responds: "I'm Out To Lick Runaway Prices." Beneath her image the same seven steps are repeated. The message clearly conveys the idea that her postwar role as an inflation fighting housewife is just as vital and patriotic as her role as a factory worker had been during the war.

Over the next twenty years, television evolved into a common fixture in the American home, and radio became a standard automobile accessory. An increasingly larger portion of advertising budgets was allocated to the electronic media, and the poster was limited to the large scale billboards and smaller versions on the pages of the printed media. When the government, in the early 1960s, became more deeply involved in a new military conflict in Southeast Asia, it chose to carry its message and its call for support to the people across the airwaves. As the war spread and its reasons became more blurred, many of the American people found it convenient just to change the station and avoid the debate. The political poster, as a simple and direct means of communication, was abandoned by the government and became, instead, the principle vehicle of the forces opposed to the war in Vietnam. As a visually effective and economically efficient means of communication, the political poster became integrated into an emerging anti-war counterculture.

As the war continued with no end in sight, with no articulated goals, and with a higher cost in human sacrifice, the anti-war poster became a visual entity with an increasingly larger audience. Rather than an image of Uncle Sam soliciting recruits, these posters encouraged resistance and forcefully told the government "Hell No We Won't Go." Woven once again into the fabric of daily life, the political poster played yet a final curtain call in determining the outcome of a war. Only this time, by abandoning a simple medium of direct communication to its people, the government abandoned a valuable resource that might have integrated national policy with the daily hopes of the average American. By overlooking a simple, old-fashioned publicity tool, the most powerful nation on earth lost the support of its people and thus the hope of victory.

Fig. 4. "America's Answer! Production." Poster Art by Jean Carlu. Distributed by the Office of Emergency Management, 1942. Collection of James Rodger Alexander.

Fig. 5. "My Girl's a WOW (Woman Ordinance Worker)." Artist Unknown. Distributed by the United States Army, 1942. Collection of James Rodger Alexander.

Fig. 6. "We'll Finish the Job!" Poster Art by James Montgomery Flagg. Distributed by the United States Army, 1945. Collection of James Rodger Alexander.

Notes

[1]"Dogs of America," *Life* 31 January 1949: 40-48.

[2]Anthony Rhodes, *Propaganda: The Art of Persuasion: World War II* 2nd ed., Vol. I (New York, London: Chelsea House Publishers, 1983) 26-27.

[3]Rhodes, Vol. I: 22.

[4]One People, One Country, One Leader.

[5]Rhodes, Vol. I: 139.

[6]Rhodes, Vol. I: 141.

[7]Rhodes, Vol. I: 141.

[8]Victor Margolin, *The Golden Age of the American Poster* (New York: Ballantine Books, 1976) 13.

[9]While today the global conflict from 1914 to 1918 is referred to as the First World War, prior to 1941 it was always referred to as the Great War. In the context of this article I will refer to that conflict as the Great War when discussing it in a context prior to 1941 and as the First World War when discussed in a context after 1941.

[10]Maurice Rickards, *The Rise and Fall of the Poster* (New York: McGraw-Hill, 1971) 26.

[11]Alan Weill, *The Poster, A Worldwide Survey and History* (Boston: G.K. Hall, 1985) 241.

[12]Weill 241.

[13]Christopher DeNoon, *Posters of the W.P.A.* (Los Angeles: Wheatley, 1987) 14.

[14]DeNoon 143.

[15]"The War Ends in Europe," *Life* 14 May 1945: 27-37.

Madison Avenue Goes to War:
Patriotism in Advertising
During World War II

Sue Hart

The World War II years. Patriotism was in the air. Americans were reminded of their duties as citizens everywhere they looked or listened. Hollywood's version of love of country played well to audiences often drawn to the theater as much by the promise of newsreel footage as by the feature film. Radio stations featured music that sang of the separations and sacrifices required on the home front—and promised a brighter tomorrow. And Madison Avenue! It may well have been the American advertising industry's finest hour.

The task of keeping enthusiasm for the war effort high, week after week, year after year, in the face of shortages and personal sacrifices, could not have been an easy one. But Madison Avenue was equal to the challenge. Advertising copywriters developed a new public relations vocabulary comprised of words like *sacrifice, duty* and *obligation* and spoke of companies being grateful and eager to contribute to the war effort. Illustrations featured war workers and Armed Forces personnel instead of more traditional models. Glamour was replaced by gunnery sergeants, and emphasis on the advertiser's product was downplayed to play up the importance of a united stand on the home front. By devoting themselves to instilling—and sustaining—a patriotic attitude toward the war effort, advertisers were able to rally the home front and keep spirits up while product supplies and personal services dwindled.

Advertisements drawn from wartime issues of *Life Magazine* (all citations are to issues of *Life*, a publication of Time, Incorporated) illustrate the patriotic tone achieved in both general-appeal ads and those more specifically addressed to the Women of America. Many major advertisers targeted the female population, perhaps 1) believing that women made up the bulk of magazine readership during the years when men were "in service," or 2) realizing that a number of women were now consumers in their own right. Either because they had suddenly become heads of household (even on a temporary basis) and thus had to make spending decisions previously left to their husbands, or because they were now "working women" (employed outside the home), women now had their own money to spend. Some companies—food producers and cosmetic makers, for example—which had always had Miss or Mrs. America as their target audience continued to address their advertising campaigns to women. Not surprisingly, the major emphasis in these ads remained on the American Homemaker, who represented, after all, one of the images the armed forces were fighting to preserve. But there

114

were subtle changes which recognized the new roles women were filling in wartime America, as well as some not-so-subtle pleas for women to become more actively involved outside the home in the war effort.

Food producers backed government-imposed rationing by urging nutrition, conservation and economy in advertising their products—or in apologizing for the absence of some familiar labels on grocery shelves. Minnesota Canning Company instructed February 7, 1944, readers "How to Eat like a Patriot":

Here are the red-white-and-blue rules of eating these days:
Eat right foods / Share restricted foods / Waste no foods
We must make every crumb, every shred, every particle of food pass on its fullest blessing to the body.
Remember, the further food goes over here, the harder food can fight over there.

Two years into the war, A&P stores reminded readers about the need to keep our armed forces well fed. An illustration of a smiling, healthy-looking soldier sitting down to a well-filled mess kit meal was identified as "The kid who used to raid the icebox." "The next time you shop for food," shoppers were asked, "keep this boy in mind...

He's the kid who used to come in late at night and 'polish off' mother's meal planned for the next day. Folks used to say he'd eat his parents out of house and home...
He's in the armed services now...along with millions of other boys.
And, of course, he and all his buddies have taken their appetites with them.
Uncle Sam knows that these fighters need the finest food...and plenty of it. And so the men of our Army, Navy, Marine Corps and Coast Guard are the best fed in all the world.
We 'stay-at-homes' must make sacrifices in support of our fighting forces. So consider this...
When you visit your A&P Super Market and learn that some favorite item is repeatedly unavailable, know that it has probably 'joined up for the duration.' And should you be asked by an A&P manager or clerk to buy only one of an item you usually purchase in larger quantity, know that it, too, is scarce because it is 'seeing service.' (25 January 1943)

The Curtiss Candy Company summed up the approach taken by most advertisers, asking for patience from customers who were feeling deprived.

We're doing our best to fill domestic orders...but with us, as with every patriotic American, the boys in service have first call.... We are grateful for the opportunity of serving our country in this greatest of all emergencies.... Every American will agree with us that Uncle Sam comes first! (25 January 1943)

Whether the target audience was the housewife trying to feed her family or the war worker trying to coax a few more miles out of worn tires, advertisers had the same goal: to remind consumers of the relationship of their product to the war effort; to keep customers loyal to products that were temporarily unavailable; to instruct consumers on the most beneficial—and least wasteful—use of scarce products; and, above all, to urge whole-hearted cooperation with the war effort. Only through a united effort could Victory—that "Someday," that "Good Day" that Madison Avenue tantalized readers with—be achieved.

While products containing materials essential to defense had an easier time explaining shortages to the public, even fringe connections to the war effort were stressed by advertisers eager to be seen as fully supportive of United States involvement in the European and Pacific theaters. And the holidays—especially wartime Christmases—offered special opportunities for companies to remind their customers not only of their quality products, but also of the necessity to give gifts that would contribute to—or at least not impede—the war effort: "Buy A Gruen Watch...But Buy A War Bond First."

Hoover, playing on its familiar slogan, told December 7, 1942, readers "Give her a War Bond and you give her the best." "For 35 years," the text reminded shoppers,

at Christmas time it has been 'Give her a Hoover and you give her the best.'
Today few Hoover Cleaners are available. The Hoover Company is not making electric cleaners now; it is making materials of war.
This Christmas a War Bond is just about the finest present we can think of.
Some day there'll be a Victory.... Some day those War Bonds will turn into U.S. Currency. Now, let them stand for the money you're saving from the things you can't buy—the money you'll have when the Good Day comes to pay for new electric cleaners and automobiles and refrigerators and stoves.
Then again we'll say when Christmas rolls 'round:
'Give her a Hoover and you give her the best.'

On this first anniversary of Pearl Harbor, Americans probably needed few reminders to be patriotic Santas, but AT&T made it clear that the advent of war brought about more than product shortages. "War needs the wires this Christmas," an operator advised. "So please don't make Long Distance calls to war-busy centers this Christmas unless they're vital" [Figure 1]. A Schenley Distillers ad summed up America's second Christmas at war by hanging a Victory V in the center of a holly wreath and commending citizens on their readiness "to give up everything needed to bring victory and lasting peace. Our gift to free peoples everywhere is this high spirit of sacrifice, the winning morale, that will achieve victory" because, the text continued, "As in every crisis, America Makes the Best of Everything" (7 December 1942) [Figure 2].

Clothing manufacturers managed to promote their products as well as patriotic civil defense activities and Bond sales in their holiday messages. On December 7, 1942, the B.V.D. Corporation urged the consumer to

Be a sentimental Santa—on the *practical* side—Buy Bonds First! This Christmas does call for sentiment...but you've got to be practical, too. You score on both counts when you give War Bonds and Stamps! Buy some for everybody on your list. Then, with the money you have left, you can add to your gift with practical Freedom Shirts...Trim, almost-military lines. Ideal to slip on when he dashes out for civilian defense duties.

The war bond message, delivered in a variety of ways, was popular with advertisers at any time of year. The manufacturers of Old Gold cigarettes challenged Americans to "Buy more War Bonds than you think you can afford"

Fig. 1. "War Needs the Wires This Christmas," Bell Telephone System advertisement, *Life Magazine*, December 7, 1942. Printed by permission of AT&T.

Fig. 2. "Spirit of '43," Schenley Distillers Corporation advertisement, *Life Magazine*, December 7, 1942. Printed by permission of Schenley Industries, Inc.

(7 February 1944). Western Electric, in an ad that proudly displayed the Army/ Navy E burgee, touted its credentials as a defense contractor and urged "Until the last enemy plane is knocked down, buy War Bonds regularly—all you can!" (7 February 1944). Chrysler reminded customers to "Back the Attack with War Bonds!" (21 August 1944). Tappan Ranges offered a "practical suggestion": "Set aside War Bonds today to purchase a Tappan tomorrow. By investing in War Bonds, families save money, help the U.S. war effort, help hasten the day when plants like Tappan will return to peacetime production" (25 January 1943). The 1943 consumer, learning to live with rationing, understocked grocery shelves, empty appliance areas in department stores and nearly-empty car lots, was reminded he would be rewarded for assisting the push toward Victory because postwar products, such as "That Tappan of the future[,] will be 'even better'! For from the designing done for instruments of war have come ideas for instruments of peace."

Nash-Kelvinator was one of many companies telling Americans that this war required the cooperation and sacrifices of all. In an effort to increase Bond sales, the company stressed the kinship of all Americans with those who were doing the actual fighting:

All that we have—in men, machines and skill—is being poured into the job to get it done...For they are our sons, too...those fearless fighters of the sky. Let's keep the battle rolling—with War Bonds and all the scrap we can collect! (25 January 1943)

P. Ballantine & Sons pointed out that "Some of us can help most in the front lines, others on production lines—all of us can buy war bonds and stamps" (25 January 1943). Their ad shows two female war workers leaving the paymaster's window with War Bonds in hand. "How *American* it is—to want something better!" the caption reads [Figure 3]. The identification of certain virtues as particularly American was a significant contribution of Madison Avenue to home front morale and resolve. Role models of "real" or "true" Americans were created by advertisers, movie makers and song writers—and the rank and file followed their lead cheerfully, for the most part.

Whatever the American at home could do to speed Victory was little enough, compared to the lot of the fighting man, and this was made clear in a February 7, 1944, National Dairy Products Corporation ad:

...Buying Bonds is hard, important, patriotic service. But it doesn't automatically make a man a hero.... Lending your money for ten years is not the same as giving your life for keeps.

Not all patriotic advertising was developed at a manufacturer's request. The War Advertising Council (WAC), with the approval of the Office of War Information, prepared United States War messages for civilians on their duties as citizens of a nation at war. A full page WAC call for conservation of materials and money ran on February 7, 1944, in space contributed by the magazine publishers of America. Under a picture of a combat-ready soldier speaking to a civilian worker holding his pay envelope, readers were cautioned about spending their wages in ways that would hamper the war effort:

How American it is... to want something better!

SURE this war-plant worker looks forward to "something better"—resuming study for her chosen career, that long-planned trip or to marriage.

That's why she's putting a healthy part of her earnings into war bonds and stamps—to speed the return of peace and all the other things which help make this "the land of something better."

Some of us can help most in the front lines, others on production lines—*all* of us can buy war bonds and stamps!

EVEN IN WARTIME, free America still enjoys many "better things" which are not available to less fortunate peoples. P. Ballantine & Sons, makers of "something better" in moderate beverages—Ballantine— America's largest selling ale.

Fig. 3. "How American it is...to want something better," P. Ballantine and Sons advertisement, *Life Magazine*, January 25, 1943. Printed by permission of Ballantine Laboratories, Inc.

Sure that Saturday night pay envelope's bulging. But let me tell you something, brother, before you spend a dime...That money's mine too!

I can take it. The mess out here. And missing my wife and kid.

What I can't take is you making it tougher for me. Or my widow, if that's how it goes. And brother, it will make it tough—if you splurge one dime tonight....

You're working...and I'm fighting...for the same thing. But you could lose it for both of us—without thinking. A guy like you could start bidding me right out of the picture tonight. And my wife and kid. There not being as much as everybody'd like to buy—and you having the green stuff.

...Stop spending. For yourself. Your kids. And mine. That, brother, is sense, not sacrifice.... I wouldn't buy a shoelace til I'd looked myself square in the eye and knew I couldn't do without. (You get to knowin'—out here—what you can do without.)

...I've got your future in my rifle hand, brother. But you've got both of ours, in the inside of that stuffed-up envelope.... Squeeze that money, brother. It's got blood on it!

Between their efforts, WAC and the nation's commercial advertisers cajoled or complimented most Americans into doing their part to speed the war's end. Women, in particular, were commended by many manufacturers for "bearing-up" through the war years. A January 25, 1943, Reliance Happy Home ad pictured women in a kitchen, looking through a War-Time Menus booklet which one of them holds. They are, the text says:

Happy...to Make the Best of It! In countless American homes, mothers and daughters are doing their part—gladly, unselfishly. They are devising new ways to keep their families healthy and happy. These patriotic women rely on fresh, practical Happy Home frocks for every active hour.

And Pacific Sheets praised the American woman for that "Half an inch...the lift of your chin":

A wonderful surge of courage brings your head up fiercely in the face of threats. A flash of your eyes measures the enemy. Sacrifice? Your answer is a short laugh. Sacrifice is a pleasure. It's something to do. It's a way to help. And you—magnificent lady—you'll help. You'll toil. You'll fight like a tigeress. We know. We've seen it in the lift of your chin.

But you won't fight alone. Across the street...down the street...far away...near away...in tiny towns, titanic towns—we're fighting. All of us. Doing our parts. (3 August 1942)

Hoffmann-LaRoche, Inc., makers of vitamins and medicines, sponsored ads that took as their theme "The more women at war...the sooner we'll win." This was a radical departure from the pre-War American aversion to women working outside the home, and the idea it introduced was probably responsible, at least in part, for the national movement of more and more women into the business marketplace which began with "Rosie the Riveter" and continues to the present. Their February 7, 1944, full-page ad pictured a new war widow, her hand crumpling a letter that began, "I hope, Mary, you will never read this..."

Tragedies like this—personal, individual tragedies—are happening every day. And they will continue happening until the great tragedy of war is over—and our victorious men start coming home. America needs millions of her women—needs you personally—to make this day of victory come sooner. You can do a vital job in ending this war quicker. You can save many and many an American soldier from fighting needless extra days. You are wanted desperately in a war job—in the armed services—in essential civilian work. [Figure 4]

On August 21, 1944, Hoffmann-LaRoche asked women to

Count these months in *lives*—not days. LIVES! Lives of American men...lives of the men of your own family...the boy engaged to that girl down the street, the freckle-faced kid who used to deliver your groceries, the youngster who whistled while he worked in the corner drugstore, the husband of your best and oldest friend...every man in a uniform. LIVES! That's the measure of time in days of war. How many of them will it cost America to win the Victory? How many will be lost?
No one knows. But this is certain: the more women who join those already at work—take a war job, enlist in the armed services—the better chance these men will have to live.... It comes right down to that!
Count these months in lives—not days—and no decent American woman will evade her obligation.

More than womanpower was needed, of course, and advertisers frequently used their public relations budgets to urge full civilian participation in the effort. "Find yourself in this picture," the Electric Storage Battery Company (Exide) captioned a combat scene.

Yes, Mr. Civilian, you're right in there, too. You got yourself into this thrilling group picture by your thoughtful buying. For thoughtful buying means: 1) that you buy nothing you can do without; 2) that when you must buy anything, it is the longest-lasting thing you can find, not likely to be needing replacing very soon. (7 December 1942)

Two years later, the manufacturers of Duo-Therm Heaters were still seeking volunteers to undertake Civil Defense, scrap collection and war bond purchasing. "Fit *yourself* into this picture *Now...*" their ad demanded in a headline over a family scene of parents, daughter and one son standing in front of a window displaying a service star.

Son Jim isn't in this snapshot—his present address is an APO. And his folks want him home again. Just as much—just as soon—as every one wants those boys back. So the whole family is pitching in to help: Dad started a car pool; speaks at War Bond drives; buys bonds. Mother is taking nurses' aide training; saves fats and tin. Jane is a school teacher; buys War Bonds; works in OCD and USO. Even Johnny helps the OCD; he's a champion scrap collector, too. That's how this whole family works whole-heartedly to win. If every family does the same, we'll gain an earlier victory...and get the boys home *Sooner!* (7 February 1944)

Fig. 4. "The more Women at War...the Sooner we'll win," Hoffmann-LaRoche, Inc. advertisement, *Life Magazine*, February 7, 1944. Printed by permission of Hoffmann-LaRoche Inc.

Often, the major contribution a civilian could make to the war effort was to do without. Companies which had previously hoped to secure new customers through their ads turned their attention to their most important customers during the war years—for once not the American Consumer. Pontiac, for example, was "building for victory," and its August 3, 1942 ad made its priorities clear: "Pontiac has many tasks but just one goal: To do everything in our power to provide American fighting men with more and better weapons for use in their struggle for victory on land, on the sea and in the air." Oldsmobile took a similar tack, quoting from an official service song, "Off we go into the wild blue yonder...Nothing'll stop the Army Air Corps!" and adding its own message—one which illustrates another important facet of World War II advertising, the bolstering of American confidence in the country's ability to get the job done, to achieve Victory:

And nothing'll stop the men and women of Oldsmobile from putting everything into their work...for these valiant fighting fliers. Every day brings new exciting news about our men who fight in the clouds.... Already they've proved that American equipment and American fliers can handle anything the enemy has shown them.... (7 December 1942)

U.S. Rubber cited "the great emergency" as a reason for placing the American Consumer at the end of the line for product delivery:

We have 3 customers: The Army...The Navy...And You. In this national emergency, the conservation and proper distribution of rubber is vital to defense. So vital, that deliveries of defense orders to the Army and the Navy must now take precedence over your orders.... [O]ur policy, from the very beginning of the great emergency in which our country finds itself, has always been one of 'all-out' willingness to do whatever is required in furthering national defense.... We have asked our dealers...to limit their orders...to actual requirements...so that we may be allowed to serve first the men who serve you....we ask you to conserve your own and your country's rubber resources. This way there will be rubber enough for all...for tanks and guns and planes and ships...for farm, factory and home. (August 11, 1941)

Not every company could boast of products that were seeing service, but most advertisers found some element of war effort on which to build their ads. Greyhound took a full page on August 21, 1944, to pay tribute to the men and women of its organization who were serving in the Armed Forces. The ad proudly displayed a Service Star with the number 5180, which was explained in the text:

The special skills and technical training of more than 5,000 Greyhound employees...have helped make them good soldiers, sailors, marines and flyers. Greyhound is going to be proud to have these men and women back, in the better days ahead, when highway travel comes fully into its own.

In a sometimes lighter vein, personal care products joined the parade of advertisers using wartime motifs in their ads. Most of them had as their underlying message the idea that, regardless of the circumstances, there was no excuse for poor grooming. Barbasol, for example, featured a leggy bathing beauty who told a group of service men on furlough, "My brother's in the service, too. His face takes a beating just like yours, from sun and wind, hard and cold water shaving. But he doesn't come home on leave with rawhide jowls and chin. He uses Barbasol" (3 August 1942).

Women's beauty and personal care products ads tended to read like mini-romances or to demonstrate that women who engaged in war work could still look their best. The makers of Jergens Lotion ("For Soft, Adorable Hands") titled one unabashedly sentimental ad "10 Days was all we had, dear."

I wasn't even sure you loved me, dear. Till you came home on that last leave.
Then you held my hands—tight. And, "Let's get married," you said.
White satin, a bride's veil? There simply wasn't time. We wanted our whole 10 days for our honeymoon.
But my hands were soft and smooth as any bride's. (You did say so, my darling.) I have Jergens Lotion to thank for that. War work, such as I do, takes the natural softeners from the skin. But—think of me always with soft hands, my dear heart. I'm faithfully using Jergens Lotion. (20 November 1944)

Pacquins, which claimed the distinction of having "More women workers in war industries use [it] than any other hand cream," pictured war workers in its ads and used such slogans as "Hands that help make bombers can still be 'smoothies'." Pacquins did not ignore the homemaker population, either, although the placement of *only* in the following sentence suggested that war work was a more important occupation than homefront KP duty. "You may make or grease 'machines' in a war-time factory—or you may only wield kitchen pans and save the grease. Either job is hard on your hands..." (7 December 1942).

Whatever their wares—beauty aids, car parts or kitchen appliances—World War II era advertisers were selling patriotism and promise first; their products second. If the apple pie which had been the symbol of America was currently out-of-stock, more and better apple pie at some future date became the war cry of the advertising industry. By telling past and future customers that new and better products—in unlimited numbers—would be available at war's end, advertisers did their part in keeping morale high and convincing consumers that "doing without" was "doing right." Gratification in terms of driving a new car or sitting down to steak on the dinner plate might have to be delayed until war's end, but Madison Avenue made Americans feel good about their individual contributions to the eventual Victory.

Whether the message urged conservation of scarce supplies or passed out commendations for efforts already made, whether the intent was to bolster confidence or ask for cooperation, Madison Avenue rallied the World War II home front to the war effort in a way that has not been seen since. When that "Good Day" of Victory finally arrived, it was in no small part due to the call to patriotism that arrived weekly in American homes disguised as magazine advertisements.

Note

All citations are to issues of *Life*, a publication of *Time*, Incorporated.

"If You're Nervous in the Service...": Training Songs of Female Soldiers in the '40s[1]

Carol Burke

In 1942 women began enlisting as WAACs, WAVES, SPARS, WAFS and Lady Leathernecks[2] in increasingly large numbers until, by the end of the war, 350,000 women had served in the military.[3] At training camps in Des Moines, the Coast Guard Academy, Hunter College, Smith and Holyoke, these women adapted popular songs by inventing verses which defined them as military women, proclaimed their enthusiasm and eagerness to serve, and voiced their frustration about the rigors of training. The verses were improvised on such familiar tunes as "The Sweetheart of Sigma Chi," "Roll out the Barrel," "Pack Up Your Troubles," "Thanks for the Memories," "Man on the Flying Trapeze," "Pop Goes the Weasel" and "California, Here We Come." The enlistees sang of "WAAC days, WAAC days, dear old break-your-back days"; they adapted "Glow Worm" to lyricize the drudgery of the barracks:

At crack of dawn, we mop the porches,
Shine our shoes by light of torches,
Shave our necks for two-inch-clearance
Still we're gigged for personal appearance.
Turn our sheets with a six-inch ruler,
Send our rings back to the jeweler,
We don't care we'll show them how,
We're in the Army now.[4]

Women did march to a few of the same songs as the male units, songs like "Gee, Mom I Wanna Go Home" ("The meat in the Army/They say is mighty fine/Last night we had ten puppies/Today we've only nine") and appended verses of their own ("The stockings in the Army/They're made of binder twine") and ("The sweaters in the Army/They say are mighty fine,/But even Lana Turner/Would look like Frankenstein").[5]

Like male soldiers in training, these women vented their disillusionment with military life. Expecting action and excitement, recruits soon found themselves bound to the domestic drudgery they thought they had left behind:

They told us we'd be soldier girls
If we would volunteer,

127

But we will be good kitchen maids
When we get out of here.

With scrubbing floors and dusting chairs
And takin' orders and how
And they all say when we complain,
You're in the Army now.[6]

But, whereas their male counterparts simply complained, women in training often tempered their grumbling with enthusiastic choruses that rationalized immediate discomforts as inevitable sacrifices. They celebrated their new identity as female soldiers and wrapped even their discontent in fervent patriotism. In the following, sung to the tune of "Funiculee, Funicla," what begins as disillusionment about joining the Army quickly rallies round to a hearty endorsement of training: the simple song of complaint is transformed into recruitment appeal:

Some join the WAACs to get a bit of glamour,
What a mistake, what a mistake!
"Let's join the WAACs and have some fun," they clamor,
Wait till they ache, wait till they ache.
We know that they will soon be making brown beds
And scrubbing floors, and scrubbing floors,
To pass a stiff inspection by some crowned heads,
And other chores, and other chores.

But we love it, we wouldn't want to change,
Civilian life to us seems very strange,
We learn to take, we learn to give
We learn new lessons every day,
If you really want to live, come join the WAACs and shout,
Hurray![7]

Women in training described themselves as tired but happy domestics, as camp followers-made-soldiers who managed if not to transform drudgery into splendor, at least to put a good face on it. In their version of "There's a Tavern in the Town," WAACs from Fort Des Moines sang of the toil of training, ameliorated by the WAAC smile:

There's a WAAC camp in Des Moines—in Des Moines,
Which we were very proud to join—proud to join,
Oh we scrub, we mop we drill for miles and miles
Our faces always wreathed in smiles.[8]

Although these songs enthusiastically endorsed the hard work of training, they also curbed any fervor women might harbor for military action. We certainly know that following training, some of these women displayed courage as well as endured hardships, some marching only twenty miles behind male combat troops in Europe, others flying supply and transport missions. But it was their humility rather than their valour that these songs anticipated.

Defensive in nature, many of these songs insisted on the modest desires of women in uniform, as if such songs were intended to quiet the fears of those who opposed the enlistment of women on the grounds that this militarization would be the first step toward arming women. In considering folk groups within institutions, we must never fail to examine the ways in which lore sanctions approved values and censures others.[9] Although some military women secretly desired to join their male counterparts in combat, they never voiced this yearning as corporate sentiment. Instead, they insisted:

I don't wanna march in the Infantry,
Ride in the Cavalry, shoot in Artillery.
I don't wanna fly over Germany.
I just wanna be a WAAC.

We're the WAACs and everyone a soldier,
To class we go, no rifle on our shoulder,
But we work to send a man who's bolder
So we'll all go free.[10]

Obviously, autonomy was to be won not only through sacrifice but also by clearly distinguishing the work of military women from the work of military men. These songs might be read simply as work songs that helped women endure the discomfort and tedium of training and that transparently communicated shared sentiments. But such a reading is, indeed, a simple one, for it fails to take into account the fact that the performances of these songs always occurred within earshot of authority. As occupational folklore generated within the total institution, these songs affirmed institutional values and transferred them, through training, on to the next batch of fresh recruits.

It might be argued, too, that these songs should be read solely in a contemporary context in which military women have demonstrated their willingness to risk their lives in the service of their country. But even as early as 1917, American popular songs proclaimed the enthusiasm for women in war:

Although I'm not a socialist
I wish they'd let the women enlist.
And if the men refuse to fight
I wish they'd give the women the right.[11]

And from another song:

If they should ever send a suffrage regiment
I'd hurry to enlist.[12]

Although popular sentiment of 20 years earlier had celebrated women's full participation in war, and although many military women were certainly willing to risk their lives in the same ways as men, these songs admitted no such radical sentiment. Instead, they often characterized the female soldier as the scatterbrained, zany girl who would somehow manage to befuddle the enemy enough to win the war:

Over there, over there
Send the word to the boys over there
That the WACs are coming, the WACs are coming
To get in everybody's hair.
We will aid in the raid
That our men make to win in Berlin
We'll be over, we're coming over
And we won't be back
Til they crack up over there.[13]

Clearly, had women serving in Europe, North Africa, and the Pacific merely gotten "in everybody's hair," overseas commanders would not have requested far more female soldiers than Washington could hope to supply.[14] The trivialization of women's labor echoed as one of the most dominant strains in these songs.

Many of these songs humorously depicted the female soldier as incompetent. "Ginny the Ninny of the Goon Platoon,"[15] forever dreaming of the Captain she would marry, moved in one direction while her company moved in the other. Tillie, another humorous incompetent, continually failed to pass inspection and perform the simple chores required of her:

Tillie joined the Army;
She enlisted in the WAACs
And soon to Fort Des Moines our Till was making tracks,
They issued her a uniform, her name was on a tag,
And with the other stuff she got,
They gave her a barracks bag.

They demonstrated how to place equipment in a trunk,
And said to her, "Aux. if you don't want to flunk
Your civies must be out of sight
Or we will surely nag.
All your personal things must go
Under your barracks bag."

Tillie went to mess hall, but the poor girl couldn't eat,
Exactly what the reason was our Till would not repeat,
But later on it all came out,
She really hit a snag,
Tillie left her false teeth
Under her barracks bag.

And then our Tillie drew K.P, in Mess No. 8,
Every time she turned around, she broke another plate,
The Sergeant said, "Now this won't do,"
Her head began to wag
So Tillie hid the wreckage

Under the barracks bag.

At Saturday inspection her hair was still too long,
The General scowled at her and said
"See here, your hair's cut wrong."
Now Tillie had a wig she wore to every ballroom shag,
Where do you think she kept it?
Under the barracks bag.

Tillie went on sick call when she caught the G.I. cold,
They gave her shots on top of that
That was worse than she'd been told.
They gave her pills and medicine that made her pockets sag,
Where do you think she put it?
Under the barracks bag.

At last Tillie died, it really was a shame,
Her funeral was military, and everybody came.
And Tillie's last request was that,
She really was a hag.
Comrades, will you bury me,
Under my barracks bag?[16]

Typically, when one of these training songs began with a spirited celebration of female professionalism, it ended with a sharp diminution of women's role. Take, for example, "Petticoat Soldiers," which called for female recruits to "stand side by side with doughboys, Marines, and sailors" in defense of liberty. It ended with these same women, obviously well behind men, having substituted make-up for guns, as if men were commissioned to wage one kind of attack and women another.

When the call to colors
Rang through this mighty land,
Our fair women answered
And took their vows to stand
Side by side with doughboys,
Marines and sailors, too,
In defending life and liberty for you.
Petticoat soldiers marching
In step to victory.
Petticoat soldiers marching
With heart and spirit free;
'Ever there's been an army,
To fight off ev'ry foe;
Now we have joined the forces
And go where-e're they go.
And you can bet we'll do
Our part for Uncle Sam,
For we're all set and keeping fit,
Yes, sir! Yes, ma'am!

We'll always serve our country
In every cause it backs.
We don't tote guns or bayonets,
Our powder comes in compact sets.
We're petticoat soldiers,
Wacky WAACs![17]

Contradiction made its way to the heart of these songs, and the oxymoronic dissonance between the title's two words, "petticoat" and "soldier" resolved itself in a kind of uneasy humor—the image of the "WACKY WAC." The efficient professional woman in training created an image of herself as the diminutive, incompetent and crazy female soldier. In one song she sang, "Yes, by cracky I'm a little WACY/I'm a little soldier girl...I fall in, I fall out, I fall asleep in class, no doubt."[18]

To comprehend how astounding this caricature was, one need only consider the background of these first female recruits. Most were between twenty-five and forty, 99% had held a job before enlisting and 90% had college training.[19] Far different, for example, were their male counterparts, who typically had no college education, and only minimal work experience prior to military service. These songs of the crazy female soldier served, then, to remind female recruits on some level of the absurdity of their predicament, of their unfitness for military work and of its temporary status. Having stepped out of socially prescribed feminine roles in response to a national crisis, they were meant to someday return to home and hearth ("I'm a rippin', snortin' *Auxie*, but I'll be a captain's wife.")[20]

But, in the meantime, women in training humorously invoked insanity and pregnancy as resolutions to their predicament. They advised:

If you're nervous in the service
and you don't know what to do.
Have a baby, Have a baby.[21]

or:

"Are you nervous in the service?
Do you want a *C.D.D.*?[22]
Are you fed up with the set up?
Come along, go nuts with me."

The popular song, "Valencia" was rewritten as "Dementia:" "Dementia/Has struck us one and all./That's why we're here on chorus call./Dementia."[23]

Just as these songs humorously depicted the tension created by women entering roles never before defined as feminine, they also explored quite literally the way in which women "fit" the image of the female soldier newly created for them by those in authority. Uniforms were often the subjects of these songs. A number of interesting controversies developed in the military over the issue of women's uniforms, a hotly contested issue even today. The question of whether to issue undergarments and robes, items of clothing not given to men, produced heated debate. The designing of WAC uniforms by tailors who had only ever clothed male bodies resulted in awkward fits in early uniforms. Had women been allowed to train in male uniforms as Oveta Culp Hobby, head of the WAC, had vociferously argued for, many hardships would have been prevented. Before their deployment to North Africa, the first 150 WACs to be sent overseas trained in the winter at Camp Kilmer, New Jersey, in short-sleeved uniforms with neither gloves nor boots because the Army had not received its order of winter WAC uniforms.[24] After much resistance on the part of the Army higherups and much illness on the part of trainees, Hobby finally succeeded in securing male coats for these women.

In her address to the first WAC officers-to-be at Ft. Des Moines, Hobby explained their change from civilian to military life in terms of their uniform:

You have just made the change from peacetime pursuits to wartime tasks—from the individualism of civilian life to the anonymity of mass military life. You have given up comfortable homes, highly paid positions, leisure. You have taken off silks and put on khaki. And all for essentially the same reason—you have a debt and a date. A debt to democracy and a date with destiny.[25]

Similarly, a few of these training songs conveyed the impression of a smart, well-disciplined female soldier, enthusiastically endorsing the uniform as a form of collective identity:

Have you heard of the girls of the Army
Who took the country by storm:
We belong to American Forces,
And we wear a smart uniform.[26]

The uniform did not erase one's femininity; it merely redefined it:

We're the WAACs, We're the WAACs.
We're the girls in the khaki,
And we think the Army's grand.
We're the girls, soldier girls,
Minus frills, minus curls,
But pretty as a picture in our suits made of tan.[27]

Many songs, however, humorously revealed the mismatch between soldier garb and the female body inside. These suits made of tan could be ill-fitting and uncomfortable, a fact to which this comic version of "Every Little Raindrop" testifies:

In my little GI shoes
I walk along the street.
In my little cotton hose,
I give the boys a treat.
My skirt looks like a barracks bag,
My hat just like a pot.
But I am in the Army now
And glad with what I got.
In my raincoat extra large,

I look just like a sack,
But I'm in the Army now
And glad to be a WAC.
The Army issues clothes alright;
They make you look an awful sight[28]

"G.I. song" describes the transformation of the young pampered recruit, whose mother made her bed, cleaned her clothes and buttered her bread, into a WAC— a GI who accepts her new image:

Then she came to camp one day
Quickly learned the WACY way
Underwear "cafe au lait!"
Oh me, oh my, strictly GI.

Hats and shoes and skirts don't fit
Your girdle bunches when you sit
Come on rookies, you can't quit
Just heave a sigh and be G.I.[29]

Female recruits forfeited stylish silks for ill-fitting khaki and sang as if to encourage other women to join them. With 78% of the American public favoring the conscription of women (according to Gallup polls at the time),[30] popular sentiment lined up behind them. But their transformation from civilian women into government issue soldiers was tentative and temporary, one meant to last only until the end of the war. And along with the construction of a G.I. self went the sentimental recollection of a non-G.I. self, to which the following harkens:

This is the song of a G.I. muse,
Lumbering along in G.I. shoes,
Sung to a sort of G.I. tune,
Under the G.I. southern moon.

G I'm loaded with GI clothes,
G I'm tired of GI hose,
G Hon, I'm sick of GI issue,
And, oh my darling, G I miss you.

G I long for a G I pass
Far from the dusty G I grass,
I'm so darn tired of GI whirls
With the usual crop of GI girls.

G I adore you, darling mine,
G I'm tired of this GI rhyme.
But G I'm happy and I'll tell you why,
Ours is love that is not GI.[31]

Notes

[1]I would like to thank Helen Allen, who sent me songs from the archives of the Women's Army Corps Museum at Fort McClellan, Alabama, as well as Jean Colby, Frank Smith and Les Cleveland, who generously shared songs from their personal collections.

[2]The acronym, WAAC (Women's Army Auxiliary Corps), was replaced in 1943 by WAC (Women's Army Corps). WAVES stood for Women Accepted for Volunteer Emergency Service, WAF for Women's Air Force; and SPAR (the Coast Guard term), for Semper Paratus—Always Ready. Women Marines were called Lady Leathernecks.

[3]Jeanne Holm, *Women in the Military: An Unfinished Revolution* (Novato, CA: Presidio, 1982) 100.

[4]*Song Book* (Washington: U.S. Government Printing Office, 1944) 25. This first verse is followed by:

> We don't care if it's ten below,
> Cold gives our face a healthy glow,
> We don't care if it rains or freezes
> We'll march along to the cadence of sneezes.
> We'll stand Reveille scantily clad,
> Wearing cotton is the latest fad,
> We don't care, we'll show them how
> We're in the Army now.

[5]*WAC Song Book* (Fort Lee, VA: Special Services, Women's Army Corps Training Center, n.d.) 2.

[6]"Soldier Girls," *WAC Songs*. From the Hazel Meyers papers, Library of Congress, Music and Performing Arts Division. This song was sung to the tune of "Solomon Levi."

[7]Hazel Meyers papers.

[8]Hazel Meyers papers.

[9]See Carol Burke, "Marching to Vietnam," *Journal of American Folklore* 102 (1989) 424-442.

[10]"I Just Wanna Be a WAAC," Hazel Meyers papers. This song was sung to the tune of "Old Gray Mare."

[11]Edgar Allen, "I'm a Regular Daughter of Uncle Sam" (New York: Shapiro Bernstein & Co., 1917).

[12]Howard Rogers and James V. Monaco, "I'm Going to Follow the Boys" (New York: M. Whitmark, 1917).

[13]"Over There," Agnes Underwood papers, U.S. Naval Academy Military Folklore Archive.

[14]Holm 30.

[15]Victoria Gotsky papers, Indiana University. Sung to the tune of "The Strip Polka:"

If there E'er was a private that was struck by the moon
Oh, it's Ginny the Ninny of the Goon platoon.
Oh, she flaunts femininity with curl and with frills,
But her mates want to choke her when she drills.
"Forward March, forward march," and she skids to the rear,
"Column right, column right," and she stalls changing gear,
But she's deaf to our curses unaware it's a crime,
That she drills, and always out of time.
For her thoughts are abstracted to a camp far away,
And she dreams of the Captain she will wed some day.
So she lists as she marches and at "Halt" bottoms up,
And her steps are all between the "Hups."
"Step it up, step it up" but unique is her rhythm,
"Slow it down, slow it down" but she isn't with 'em.
For she's off in a dream-world and her bliss is sublime.
So she drills, and always out of time.

[16]*WAC Songbook* 17-18.

[17]"Songs for Singing on the March," Fourth WAAC Training Center Special Service Office, publ. 154, n.d.

[18]Eleanor Moffett, "Yes, By Cracky," in the personal papers of Jean Colby, Las Vegas, NV.

[19]Holm 28.

[20]"I Got Tags," Jean Colby. This song is sung to the tune of "Jingle, Jangle, Jingle:"

I got tags that jingle, jangle, jingle
As I go marching merrily along.
I got shots that tingle, stingle, tingle
But in my heart I always have a song.
Oh, Army life, with care and strife;
I'm a rippin' snortin' Auxie,
But I'll be a Sergeant's wife.
I got tags that jingle, jangle, jingle,
As I drill and so gaily march along.

[21]Both this verse and the fuller verse that follows were contributed by Jean Colby. Some may be more familiar with this in its male form:

If your baby has a baby
and she blames it on you—
Leaky rubber, leaky rubber.

[22]C.D.D. refers to a "Section 8," or discharge for insanity.

[23]Jean Kritzer, "Dementia," in the personal papers of Frank Smith.

[24]Helen Rogan, *Mixed Company: Women in the Modern Army* (New York: Putnam, 1981) 132.

[25]Rogan 131.

[26]"The U.S. Army WAC," *Songbook* 18. The verse continues:

We're drilling and training and learning
To master the true Army way.
And take the place of the soldiers
Who are needed for the fray.
    Chorus
At duty's call, we offered all.
We're the U.S. Army WAC.
Releasing men to fight and win
With a mightier attack.
We're in to stay until the day
Our boys bring the Victory back.
Among the brave, our banners wave
We're the U.S. Army WAC.

[27]From the personal papers of Frank Smith.

[28]"In My Little GI Shoes," *WAC Songbook* 6. Sung to the tune of "Every Little Raindrop."

[29]"Oh, Me! Oh, My! That Ain't GI," *WAC Songbook* 22.

Rosie the Riveter and
the Eight-Hour Orphan:
The Image of Child Day Care
During World War II

Rose M. Kundanis

A new, if temporary, way of life in America is coming up like thunder out of Pearl Harbor and Singapore. Homebodies, young mothers who had never contemplated working outside their own kitchens, suddenly lured by patriotism and dollars, are clamoring for factory jobs. And everywhere the cry arises, "What about the children?" (Barnard 107)

One of the first magazine articles on child care after December, 1941, used the above war imagery to describe the change World War II had in store for families. No image of the working woman during this time was more pervasive than Rosie the Riveter. Sometimes, however, Rosie, rivet gun in hand, was pictured with a child in a backpack (See Figure 1). It was evident to many observers, however, that "The hand that holds the pneumatic riveter cannot rock the cradle at the same time" (Wetherill 634). Popular magazine articles during the war years typically tried, then, to answer the question: What would happen to the children when Rosie took off her backpack?

Although child care was not new, the way it would be used during the war emergency was. There had been extensive child care for poor working mothers during the pre-war period. But the war situation "intensified and enlarged the need to dimensions sufficient to require official action" (Taba 197). Now middle-class women also needed child care, women who volunteered as well as women who had to work while their husbands were overseas. It was then that the term "day care" was coined. At the same time, searching for phrases that would be acceptable to a wider audience, a *Parents' Magazine* article described a "child care center" as "the wartime name for [the] all-day nursery school,..." (Danziger 20). World War II was providing new words to describe child care and ways to talk about it.

There is in America today a strong legacy of child care images from World War II popular magazines.[1] The innovation of child "day care" and its communication (to the American public) through popular magazines during World War II are, indeed, key elements in the diffusion (Rogers and Shoemaker) of the idea of child care in this country. Some popular magazine articles encouraged consideration of child care by simply informing the readers, while others gave advice about the specifics of the child care dilemma (Carlson and

Fig. 1. Rosie the Riveter with Child, unsigned illustration from G.G. Wetherill, "Health Problems in Child Care Centers," *Hygeia*, (September 1943) 635.

and Crase). Child care was also viewed as both a safe place for children and as a developmental and educational experience (Steinfels).

Historical Setting and Context

How could a society that had believed the best place for a child was in his or her own home (Mackenzie, "Home" 22), even consider giving "outside" child care a second look? One reason was clearly patriotism. A *Business Week* article during 1943 described how much the lack of child care could cost the war industry. Quoting the West Coast Aircraft War Production Council, the magazine noted:

One child-care center enabling 40 mothers to work full shifts adds up to 8,000 man-hours a month; in...ten weeks, [that is] equal to one four-engine bomber. Lack of 25 child-care centers can cost ten bombers a month. ("Women Drop Out" 88)

Popular magazines had, at first, sought to promote women's contributions to the war effort solely as an emergency measure. When it became evident, however, that women were needed to work full-time, adequate child care became paramount. Altered existing institutions and many innovations were the result. Though some nursery schools closed during the war because their ill-sited locations caused commuters to worry about gas and tire rationing or increased taxi fare, most changes showed increases, and many schools lowered their entrance age ("Are Nursery Schools" 24) and extended their days from six to eight hours (Mackenzie, "Wartime"). Public schools also extended their hours and occasionally gave space for the pre-schools within their already existing buildings.

Uncle Sam was described by one source as "...one of his own largest nursemaids" ("While Mothers Work" 22), even though the federal government never had a child care bill pass during World War II. Not until 1943 did the administration allow funds from the Lanham Act, passed initially to construct wartime facilities, to be used for day care centers (Chafe 166). An alternative piece of legislation, the Thomas Bill, was considered in 1943 but did not pass Congress (Close, "Day Care" 197). The first cooperative nursery school did not receive an official rating from the Office of Civilian Defense as a war project until 1943 (Ross 32).

Yet interest in the Thomas Bill, combined with the availability of Lanham Act funds, did support a peaking of child care articles in 1943, when 42% of all articles for the war period were published. The number declined by half in 1944 to 22%, and, in 1945, the number declined even further to 15%. This finding supports other research that has found peak years for child care articles to correlate with the political history of child care in the United States (Perry-Sheldon and Fairchild).

The themes of the World War II child care articles reflect the hopes and fears of the dilemma of child care in the war years—the struggle for acceptance, Yankee ingenuity, the horrors of inadequate care, democratic images and visions of the future. The push to win the war meant the mothers' need for child care was an issue in the popular journals.

The Struggle for Acceptance

With the war seemingly at the root of the problem of child care, war imagery was used to depict child care in a positive light. Why are we fighting this war anyway if it's not for the children? was a question asked and answered in many ways. In the photographs in one article by F. Duncan, children are juxtaposed to the flag (See Figure 2), and the reason for fighting is given: "To take care of children whose fathers and mothers work day and night turning out war materials is vitally important. For it is to keep them free that we are fighting" (10). But an appeal to patriotism alone was not sufficient for mothers considering employment.

Parents had to accept child care for it to be successful (Kellogg). To encourage greater acceptance, articles discussed the advantages of cooperative day care, nursery schools and play groups. These arrangements were not for full-time working parents but for those who worked part-time or did volunteer work in the war effort. Cooperative and part-time child care were easier for some mothers to accept than full-time care. It was difficult for some to see child care as commercial, involving an exchange of money for services. Cooperative child care was attractive because money was not an issue. By keeping money out of the picture, there was less chance of exploitation of children.

Even in the early literature, an effort was made to distinguish custodial arrangements that were makeshift from those with educational standards. "For these defense nurseries...are not mere baby-minding stations. Rather, they are planned to approximate nursery schools, real educational institutions for young persons from eighteen months to five years old" (Barnard 107). Much of the literature during the war aimed to encourage use by showing the educational strengths of nursery schools. *School Arts*, for instance, after providing a lengthy discussion of creativity in selected schools, added:

It is hoped that the foregoing glimpse of nursery school techniques will encourage those thoughtful people who shrink from the idea of group care of small children to investigate more fully the sound educative principles upon which every quality nursery school program is built. (Kiskaddon 292)

The appeal to educational advantages showed that the needs of children as well as parents were being addressed.

The working mother who hoped to contribute efficiently to the war effort needed information about safe places for her children. The popular magazine sources acknowledged that child care must be convenient and capably run if the mothers were to become reliable workers (Stolz 20). Kaiser shipbuilders in Washington found "two things about working mothers: that they must be educated in the use of group care for their children and that they will not enroll their children in any institution until they have seen it in operation" ("Kaiser's Children" 351).

By 1943, part-time child care could not meet all the war needs. Women no longer were encouraged to stay home (Close, "Day Care" 194). Many realized that, to win the war, women must be in the work force full-time. It was acknowledged that mothers could not work and care for children at the same

ED PHILLIPS

● To take care of these children under the American flag that we whose fathers and mothers work are fighting. Your community day and night turning out war can do just as well as Burbank materials is vitally important. For does if you're intelligent, ener- it is to keep them free and happy getic and interested in children.

Fig. 2. Child Care and the Flag, Photography by Ed Phillips in F. Duncan, "While Their Parents Build Planes," *Women's Home Companion*, (March 1943) 10.

time. More important was the admission that the mother's peace of mind was important to her productivity on the job. "It is not fair, it is not wise from the standpoint of production to ask women to work in war industries and not give them peace of mind about their children" (Benedict 11).

Although most popular journal articles stressed the needs of mothers, some also referred to the needs of fathers. One article even proposed that fathers who missed their children might spend time with them at nursery school canteens during their leaves. Roger Sturtevant, one of the few male journalists writing on the subject of child day care, thought men might take advantage of the opportunity to play with children and provide some "father love" that so many children were missing (8). It was necessary for fathers to accept day care if it were to succeed, so it was not unusual to find fathers quoted as endorsing child day care too. "'I think nursery schools are good for all children'," wrote one dad in 1945 (Cook 20).

What made the nursery schools good were the teachers and caregivers, who were lauded in many articles. In one case, caregivers were depicted as goddesses "trained to know what makes children tick" (Barnard 107). One 23-year-old caregiver even was quoted as saying she could have prevented World War II: "You know,...sometimes I think if I'd had Hitler in nursery school at the age of two, I could have done a job on him. I mean, you know, there wouldn't have been any war and all that sort of thing" (107-108). The power of education for the very young was seen by this caregiver as strong enough to have changed history. Companionship (Aschmann), nutrition and safety advantages also were described.

Yankee Ingenuity and Child Care

Uncle Sam funded some day care, but entrepreneurs and corporations also made contributions and innovations. At the Los Angeles Gale Manor Apartments, for instance, the mother of a soldier and a single parent herself decided to convert one of the floors of an apartment building into a child care center renting only to working parents with children (Pope 24).

Perhaps the best known corporate child care of the period was Kaiser's two child-care centers in next-to-plant sites in Portland, Oregon. Though the U.S. Maritime Commission supplied the $750,000 needed to build the two centers, allowing Kaiser to bypass the federal government's red tape under the Lanham Act, it was the company which designed and constructed the sites without government direction ("Kaiser's Children" 40).

Kaiser's primary purpose was making a profit, and that meant the "stabilization of the woman shipyard worker" (Lowenberg 77). To accomplish this end, the centers provided 24-hour and holiday care, a children's infirmary and "home-service food." While the first two may be seen in child care needs today, the "home-service food" may have been the predecessor of fast-service food and McDonald's. Nutritionist Miriam E. Lowenberg described how a mother could pick up a main dish and dessert, food that took a while to prepare, for her whole family when she picked up her child after work (76).

Kaiser saw the nurseries as good public relations. In November of 1943, the Consultant Director of the Child Services Department at Kaiser Corporation wrote in the *New York Times Magazine*: "the staff...is preparing to make

Portland the focal point of the nation in the care of working mothers' pre-school children" (Stolz 39). The child care professionals involved also saw an opportunity to educate industry. The Chief Nutritionist in the Child Services Department of Kaiser wrote in the *Journal of Home Economics*: "we feel that we have an excellent opportunity to demonstrate to an industrial organization what adequate care of young children really means" (Lowenberg 77). The architects, Wolff and Phillip, published their plans for the child care facilities in *Architectural Record* and lauded Kaiser for the boldness of locating child care next to the site of the plant.

The Horrors of Inadequate Child Care

Although most of the magazine coverage was positive, fears of inadequate child care were fueled by a few articles. War imagery was used to describe the negative effects of no care and bad care. "Long range guns which can shoot twenty years into the future are now firing on the United States in a war potentially as destructive as that being fought around the world today" (Allen, Davis and Olivier 20). In an exposé of inadequate child care in the United States, the *Saturday Evening Post* used the phrase "eight-hour orphans" (Allen, Davis and Olivier; Pope) for children whose parents worked all day.[2] Mothers who neglected their children were castigated. Several incidents were described in which children were neglected while mothers were working. In one incident, nine children and four dogs were chained while parents worked all day. In another situation, four children slept in the car parked near the window of their mother's job during the graveyard shift (Allen, Davis and Olivier 21).

Child care by strangers became a problem for some families and led to some of the horrors of bad care reported in the popular magazines. There was little if any regulation of child care during the war, yet good care was needed for those workers who relocated to work in war industries and were separated from extended family and familiar support services. The following example of bad care led to changes in the state of Washington, where many workers resettled for the war-related work available:

In Seattle last month there was a murder trial. Chief witnesses for the prosecution were a young couple, war workers, who had answered a newspaper ad when they had to find some place to leave their nine month old child while looking for a place to live. They did not know they were dealing with an unbalanced woman, whose impatience would result in the baby's death. (Close, "Day Care" 194)

Though very few child care articles were negative, those that were seemed to be aimed at reenforcing the fears of many mothers and reinforcing the prejudices of those who opposed mothers working outside the home.

By 1945, it was clear that not all criticism of child care was well-founded. Early criticism of child day care by communities before it even was established "...disappeared almost entirely as soon as the preliminary problems of getting the centers organized and properly equipped was accomplished" (Kellogg 9).

Democratic Images

Democratic images were the antidote for the fears of war and its consequences. Before the war, one researcher found that images of child rearing could be democratic or not. Strathman noted a parallel between war fears before World War II and views of child rearing in some popular magazines: "War fears were already evident in 1938, even in *Parents' Magazine*, and family structure and child rearing habits were already being implicated as breeding grounds for either democratic or fascistic tendencies" (25). Similarly, the move toward cooperative child care among mothers during the war was described as "democratic": "The play groups are conducted in such a democratic way that each mother has a chance to make her contributions, and feels herself of real value because her ideas are accepted and tried" (Taylor 323). For many, the values of good child care were a microcosm for the democratic values that were being defended during the war.

The dilemma of being mother and worker crossed class and socio-economic lines during the emergency of World War II. The pre-war image of child care had been as a service for the well-to-do and the very poor. There was not necessarily more child care during World War II than during the depression that preceded it. In fact, *Business Week* reported that there were fewer nurseries operating in 1943 than the Works Progress Administration had operated during the peacetime pre-war period. But the war image of child care differed in that child care was seen as a service for everyone regardless of background: "here in the nursery all class distinctions disappear" (Stewart 39).

It is interesting to note that, in a period of racial segregation in the United States, references to racial integration were found in at least four articles (Budd; Marshall; Cook; Close, "After Lanham"). "Here you see democracy in action. Children of every race and creed learn to get along well together," boasted a *Women's Home Companion* article in 1942 (Budd 58). "It does one's heart good to see the youngsters of all races playing peaceably—the Mexican boy with the Chinese girl, the Negro and the little Jewish child" (Cook 58). Racial integration was depicted in some of the photos as well (Close, "After Lanham" 133-134).

Visions of the Future and Legacy of Child Care Images

While a positive image of child day care was a way to promote women's contribution to the war effort, some writers hoped that child care would die with the end of the war. They predicted that child day care would have to be reconsidered, since it was allowed only because of the emergency ("Kaiser's Children" 351). But others hoped the innovation would survive to become a permanent legacy: "And after the war, because we have acquired this habit, it may be that all of the children, all of the time, may have the food they need, the health care they need, to become the best person each of them can be" (Langdon 64). It seems that, at least for some, association with child care was considered a plus.

Once the emergency was over, the predominantly custodial child care image did not mandate education for pre-school children. After the war, much of the child day care for working mothers disappeared with the end of federal funding. However, the legacy of the child care images of World War II can be seen in the extensive adoption of kindergartens in public school systems throughout the country (Kundanis).

The authors of child care articles during World War II encouraged consideration of child care innovation by both informing and giving advice. There were some differences in types of magazines. Women's magazines[3] and educational magazines[4] usually gave working mothers advice about child care, while general circulation[5] and professional[6] magazine articles were largely informative rather than prescriptive.

Depicting child care as educational may have been too threatening to the traditional home. Two-thirds of all World War II child care articles consulted depicted child care simply as a safe place for children to be while their mothers were working rather than as an educational experience. The predominance of the custodial image meant that, when the custodial need disappeared, so did the child care.

We do have a child care image legacy from World War II popular literature. Child care as a need and a problem for all classes of people was first established then, and the language and images of child care have endured. Democratic advantages were noted in integrated child care facilities well before racial integration in many parts of the United States. The growth of child care in the last 20 years has been the result of different economic needs than those of World War II. But the image of Rosie the Riveter with a child strapped to her back captures the dilemma of the working mother, informing us and inspiring us today.

Notes

[1] The sample considered for this research included 60 articles indexed by the Readers Guide to Periodical Literature from 1941 to 1945. The sample came from 22 journals.

[2] The children were also sometimes referred to as daytime orphans ("While Mothers Work" 22).

[3] The women and family category included 14 articles in five journals: *American Home, Good Housekeeping, Independent Woman, Parents' Magazine,* and *Women's Home Companion.*

[4] The education and library category included 13 articles in four journals: *Education for Victory, Elementary School Journal, Library Journal* and *School Arts.*

[5] A third of the articles came from the general circulation category, which included two newspaper magazines (*Christian Science Monitor Magazine* and the *New York Times Magazine*); *Newsweek, Colliers, Saturday Evening Post* and *Survey Midmonthly.*

[6] The profession and organization category included 13 articles in seven journals: *Architectural Record, Business Week, Catholic World, Hygeia, Journal of Home Economics, Recreation,* and *Rotarian.*

Works Cited

Allen, Grace Thorne, Maxine Davis, Warner Olivier. "Eight-Hour Orphans," *Saturday Evening Post* 10 Oct. 1942: 20+.

"Are Nursery Schools and Kindergartens Affected by the War?" *Education for Victory* 15 July 1942: 24.

Aschmann, Helen T. "Wanted, a Playmate," *Parents' Magazine* Aug. 1943: 31+.

Barnard, Eunice Fuller. "Definitely Woman's Work," *Independent Woman* April 1942: 106-08.

Benedict, Agnes E. "Starting a Nursery School," *Independent Woman* Jan. 1943: 11+.

Budd, Dorothy. "While Mothers Work," *Women's Home Companion* July 1942: 58-59.

Carlson, Colleen Lonergan, Sedahlia Jasper Crase. "A Content Analysis of Childrearing Information in Popular Magazines," *Home Economics Research Journal* 11:3 (1983): 223-233.

Chafe, W.H. *The American Woman, Her Changing Social, Economic, and Political Roles, 1920-1970.* New York: Oxford UP, 1972.

Close, Kathryn. "Day Care up to Now," *Survey Midmonthly* July 1943: 194-97.

——— "After Lanham Funds—What?" *Survey Midmonthly* May 1945: 131-35.

Cook, Jean G. "Books for Nursery-Schools," *Library Journal* 70 (1945): 18-20.

Danziger, Juliet. "What are Child Care Centers?" *Parents' Magazine* Aug. 1944: 20+.

Duncan, F. "While Their Parents Build Planes," *Women's Home Companion* March 1943: 6+.

"Kaiser's Children," *Survey Midmonthly* Dec. 1944: 351.

Kellogg, Rhoda. "Extended school services—An 'accepted part' of the school program," *Education for Victory* 3 Feb. 1945: 9-10.

Kiskaddon, Louise, Florence Harris, Helen M. Reynolds. "Creative Activity in Nursery Schools," *School Arts* May 1943: 291-292.

Kundanis, Rose M. "Where Did All the Child Care Go? The Post World War II Image of Child Care in Popular Magazines." Northeast Popular Culture Association Conference. Amherst, MA, 5 Oct. 1990.

Langdon, Grace. "Uncle Sam Takes Care of his Youngest," *Parents' Magazine* Jan. 1943: 34+.

Lowenberg, Miriam E. "Shipyard Nursery Schools," *Journal of Home Economics* 36.2 (1944): 75-77.

Mackenzie, Catherine. "Home vs. Nursery Child," *New York Times Magazine* 27 June 1943: 22.

——— "Wartime Nursery School," *New York Times Magazine* 31 Jan. 1943: 28.

Marshall, Jim. "Babies Aweigh," *Colliers* 29 Aug. 1942: 58.

Perry-Sheldon, Barbara, Steven H. Fairchild. *Educating the American Public: A Survey of Child Care Articles in Popular Women's Magazines, 1959 to 1981.* Paper presented at Annual Meeting of the Eastern Education Research Association. ERIC ED 229 149, PS 013 506.

Pope, Vernon. "One Way to Care for our Eight-Hour Orphans," *Saturday Evening Post* 10 April 1943: 24+.

Rogers, Everett M., F. Floyd Shoemaker. *Communication of Innovations: A Cross-Cultural Approach.* 2nd ed. New York: The Free P, 1971.

Ross, Ann. "What Seven Mothers Did," *Parents' Magazine* May 1943: 32+.

Steinfels, Margaret O'Brien. *Who's Minding the Children? The History and Politics of Day Care in America.* A Touchstone Book. New York: Simon and Schuster, 1973.

Stewart, George. "Check Your Child?" *Rotarian* Oct. 1942: 38-39.

Stolz, Lois Meek. "The Nursery Comes to the Shipyard," *New York Times Magazine* 7 Nov. 1943: 20+.

Strathman, Terry. "From the Quotidian to the Utopian: Child Rearing Literature in America, 1926-1946," *Berkeley Journal of Sociology* 29 (1984): 1-34.

Sturtevant, Roger. "A Barrel of Fun at the Nursery Canteen With Kids Like the Ones you Left at Home," *American Home* Dec. 1943: 4+.

Taba, H. "Developing Child-Care Centers," *The Elementary School Journal* 43 (1942): 196-198.

Taylor, Katherine Whiteside. "Co-operative Play Groups," *Journal of Home Economics* 36.6 (1944): 321-326.

Wetherill, G.G. "Health Problems in Child Care Centers," *Hygeia* Sept. 1943: 634-635.

"While Mothers Work," *Rotarian* Aug. 1943: 22-24.

"Women Drop Out," *Business Week* 21 Aug. 1943: 88.

Told Without Bitterness:
Autobiographical Accounts of the Relocation of Japanese-Americans and Canadians During World War II

M. Paul Holsinger

Japanese bombs had barely stopped falling on Pearl Harbor, Manila or Hong Kong before the governments of the United States and Canada began the process which would result in the forceful removal of nearly 135,000 Japanese residents from homes up and down the Pacific Coast.[1] It made little difference to most officials whether these persons were citizens or not;[2] what primarily determined the decision of who would move and who would not was skin coloration. As the armies of Japan roared victoriously through the Pacific theater, both nations slipped into what, some years later, a perceptive justice of the United States Supreme Court was to call "the ugly abyss of racism."[3]

Thanks to President Franklin Roosevelt's infamous Executive Order 9066 and the belief of the Army commander in charge of the West Coast that "a Jap's a Jap" irrespective of citizenship, orders were soon issued to remove from their homes and businesses all of California's, Oregon's and Washington's Japanese-American settlers. Canada was not far behind. Reacting to the fear and intemperate bigotry expressed by many of the province of British Columbia's white leaders, Prime Minister W.L. Mackenzie King soon put the Royal Canadian Mounted Police in charge of removing, and relocating, the huge number of Japanese-Canadians living in Vancouver and the southern coast of that area.

The two neighbors differed only in degree in the approaches they took. In the United States, all Japanese were first moved to huge assembly sites, including many unused race tracks, and then to ten newly built "relocation centers"—the name euphemistically given for this nation's concentration camps. There, for the next three years (1942-1945), the bulk of Japanese-Americans were kept behind barbed wire under Army guard.[4] Canadians had a slightly different response. While they imprisoned those many young men whom they felt, justly or unjustly, to be disloyal, the majority of the country's Japanese were sent to the foothills of the Rockies nearly seven hundred miles from their former homes. Like their American counterparts, the R.C.M.P. held its evacuees as virtual prisoners for the duration of the war.[5]

Long before the last residents of these various centers returned to the freedom of the "outside," government officials on both sides of the 49th parallel were already publishing book-length justifications for their actions. The end of the war accelerated this publication record, nearly all of which pictured the relocation process in a positive light.[6] Few publishers, on the other hand, seemed willing to hear the side of those persons most intimately affected—the Japanese. One brief, heavily illustrated volume, Mine Okubo's *Citizen 13660*, a memoir of her days at both the Tanforan Race Track and the Topaz, Utah relocation center, *was* published in 1946, but the majority of American or Canadian publishers showed little interest in bringing the day-by-day details of Japanese relocation to their readers.

In 1953, Boston's Little Brown and Company issued Monica Sone's *Nisei Daughter*, one of the first serious autobiographies of a second-generation Japanese young woman, but it was not until the early 1970s, in the midst of the Vietnam War, and later that readers were able to study in any depth Japanese relocation from the participants' point-of-view. Some of the new volumes, notably Yoshiko Uchida's children's book, *Journey to Topaz*, and Jeanne Wakatsuki Houston's *Farewell to Manzanar* were widely circulated and drew much praise from their reviewers. Others, like Estelle Ishigo's emotionally written *Lone Heart Mountain*, an excellent—but privately published—volume, were barely noticed.

In Canada, a similar phenomenon was occurring. Beginning in 1971 with a children's book, Shizuye Takashima's almost lyrical semi-fictional autobiography, *A Child in Prison Camp*, Canadian readers were also slowly able to see the other side of their government's policies toward the Japanese during World War II. Takashima's book was followed by the published wartime diary of Takeo Ujo Nakano, *Within the Barbed Wire Fence* (1980) and then by Joy Kogawa's powerful autobiographical novel, *Obasan* (1981), based in part on the real-life experiences of Muriel Kitagawa. These various books, along with Uchida's later *Desert Exile: The Uprooting of a Japanese-American Family* and Kogawa's small children's book, *Naomi's Road*, provide the basis for this study.

The authors of these ten volumes offer a wide cross-section of backgrounds. Okubo, Sone, Uchida and Wakatsuki were all citizens of the United States at the time they were forced into the relocation centers. Takashima, Kitagawa and Kogawa's heroine, "Naomi Nakane," held Canadian citizenship. Okubo and Kitagawa were both young adults at the beginning of the war; Sone was a teenager just recovering from a bout of tuberculosis. Uchida was eleven; Wakatuski, seven and Nakane, only five. At the other end of the spectrum was Nakano, an already middle-aged laborer in the lumber industry just north of Vancouver. Even more unique was Ishigo. A Caucasian and the daughter of a Union Army veteran of the Civil War, she had married a Japanese-Californian in 1928, and, when his evacuation was ordered at the start of the war, she willingly went to suffer with him. Hers is the only "white" vision of the life of a prisoner, but it offers a fascinating point-counterpoint to ethnic Japanese views.

Even before the first Japanese-Americans were sent to the first assembly center, the United States Army quickly moved to depersonalize all the evacuees by assigning each family a separate identification number—a number which, for the rest of their incarcerations, became the family "name" as far as the government was concerned. Mine Okubo became Citizen 13660—the title of her memoirs; Yoshiko Uchida and her family, 13453; Monica Sone, 10710 and so on. As groups gathered with the few belongings that they were allowed to take with them to camp, everyone and everything was required to have one white pasteboard label with the assigned number on it for all to see. Even now, nearly fifty years after the war's conclusion, the image of being forced to become a "number" remains to haunt each and every American Japanese writer in exactly the same way as Nazi S.S. tattoos on Jewish arms bring back vividly the horrors of those camps throughout Europe.[7]

Because of the maddening rush to move Japanese families away from the Pacific Coast, both countries hurried them into the largest assembly areas possible—areas behind well-structured fences that could be carefully guarded to prevent the sabotage that officials illogically assumed would break out at any minute. Race tracks and state fairgrounds were "naturals" for such sites. The Santa Anita race track outside Los Angeles housed more than 18,000 Japanese residents for almost six months in early 1942; thousands of others were at the Tanforan track in San Bruno just south of San Francisco. In Washington State, officials requisitioned the state fairgrounds in Puyallup, and, in British Columbia, the Canadian government took over the huge Pacific Exposition grounds in Vancouver's Hastings Park and moved in thousands of single men over the age of 18 as well as various families and older adults unable to take care of themselves.

In every case, authorities seemed unwilling to consider whether "Japs" ought to be granted a decent standard of living. It was a common sight for entire families to be moved into just recently vacated horse stalls, the smell of rotting manure still permeating everything. Occasionally, there had been a crude attempt to paint the stall but, because of the rush, little could be done to disguise the obvious. Mine Okubo, arriving at Tanforan with her brother, found their new home, "Stall 50." "Spider webs, horse hair, and hay had been whitewashed with the walls.... A two-inch layer of dust covered the floor, but on removing it we discovered that linoleum the color of redwood had been placed over the rough manure-covered boards" (35). Yoshiko Uchida's family, also at Tanforan, had the same experience. Assigned to "Barrack 16, Apartment 40," they finally found, after much searching, that they were to live in a stable reached only by way of "a broad ramp the horses had used to reach the stalls. Each stall was now numbered and ours was number 40. That the stalls should have been called *apartments* was a euphemism so ludicrous it was comical" (*Desert Exile* 70). Monica Sone's entire family from Seattle found dandelions pushing up between the cracks in the floor boards of their new home at the Puyallup fairgrounds. Monica's mother, refusing to be discouraged by the incongruity of the strange setting, ordered her husband and children to let the flowers grow, since they were one of the few beautiful things remaining in an increasingly ugly world (174).

The Canadian setting was not much better. Japanese families and other individuals were so rapidly pushed into the exposition grounds' Livestock Building that piles of manure had not even been cleaned from the animals' stalls. Wood planking had simply been placed over the debris with no thought for sanitation. When some of these boards were removed, "it was the most stomach-turning, nauseating thing [with] maggots...still breeding" throughout the manure (Kogawa, *Obasan* 99). When eleven-year old Shizuye Takashima and her mother visited friends on the grounds "a strong odor hit us as we enter[ed]: the unmistakable foul smell of cattle, a mixture of their waste and sweat. The animals were removed, but their stink remain[ed].... It seemed as if we [were] visiting the hellhole my Sunday School teacher spoke of with such earnestness" (7). And Takeo Ujo Nakano, confined to the same stables and unable, even with his head under the bedclothes, to escape the all-pervasive smell, found himself putting into classical Japanese *tanka* his feelings:

> Reek of manure,
> Stench of livestock,
> and we are herded,
> Milling—
> Jumble of the battlefield. (13)

Everyone understood, however, that, no matter how inadequate or disgusting the various stalls, stables or other small shacks were in the spring and early summer of 1942, they were temporary. Both American and Canadian governments were determined to move their Japanese residents away from the coastal areas as soon as "permanent" locations could be provided. In British Columbia, the government designated a number of old mining "ghost towns" for Japanese family relocation. Single men as well as most Japanese alien male heads of households were at first not allowed to join their families but were assigned to work on various road gangs building highways and bridges through the eastern sections of the province. "Disloyal" men—and the Canadian government used a perverse standard to determine such designation—were sent to a former P.O.W. camp north of Lake Superior in Angler, Ontario. Takeo Nakano was one of the latter. Though his only concern was to be reunited with his wife and small daughter, Nakano was to spend twenty-one months apart from them. Not until December, 1943, were they able to live together as a family.[8] Six year-old Naomi Nakane, the heroine of both Joy Kogawa's adult novel *Obasan* and her children's book *Naomi's Road*, got to see her father for only a few days after early 1942. Even when, three years later, she and the rest of her family were moved to the southern Albertan sugar beet fields to work, Naomi's father was not allowed to join them. Not until 1950 did the family, via a coldly impersonal bureaucratic letter, discover that he had died some years before while undergoing an operation.

For those who were sent to eastern British Columbia, however, the government did attempt to make the move at least sound appealing. The Takashima family went to New Denver, with all the promise of a bright future "in one of the most beautiful spots in British Columbia" (9). To their horror, they discovered that none of the buildings had running water, electricity or adequate heating facilities. Mr. Takashima, who, as a naturalized citizen, was able to be with his family, constantly complained to authorities but to no avail. His increasing bitterness at this and his relatives' treatment came close to convincing him to renounce Canada and return to Japan.

The United States Army, in selecting the sites for its relocation centers, took the opposite approach to the matter. Far from looking for scenery that could be called "beautiful," government officials selected the most desolate, isolated locations that it could find. When they remember their days of imprisonment, all writers include the vividly depressing initial image of their future homes. Yoshiko Uchida and her family were, at first, temporarily lulled by the government's assignment to Topaz, Utah. "Such a beautiful golden name,"

Yoshiko's mother said. As the busses sent to the train station in Delta to pick them up neared the site of the center, however, the reality proved shocking.

Gradually the trees and the grass and the flowers began to disappear. Soon there was no vegetation at all and they were surrounded by a gray-white desert where nothing grew except dry clumps of greasewood.... And [then] there in the midst of the desert, they came upon rows and rows of squat tar-paper barracks sitting in a pool of white dust that had once been the bottom of a lake. They had arrived at...their new home. (*Journey to Topaz* 94, 96)

Okubo, sent to the same camp, and not nearly so naive as to believe the government designation of Topaz as the "Jewel of the Desert," still confessed her depression at viewing the "desolate scene" of the camp from the bus window (121-122).

To the north, at Minidoka, Idaho, conditions were virtually the same for Monica Sone and her family. Approaching the camp north of the Snake River, "I could see nothing," she remembered ten years later, "but flat prairies, clumps of greasewood and...jack rabbits" (192). For self-imposed exile, Estelle Ishigo, Heart Mountain, Wyoming "stood in cactus-covered sand on ancient, weirdly jagged wasteland that spread far into the wide horizon" (19), and in the barren Owens Valley of California, Manzanar seemed to young Jeanne Wakatsuki to spread for miles across a plain of sand (14).[9]

Such inhospitable natural settings boded ill for the thousands of Japanese families from lush regions along the Pacific Coast. The Army Corps of Engineers, responsible for the construction of the ten centers, had systematically bulldozed down all trees and most vegetation in the regions around the new barracks. The result was swirling, often blinding, dust storms which seemed to blow up at any time of the day or month. Okubo remembered it looked "as if we had fallen into a flour barrel" after one such storm (123). Uchida, who had thought the dust in the early weeks after she arrived in Topaz bad, was unprepared for the "ominous strength" of one storm which

swept around us in great thrusting gusts, flinging swirling masses of sand in the air and engulfing us in a thick cloud that eclipsed barracks only ten feet away.... [E]ven inside, the air was thick with dust.... We waited more than an hour, silent and rigid with fear, but the storm didn't let up. (*Desert Exile* 112)

In Minidoka, Sone remembers feeling "as if we were standing in a gigantic sand-mixing machine as the sixty-mile gale lifted the loose earth up into the sky, obliterating everything. Sand filled our mouths and nostrils and stung our faces and hands like a thousand darting needles" (192).[10]

Evacuees arrived at camps which were poorly constructed and, in nearly every case, unfinished. Though tar paper had been nailed on the outside walls of the various barracks, life in the camps, as Jeanne Wakatsuki notes, "was pure chaos.... The evacuation had been so hurriedly planned, the camps so hastily thrown together, nothing was completed when we got there, and almost nothing worked" (21). At Topaz, "many internees found themselves occupying barracks where hammering, tarring, and roofing was still in progress, and one unfortunate woman received second-degree burns on her face when boiling tar seeped through the roof onto the bed where she was asleep" (*Desert Exile* 111).

No inner sheetrock walls or ceilings had been installed [Uchida remembered years later], nor had the black pot-bellied stove that stood outside our door. Cracks were visible everywhere in the siding and around the windows, and although our friends had swept out our room before we arrived, the dust was already seeping into it again from all sides. (*Desert Exile* 109)

Not until winter in all its fury hit Idaho did the government make any attempt to cover the inside walls of the barracks apartments at Minidoka. "Until then," Sone notes, "our four walls had looked like skeletons with their ribs of two by fours bare and exposed" (196).

At both assembly camp and relocation center, no one gave much thought to the physical comforts of the evacuees. Mattresses often consisted of bags of ticking and all the straw residents wished to stuff into them. No blankets or sheets were furnished, and many families found themselves forced to improvise with anything they could find in order to stay warm (Okubo 44-47). Partitions between the stable stalls in the camps usually did not reach to the ceilings, so the possibility of privacy was virtually non-existent. Even after residents came to the relocation centers, walls between the barrack rooms were almost paper-thin creating similar situations. Indeed, privacy was at the bottom of the Army's priorities. "Men's and women's latrines were ranged in fully exposed rows, shocking the decency of everyone" (Ishigo 9). Communal showers were built back-to-back, and, though they were, of course, segregated by sex, many women were especially "very self-conscious and timid about using [them]" (Okubo 75).

Food, too, was at first poorly planned and haphazard. Early in the relocation period, "the diet was mostly cereal, rice, bread, bread-pudding, beans and hot dogs with canned tomatoes. Once in a while there was stew with an extremely small amount of meat" (Ishigo 10). Though food unquestionably did get better as the years passed, no one remembers it as anything more than adequate. Lines were everywhere and became a part of every evacuee's daily life. "We lined up for mail, for checks, for meals, for showers, for washrooms, for laundry tubs, for toilets, for church services, for movies. We lined up for everything," remembered Mine Okubo (86).

Though to the north Japanese-Canadian evacuees could, and frequently did, comment on the singular beauty of the mountains and lakes of eastern British Columbia, most rapidly realized that Canada had forced them into that region to appease the racist fears of their white neighbors in the west. Kogawa quotes "Emily Kato" (Muriel Kitagawa): "We were therefore relegated to the cesspools...just plopped here in the wilderness. Flushed out of Vancouver like dung drops. Maggot bait..." (*Obasan*, 118). Without adequate public services, most evacuees suffered endlessly. When Shizuye Takashima's father finally exploded in anger at one government official because of his family's treatment, he was bluntly told: "You are in camps. Therefore you are considered enemies. You have no rights" (40).

All the Japanese, on both sides of the border, were, from time to time, depressed at the treatment they received. Estelle Ishigo remembers "the horror of exile," the despair "of being excluded, isolated, forced out from the rest of humanity into lonely imprisonment" (16). To Jeanne Wakatsuki, even years after the war, there remained the "shame for being a person guilty of something enormous enough to deserve [incarceration, a] sense of unworthiness" (133, 140). Uchida remembered "the general sense of malaise and despair" which governed the lives of most of the evacuees (*Desert Exile* 111), and Monica Sone could not forget the "pall of gloom" that enshrouded her family at various times (158).

Canada's Japanese experienced the same feelings. "Emily Kato" writes about the "humiliation" of being forcibly relocated, a humiliation that ultimately turns to "helpless panic...not the hysterical kind but the kind that churns round and round going nowhere" (*Obasan* 93). Takeo Nakano repeatedly notes in his diary how the "uncertainty and irritability" at being rounded up and treated like the enemy eventually brought him and others "to the point of pondering death" (13, 21). After being sent to Angler, Ontario, he added that he and his fellow prisoners were

stripped of all that determines [a] positive self-image. I myself had a taste of the lowest point of human existence, the powerlessness and the shame.... I was able, for the first time, to empathize with people who live life at the rock bottom. (48)

Takashima also remembers her father's outspoken, bitter (and useless) protests at being "treated like dogs" and at having been stripped of all "human dignity" by white Canadian officials (29, 14).

It was very hard for many traditional Japanese families to remain together emotionally as units during the evacuation period. The communal life-style in all the camps as well as the absence, in many instances, of a strong father-figure tended to destroy the role played by elderly parents or grandparents. Many young, second-generation *Nisei* took out their anger at being relocated on their parents' "Japaneseness." They refused to consider themselves Japanese at all, reserving such a designation only to those minorities who were resident aliens. Monica Sone was one such person. Rejecting her ancestry, she jumped at the opportunity to leave Minidoka and take a job in Chicago, putting her past behind her. Only after two years away from her parents, who remained in the center, did she come to see how foolish such an exclusionary attitude was. Returning for a visit early in 1945, she was finally able to say: "It's really nice to be born into two cultures, like getting a real bargain in life, two for the price of one.... I used to feel like a two-headed monstrosity, but now I find that two heads are better than one" (236). Jeanne Wakatsuki buried her memories of Manzanar, married a Caucasian and tried desperately "to live agreeably in Anglo-American society" for almost thirty years before finally coming to grips with her Japanese heritage (133-145).

Japanese-Canadians also rejected their ancestry, often straining family relations to the breaking point. Takashima, realizing on one occasion that she and her family were doomed to exile as long as the war continued, suddenly said: "Damn Japs! Why don't they stop fighting?" Her father, overhearing her, screamed back: "What do you mean 'Japs'? You think you're not a Jap? If I hear you say that again, I'll throttle you" (46). Years later, that same alienation had not gone completely away.

Both governments, despite overwhelming evidence to the contrary, always doubted the loyalty of their Japanese residents and encouraged the evacuees to consider repatriating to Japan whenever possible. In the United States, even as late as 1944, the government insisted on getting signed loyalty oaths from everyone. All evacuees still in the camps were required to pledge to fight for the country if called on *and* to forswear all allegiance to the Emperor of Japan or any other foreign leader. Any one who refused to provide immediate "Yes, Yes" responses was segregated as disloyal and shipped to the Tule Lake, California center for eventual repatriation. Looking back on this experience years after the event, many Japanese-American authors still remain bitter at having to demonstrate their love for America again and again.

Eventually, both the American and Canadian governments did allow the evacuees in the various camps to return to the "outside" world as long as it was away from the Pacific Coast. Okubo, Uchida and her sister, and others made the move to New York City; Sone went to Chicago; Nakano, to Toronto; the Takashimas, to northern Ontario. Authorities on both sides of the 49th parallel championed their ability to help create these and similar moves, but the patina of happy, enthusiastic evacuees willingly selecting new homes for themselves in other parts of their nations, obscures the truth. Many older, first-generation *Issei* felt trapped in the camps, rootless, yet unable to move until government officials required it. The Nakane family, featured in Kogawa's two books, were forced out of their home in Slocan, British Columbia and forcibly sent to Granton, Alberta, "a dusty, lonely place" with almost no trees, dust and endless flies. "I hate it here," little Naomi wrote to a Caucasian friend back in British Columbia, "I hate it here so much I want to run away" (*Naomi's Road* 63-64). But she did not, and, as Kogawa noted in her adult *Obasan*, Granton, for better or worse, became the family's "exile from our place of exile" (197).

Perhaps Estelle Ishigo and her husband, Shigeharu, more closely typified the "real" evacuee as the camps began to close down. When neither was willing to leave Heart Mountain to take domestic or farm jobs (Shigeharu had worked for the Hollywood movie industry before the war; Estelle had been an artist), they were placed under tremendous pressure to relocate on their own. When they chose to remain in Wyoming with others reluctant to reenter "society" with little to their name, the War Relocation Authority threatened all sorts of dire consequences. Their barracks were allowed to deteriorate and, even after winter storms had ripped off tar-paper sheathing, nothing was done to repair the damage. Heating fuel was kept to a minimum, and, finally, when even this failed to budge them, the Ishigos and others were given twenty-five dollars each, transportation to any site of their choosing, and the government's assurance that its mission was complete. "Most of us had no place to go," Estelle wrote in her memoirs thirty years later. All our personal property "had been stolen or destroyed. The twenty-five dollars we had received upon leaving camp was not enough to get a place to live and provide food and clothes" (92-94). Not until 1947, after living in crowded trailer parks and working in a fish cannery, was Shigeharu able to find permanent work.

Even those many Japanese who "successfully" made the transition from prisoner to citizen suffered in other ways. Jeanne Wakatsuki's father was "too old to start over, too afraid of rejection...too stubborn and too tired to travel [far] and finally too proud to do piecework on an assembly line."

Papa did not know which way to turn. In the government's eyes a free man now, he sat, like those black slaves you hear about who, when they got word of their freedom at the end of the Civil War, just did not know where else to go or what else to do and ended up back on the plantation, rooted there out of habit or lethargy or fear. (95-96)

Wakatsuki returned to southern California, but, as one business venture after another failed, he began to drink heavily. Before the war, though "not a great man,...he had held onto his self-respect, he dreamed great dreams, and...whatever he did had flourish" (42). But no more. When he died several years later, he had never been able to make the abrupt transition expected of him. The same story could be written again and again for hundreds of others.

Yet, surprisingly, despite the denial of their rights, the lost property and the often shattered lives,[11] the majority of the Japanese evacuees "endured the hardship of the evacuation with dignity, stoic composure, disciplined patience and an amazing resiliency of spirit. I think they displayed a level of strength, grace, and courage," Uchida writes, "that is truly remarkable" (*Desert Exile* 148).

All of the personal accounts of Japanese relocation express neither rancor nor bitterness. In many ways, each is a catharsis, a cleansing of the past, for the participants. "It has taken me twenty-five years to reach the point where I could talk openly about Manzanar," wrote Wakatsuki in the forward to her best-selling memoir (ix). For others, it was even longer, but, in putting down the truth as they remembered it, every person has been able to deal finally with his or her own personal suffering.

On the other hand, nearly all the autobiographers stress a deep personal commitment to telling the story in the hope that it may guarantee an end to such bigotry in the years ahead. Uchida, for instance, in her role as a renowned writer of children's stories, often encounters youngsters who have never heard of "America's Concentration Camps." Her books on relocation, then, have been written because, "as painful as it may be to hear, [the story] needs to be told and retold and never forgotten by succeeding generations of Americans" (*Desert Exile* 154). Mine Okubo says essentially the same thing. "I am not bitter," she writes in a 1983 reissue of *Citizen 13660*, but "I hope that things can be learned from this tragic episode" so it cannot happen again (xii, U of Washington P, 1983).

Far from bitterness, indeed, nearly all the Japanese-American/Canadian reminiscences of the war preach a theology of forgiveness. Joy Kogawa, perhaps, captures that spirit best when, in *Obasan*, she has one of her characters pray: "Father...we are abandoned yet we are not abandoned. You are present in every hell. Teach us to see Love's presence in abandonment. Teach us to forgive" (243). Such a prayer is a coda that repeats itself in every one of the autobiographies or autobiographical fictions written by, or about, Japanese-Americans or Canadians and the terrible days they spent as enemies of their own land.

Notes

[1]There were, according to United States Army records, just over 110,000 persons of Japanese ancestry removed from the three Pacific Coast states during the war years. Canadian statistics show that country removed 21,975 persons from western British Columbia.

[2]In Canada, according to the 1941 census, 13,600 of the 23,450 persons of Japanese ancestry (58%) were native-born citizens. Another 3,650 were naturalized—a total of 73.6% in all. In the United States, where, under law, naturalization was forbidden, 79,642 of 126,947—62.7% were native born citizens. Combining the two countries' statistics, 64.4% of the "Japanese" were citizens of their respective nation, though this did not prevent their deportation.

[3]*Korematsu v. United States*, 323 U.S. 214, at 242 (1944).

[4]There have been dozens of books written about the relocation of the Japanese in the United States. Among the best are Roger Daniels, *Concentration Camps, U.S.A. Japanese Americans and World War II* (Hinsdale, IL: Dryden, 1971); Audrie Girdner and Anne Loftus, *The Great Betrayal: The Evacuation of the Japanese-Americans during World War II* (New York: Macmillan, 1969); Morton Grodzins, *American Betrayed: Politics and the Japanese Evacuation* (Chicago: U of Chicago P, 1949).

[5]Among the best comprehensive studies of the removal of Japanese Canadians are Ann Gomer Sunahara, *The Politics of Racism: The Uprooting of Japanese-Canadians during the Second World War* (Toronto: Lorimar, 1981); Patricia Roy, et al., *Mutual Hostages: Canadians and Japanese during the Second World War* (Toronto: U of Toronto P, 1990).

[6]See, among many, United States, Department of Interior, *W.R.A.: A Story of Human Conservation* (Washington: GPO, 1946) or United States, Department of the Army, Western Defense Command, *Final Report. Japanese Evacuation from the West Coast, 1942* (Washington: GPO, 1943). Two popular children's books of the era: Robert L. McLean, *Tommy Two Wheels* (New York: Friendship, 1943) and Florence Crandell Means, *The Moved-Outers* (Boston: Houghton, 1945) also offered justification for the evacuation by having Japanese-American characters express their willingness to be moved for the sake of America.

[7]All the various authors, though more than willing to talk in terms of "concentration camps" in the American west, are very careful to emphasize that in no way were the United States camps comparable to those in eastern Europe or Asia. For all its failings, the United States did try to make life in the relocation centers as bearable as it could.

[8]Nakano was placed in the Angler camp along with a huge majority of Japanese nationals whose loyalty was with Japan. When he eventually got permission to leave and work in Toronto for a packing firm, he was treated as a traitor by his fellow Japanese. Many years after the war, Nakano applied for and received Canadian citizenship.

[9]Florence Means' fictional heroine, Sumiko Ohara, on seeing the center at Amache, Colorado just west of the Kansas border, has the same reaction. "This is the worst moment of all," she notes. "It's so ugly, so dull, so dry." To a Californian friend she writes: "I never dreamed how it would be. To have everything drab, even the air, with the sand in it, why it's like a dead world. No green; no fragrance" (*The Moved-Outers* 89, 93).

[10]As a common theme, Means also has the Oharas experience the same problems with sand and dust everywhere and on every thing.

[11]The Canadian government has never seen fit to apologize to its Japanese residents for their relocation and mistreatment during the war years though in 1964 former Prime Minister Lester Pearson did personally express regret at what had transpired. For years, the United States also tried to avoid its responsibilities. It did agree to pay minimal amounts for destroyed personal property—Uchica received the grand sum of $386.25 (*Desert Exile* 150)—but, not until 1990, did Congress finally approve a monetary sum of $20,000 for each remaining evacuee as a belated apology for the Government's actions nearly fifty years ago.

Works Cited

Houston, Jeanne Wakatsuki and James D. Houston. *Farewell to Manzanar*. Boston: Houghton, 1973.

Ishigo, Estelle. *Lone Heart Mountain*. Los Angeles: n.p., 1972.

Kogawa, Joy. *Naomi's Road*. Toronto: Oxford UP, 1986.

——— *Obasan*. Toronto: Lester, 1981.

Nakano, Takeo Ujo with Leatrice Nakano. *Within the Barbed Wire Fence: A Japanese Man's Account of His Internment in Canada*. Toronto: U of Toronto P, 1980.

Okubo, Mine. *Citizen 13660*. New York: Columbia UP, 1946. Reissued Seattle: U of Washington P, 1983.

Sone, Monica. *Nisei Daughter*. Boston: Little, 1953.

Takashima, [Shizuye]. *A Child in Prison Camp*. Montreal: Tundra, 1971.

Uchida, Yoshiko. *Desert Exile: The Uprooting of a Japanese-American Family*. Seattle: U of Washington P, 1982.

——— *Journey to Topaz: A Story of Japanese-American Evacuation*. New York: Scribner's, 1971.

An Absence of Soldiers:
Wartime Fiction by British Women

Laura Hapke

The men who produced fiction in World War II Britain had a predictable fascination with the soldier—his psyche, his trials, his sacrifices. "Books," an English aristocrat once remarked, "are weapons of war," and combat-oriented works by male writers certainly generated respect for the war effort and countered the enemy's version of events. But, in so doing, such fiction reinforced traditional gender roles by extolling manliness as battleground heroism, womanliness as homefront self-sacrifice.

To be sure, without rejecting the importance of the anti-Nazi effort, some writers questioned the code of the military man and even the nobility of war itself. But war was clearly the occasion for their fiction in a way that works by female authors were not. Describing her own collection of tales, Elizabeth Bowen spoke for many women writers of the time. "These are all wartime, none of them war stories," she explained. They "are, more, studies of climate, war-climate, and of the strange growths it raised" (*Ivy* viii).

Many of the best female novelists of the period took Bowen's approach to the subject. True, none of them was considered the voice of homefront England that Jan Struther was for her fiercely patriotic *Mrs. Miniver* (1940). But other talented authors offered compelling tales of wartime non-combatants. One group in particular, writing during or soon after the war—E.M. Delafield, Stella Gibbons, Betty Miller, Pamela Frankau, Mollie Panter-Downes and Bowen herself—presented a collective critique of the male military vision.[1] Although they were not the only writers to do so, they were certainly among the most important.

Once popular with a fairly wide readership, these women gave what a *Times Literary Supplement* review of Bowen's fiction praised as "imaginative interpretation[s] of the effect of war on the manners, morals and emotions of those not directly engaged in the fighting" (152). Yet, to see their texts primarily as feminine contributions to the war effort is to obscure the meaning of the works. Analyzing war's impact on the heterosexual relationship, on woman's role in the family and the workplace, and on the feminine self-image, these authors did more than mirror the rearrangement of male-female relations characteristic of World War II British society.

On the surface, E.M. Delafield, Stella Gibbons and Mollie Panter-Downes seem traditionalists of the "Mrs. Miniver" school. Yet, unlike Struther's conventional matron, in one way or another their heroines question the role of the cheerful, patriotic helpmeet awaiting her master's return. Male absence, both literal and figurative, whether as soldier or non-combatant, affects the protagonists of all these texts, empowering some and disappointing others. Characters as diverse as Delafield's commanding matrons or Panter-Downes's dissatisfied ones, Gibbons's power-grabbing spinsters, Miller's embittered soldier wives and girlfriends, and the betrayed but strong-minded heroines of Bowen and Frankau, all suggest a far different imagining of women's response to their men than is usually associated with the feminine literary effort of wartime England.

Before re-evaluating the fiction in such revisionist terms, however, it would be well to suggest how it was perceived in its day. However much Delafield, Gibbons and their contemporaries offered a response to the Stiff-Upper-Lip school of war fiction, in their time they were thought to exemplify it. One reviewer's judgment of Miller's work might have applied to all of the novels under scrutiny. She was, in his sex-stereotyped view, merely applying "feminine shrewdness about people" to the trying conditions of wartime England ("Wartime Village" 113). What may also have shaped period responses to these writers was that they all came from reassuringly English middle-class or, in Bowen's case, Irish upper-class backgrounds and shunned the image of the New Womanish author challenging the male literary establishment. Bowen, it is true, earned great distinction as a writer, but she followed her husband where his career took him. All but Frankau, herself a seasoned contributor to women's magazines, lived the dual life of author and helpmeet wife.[2] Perhaps none of the others imitated Miller's rather extreme example of whisking her papers and writing materials away the moment her husband's key was heard in the door. But they all encouraged the public perception of them as writers who found comforting material for wartime stories in the occasions of feminine life. To that end, as Stella Gibbons put it in the early 1940s, she sought out "church[es], hospitals, school prize-givings, and social service committee meetings" (Simmons, "Gibbons" 470), locales familiar to the protagonists of Delafield and Panter-Downes as well. To characterize Bowen and Frankau's subjects, Gibbons might simply have added the newly legitimized feminine war work. Even as chroniclers of what a 1940 propaganda text called woman's "entirely unprecedented set of [work] circumstances," these writers seemed anything but threatening (Goldsmith, *Women at War* 10). By the early 1940s, in an "unmatched mobilization effort," half of all British women were at work (Costello, *Virtue* 5). One-third of them were in war work: even bourgeois matrons aided in Blitz relocation, took in refugees, and worked alongside men as Air Raid Wardens (Campbell, *Experience* 152). By 1941, all single women over 20 were required to register at government employment agencies as "mobile" labor for war factories, and it was routine for women to staff Government departments or work in technical positions in the WRENS, the WAAF, ATS, and the Land Army.[3] Even a typical ad in *Picture Post*, a British version of *Life* magazine, acknowledged the "new" working woman. Placing the homemaker in significant last place, the ad urged women to purchase the product, "whether the job you're doing is in or out of uniform, whether you serve in a factory, an office, a shop or in a home..." (4).

Delafield, Gibbons, Miller, Bowen, Frankau and Panter-Downes offer a composite portrait of women in such new roles. Delafield's comic gallery includes harried Red Cross workers, outspoken ambulance drivers, mannish female officers, canteen workers from their teens to their sixties, and showy Lady Bountifuls turning their homes into aid centers and hospitals. Gibbons's characters range from an attractive widow with a job at the Ministry of Applications to an affluent young woman turned factory girl who wears an armband with the apt motto "Front Line Service" as she works in the dangerous Royal Ordinance factory. Miller paints a world in which female military personnel and base nurses seem less interested in work than in men. They compete for the attention of the officers, sometimes edging out the wives and civilian sweethearts excluded from staff dances and parties. Bowen's less man-centered heroine is "employed, in an organization better called Y.X.D., in secret, exacting, and not unimportant work, to which the European position since 1940 gave ever-increasing point" (*The Heat of the Day* 17). Bowen also offers a number of secondary and minor characters, including a not-too-bright factory girl longing for her soldier husband and a boisterous air raid warden who attacks her work with missionary zeal. Frankau's female workers are military: her elegant protagonist moves from the prewar Shakespearean stage and Bloomsbury trysts with her surgeon lover to a post as platoon officer with the ATS, surrounded by "women in khaki" (*The Willow Cabin* 162). And Panter-Downes refers to the finest time in the life of a promiscuous working-class girl as when she was "buttoned...into the WAAF uniform" (*One Fine Day* 70). She mentions, too, the women who had "flown aeroplanes [and] been bombed on gun sights" (145), references to women's ATS work,[4] though her real subject is the "other women [who] sat stitching and folding" (115), making sure domesticity was still there when He returned Home.

It is not surprising that the popular and critical response to works like Delafield's *Diary of a Provincial Lady in Wartime*, Gibbons's *The Bachelor*, or Frankau's *The Willow Cabin* was that, in the words of one extoller of the *Diary*, they wove "a tapestry of England's reactions that flow[ed] with...color...[and] essential truth" (*New York Times*, 7 April 1940, 9). But what these novels did with the "essential truth" of the Englishwoman doing her part for the war effort was not simply verisimilitude in the name of patriotism. Rather, these works integrated social-historical depictions of women's new roles into a critique of male behavior. To sample the diversity of these texts as well as the uniformity of war response to wartime myths of manliness, we now turn to the novels themselves.

E.M. Delafield's *Diary of a Provincial Lady in Wartime*, published in 1940 as the sequel to her long line of lightly comic "Provincial Lady" adventures, is, on the surface, unconflicted traditionalism itself. Much of the humor issues from the matronly protagonist's ladylike tussles with the moody cook, the flighty parlor maid, the Daily, Weekly and Sometime help who, if "managed," enable the complacent lives of the upper-middle class to run smoothly. Beneath the situation comedy about the servant problem, however, the book is the Lady's fantasy of escape from domestic responsibility into the world of work. From the moment the narrative in rambling diary form opens, the otherwise unnamed "wife of Robert" is determined to leave for London to help with the war effort. She is not put off by her husband being an Air Raid Warden, her own activity in village war relief, or the fact that she has just taken her city-fleeing aunt, two child-refugees, and the children's nurse into her home for the duration of the war. Only three days after England declares itself at war with Germany, she contends that, both as a patriot and a writer (significantly, of novels like Delafield's), she is unable to "remain out of touch with current happenings in London" (16). Thus this provincial matron, mother of two, foster mother of two more, and wife of a taciturn man who, as she breezily notes in an earlier book, minimizes her writing when he is not hiding behind a *Times* crossword, escapes. Moving in with a girlish canteen worker, she joyfully occupies a tiny top-floor flat "well within [the] official danger zone" (50) to give life a piquancy it definitely lacked at home.

When the novel appeared, Delafield's readers, many of them women expected to accept without complaint the solitude of the war wife or the clamor of refugee boarders, hugely enjoyed the matron's adventures. In peacetime, the same audience would have questioned such straying from woman's prescribed role, but, as the Lady repeatedly points out, the need for volunteers legitimized her makeshift London existence. Hence the new woman-filled world of the underground canteen where she looks for work.

Delafield's narrative focuses on feminine energy, for, though the city is filled with anonymous "men in armlets," it is women—ambulance drivers, military personnel, canteen workers—who dominate the landscape. The Lady is a 1940s version of the Supermom on the (deliberately?) rare occasions when she returns to the provinces to check up on her household, joke with (and about) the vapid Robert and return to London with as much dispatch as possible. In the city, though, she is independence itself. She glories in working the cafeteria graveyard shift, walking home through potentially dangerous streets, naughtily eating bad food (while her servants follow the sensible menus she has left for her country family), and hearing the romantic problems of unattached young women pursued by London's bachelor officers. What heightens the sense that this woman is bent on liberation is the way in which she and her creator shunt men to the margins of the narrative. For all her patriotic fervor and emphasis on serving the "Allied cause," she makes only passing reference to soldiers at the front and her husband back in the provinces.

Women are officers and men, so to speak, in Delafield's world. Robert-back-at-home, in contrast, is relegated to women's tasks. Hardly the soldier—it is never explained whether he is too old or unhealthy for combat—he is the World War II version of the remote, mulch-obsessed farmer-gentleman of her 1927 novel *The Way Things Are*, but with a difference. In that book, Delafield's frustrated 20's wife broods that, after marriage with Alfred, "she wanted an emotional life" (8), but her attachment to provincial respectability keeps her home with him and the cows. "Mrs. Robert," in contrast, leaves Robert and thoughts of him behind, consigning her passive spouse to the role of managing the servants, the schedules and the home.

Having her heroine unman one Englishman, Delafield protects the protagonist (and herself) against charges of subversive feminism by sprinkling the narrative with disapproval of assertive women. Such attacks on less conventional woman obviously reveal her ambivalence about feminine freedom. But they do not negate the fact that in her vision of male-female relations, to keep a husband at home while one lives in daily expectation of the Blitz is far more satisfying than occupying the traditional feminine role. One pays lip service to female subordination and masculine dominance, the book implies, but one lives in a real world of strong women and weak men.

In her wartime novel of a strong-willed female and an inconsequential male, Stella Gibbons is another traditionalist who plays with role reversal. Her well-received and probably misunderstood 1944 novel, *The Bachelor*, appears to commiserate with Kenneth Fielding, the title character, who is totally under the sway of his sister Constance. It is she who dictates what the household is prepared to do for the war effort. It is not much. She will take in only pliant refugees who will act as servants, or grateful female relatives who will be away at work and are paying guests in any case. Like Delafield, Gibbons cloaks her portrait of a Woman in Command in comedy: "whereas Miss Fielding's mother had been large, handsome, and clever, Miss Fielding was only large and handsome," and: "If other people chose to notice the War, Miss Fielding did not propose to dissipate her energies by pointing out to them how misguided they were" (43). But, satire on this officious spinster notwithstanding, that is exactly what Miss F. does throughout the book. For as men must war—or in Kenneth's case, be part of the Home Guard—Miss Fielding certainly does not weep. She willfully avoids directing her formidable energies to the volunteer work which absorbed so many middle-aged and older single women. She taunts her brother for putting up blackout curtains, invites pacifists to stay with her, puts on home-centered "revels" and festivals by dragooning family friends as if it were prewar, indeed Victorian, England, and generally bullies her way through the book with no significant opposition. None, that is, from anyone but the little refugee she eventually dismisses from her employ.

In an uncharacteristically chivalric moment, the passive Kenneth rebels and, to Miss F's astonishment, weds the little servant girl. But his proposal is really one woman's triumph over another, for now Miss Fielding is not the only empress of the bourgeois domestic realm. The young wife invites her relatives to live with them, obtains the keys to the linen closet, and soon engineers Miss Fielding's relocation. What critics described as a "traditional, well-constructed book" and the author termed "making ordinary people laugh" ("Gibbons," *Contemporary Authors* 472) is, if one looks deeper, a study of one woman's attempt to impose feminine will on the masculine situation of wartime. Unlike Delafield's London-craving women, Miss Fielding has no provincial marriage to rebel against. War, indeed, can give her no precedence she has not had before. As one who manages the accounts and members of her prosperous household, she struggles against the accidents of history which might—and finally do—dislodge her.

The two sisters at the center of Betty Miller's mordant 1945 novel of life in a Cotswold village and neighboring military hospital also have little patience with the war. But the protagonists of *On the Side of the Angels* are far more dependent on male approval and, often, economic support, than are the Miss Fieldings of this world. Miller takes on the clichés of patriotic fiction—the devoted family man or boyfriend who reluctantly leaves for the front; the uncomplaining wife or sweetheart who cheers him on. Instead, in Miller's world, men treat women as encumbrances or transient sexual comforters, only to leave them in times of crisis. Indeed, all of the men in the novel long for the simplicity of a "male world, without loyalties outside the rigid artifacts of military life" (39) for reasons they half understand: adolescent ideas of glory, flight from women and responsibility, escape. As the book opens, young Mrs. Carmichael, a mother of two whose first name, significantly, is Honor, suffers from neglect by her boyish physician husband Colin. An RAMC captain, he spends his free time listening to pep talks on the machismo of overseas medical duty from Colonel Mayne, his misogynistic commanding officer. Miller explores how Mayne plays sexual politics in the name of wartime manliness. Honor and her sister Claudia have gone to find Colin in the town, where they see him walking devotedly with Mayne and a group of young officers. Mayne taunts:

> "Well, Colin—?" "Sir!" "What's it to be? Are you coming along with us for that drink, or—" he paused imperceptibly, he turned toward Honor, the smile of false jocularity lit his face again: "—or is your wife going to carry you off single-handed to attend to your domestic duties?" (43)

As Colin, in a fleeting moment of responsibility, walks off with his wife and her sister Claudia, Claudia looks at Colin and is "startled...It was a long time since she had seen such an expression of open frustration on the face of an adult" (44).

Claudia has chosen no more wisely than her sister: her fiancé, a shell-shock victim, takes out his frustrations on her because he cannot return to combat. And a dazzling commando stationed for a while at the base, who turns out to be a complete fraud, taunts her with the inferior courage of women. The battle lines in Miller are those of gender. The actual war is an occasion for men to take what they wish for as long as they wish from women, and flee. The novel is dedicated to Miller's heroic brother, missing and presumed dead, but no man in it can see beyond the narcissistic pursuit of manliness, and thus none seems capable of frontline activity, much less heroism.

Like the other novels under scrutiny, in its time the Miller book was judged for its fidelity or lack of fidelity to wartime life. Its dark vision prompted one representative reviewer to charge that it was unrealistic, lacking "substance" (*Times Literary Supplement*, 10 March 1945, 113). Nothing is farther from the truth, for the novel is an indictment of the myth of soldiering as the only true form of manhood. In its name, Colonel Mayne can bully and taunt his men and insult their women; a disturbed man can flee his bank manager job, wife and children to masquerade as "Captain Herriot" and seduce the women who come his way; and an insecure Colin Carmichael, convinced that a medical posting to the Sudan will win him acceptance in the community of men, can forsake his own family without regret. Although it is unlikely that any of these posturers or escapists will see combat, the novel makes a larger comment on the way men wedded to the "soldier mentality" turn their women into the real enemy. Thrusting women into positions ranging from transient plaything to family head, men, Miller writes acerbically, are "humiliated by [women's] presence" (39) on all other male-bonding occasions.

Two other writers whose novels appeared shortly after the war, Elizabeth Bowen and Pamela Frankau, also question wartime truths of gender-related conduct. Their respective works, *The Heat of the Day*, published in 1948, and

The Willow Cabin, in 1949, focus on single women involved in war office or military work and the shadowy lovers who fail them. Both works demonstrate that even the woman who lives for passion, making no marital or domestic demands on her military lover, can be disappointed by his inability to conduct himself honorably, or even competently, in romantic and military roles alike.

When *The Heat of the Day* appeared, reviewers paid homage to it as a work which "illuminate[d] the landscape of war," most notably the tense London of the Blitz (*Book Review*, 19 Oct. 1947, 10). The *Times Literary Supplement* remarked that one of the most respected writers of her time had captured the way characters responded to the dangers and consolations of the war-torn city. The reviewer aptly commented that Bowen "interprets war through love," in this case the affair between an attractive widow, Stella Rodney, and Robert Kelway, an officer she learns is spying for the Nazis ("Climate" 152). Significantly, the review faults the book for not fleshing Kelway in more as a character, for a "vagueness surrounding his personality" (152). The *New York Times* found Kelway more credible, ingeniously explaining that the retreat at Dunkirk had soured Robert on British effectiveness, luring him to the wrong side (*Book Review*, 19 Oct. 1947, 10). What both reviewers failed to notice, however, is that Stella, not Robert, is the center of the narrative: his "vagueness" is a foil for her vividly etched personality. If he is shadowy, it is so Stella, capsuled by her creator as "on happy sensuous terms with life" (17), may be viewed all the more clearly.

Stella's womanliness and responsiveness to experience are not the least of her attributes. As a self-supporting woman living in a dangerously Blitz-ridden London, she handles herself gracefully with a series of manipulators, among them the slimy Harrison, assigned to catch Robert, and the female Kelways, vivid in their hostility to her and their controlling attitude toward the son of the house. As the novel opens, Bowen focuses on Stella's response to the intelligence officer who is both hounding her for news of Robert and suggesting that her sexual favors can distract him from the task. Although Stella is increasingly convinced that Robert is a traitor, the novel does not shift to an analysis of his motives. What little the reader does learn of Robert comes, significantly, from descriptions of his house-proud mother and noisily patriotic sister, as if in proclaiming the values of bourgeois materialism and English supremacy they had obliterated him as a person and prevented him from believing in anything but what they held in horror. Typically, however, Bowen shifts from Robert's reasoning to Stella's conduct: her decision to try to help him escape his pursuers rather than his response to the fact that he has been discovered. Bowen compels respect for Stella's decision not because Robert deserves such help but because Stella offers it. She is not just a woman in love with a distant, enigmatic man but the stronger personality in the relationship. Indeed, Stella's love comes to seem not an infatuation with a quisling but an act with its own validity; she loved Kelway before the discovery that he was a traitor, and sees no reason to stop.

Robert's conduct as the remote lover, the man of masks, is an allegory of his betrayal of England. As an elusive male figure, however, he is no different than the other men in the novel—Stella's withdrawn son, the rather androgynous Roderick, who is home for weekend leave from the Army, or the spy-hunting Harrison, who hides behind the questions of the seasoned investigator.

Pamela Frankau's Michael Knowle in *The Willow Cabin* is an even weaker reed than the elusive Robert, the tentative Roderick, or the faceless Harrison. War brings to a head his problems with identity. In this case, the reader can witness his struggle to master life in the years prior to the war, for the novel begins in 1936, when Caroline first meets Michael, a surgeon estranged from his strong-willed and wealthy wife Mercedes, whose neurotic hold on him he seems unable to break. Caroline Seward is rather like the tough, glamorous, but forgiving heroines of the 1940's Hollywood tear-jerkers, in which a Bette Davis or a Joan Crawford must choose between an indecisive, often married, man (whose personality hers overshadows) and a promising career. Caroline sacrifices her acting to wait for Michael in various flats and hotel rooms, while he snatches time from the operating room or from disputes with Mercedes. In 1939, he is called up, and Caroline joins the women's Auxiliary Territory Service to be closer to him, becoming an officer and training instructor. There are other Hollywood elements in this novel, which was avidly read by a romance-prone female audience. Michael is as mysterious a figure in the Army as he was before it. Frankau was a veteran women's magazine contributor, and Knowle is reminiscent of the hero of the women's romance magazine: sexy, haunted, mysterious, dangerous. Yet he is also self-destructive, insecure, frightened of life. In a sense, the novel concerns Caroline's obsessive drive to keep herself from acknowledging the deeper truths of her hero's nature, that he is in flight from himself, looking to profession, the military, and impressionable young women to assuage his pain. His suicide from a pill overdose in 1943 is evidence enough that he is unable to flee that self.

What is so interesting about the book, however, and makes it so readable, both on the "Hollywood" level of the doomed adulterous affair and on the level of serious fiction, is that Caroline reacts to this weak man in death as she did in life, by idealizing him. Like the widow of a much-decorated soldier husband, she cares only to retain an untarnished memory of her lover. She even spends the postwar years carrying on an imaginary conversation with the lost Michael, trying to satisfy herself that his death had a logical reason. The truth which she, but not the reader, avoids is that she is simply the stronger one, able to meet adversity, including wartime dislocation, head on.

On the surface, Mollie Panter-Downes seems to resist the revisionist view of wartime gender relations applied to the other authors studied here. In stories like her 1941 "Goodbye, My Love," the men go resolutely off to combat. The women cheer them and England on, choking back tears, not resentment or doubt. Yet, in the 1946 novel *One Fine Day*, even so orthodox a chronicler of the fighting spirit paints a portrait of a tired-out, alienated officer home from the battle. On one level, such a portrait typifies the fatigued wartime returnee but, like other women writers of the day, the author sees men as distant and emotionally unavailable rather than as heroic figures. And she, too, places the male character in the blurred background of the narrative and foregrounds the wife, making her a symbol of postwar adaptation to economic deprivation and marital dissatisfaction alike. One period review of the novel was aptly titled "Laura Sees It Through," for the book concerns Laura Marshall's ability to cope with the difficulties of a pinched postwar existence—unappetizing food, a servant shortage, a taciturn husband who is distant from his wife and schoolgirl daughter.

Stephen Marshall is back from war, but he is absent too. Sleeping poorly, angered if the house is disorderly, envying the men who had slipped right back into their professional routines and who could say "[t]his is what I missed all these years [away], this is what I dreamed about" (210), Marshall does what is expected of him. He takes the commuter train to London, supports his family, tries to slough off postwar fatigue, but he is removed and remote. "If they could be quiet together for a little while, with a hill to walk on and a sea to swim in," Laura reflects on their silent marriage, "might not something come back?" (191). The novel provides no answer. For Stephen's fatigued, uneasy re-entry is a parable of the mental state of England, and the book is at pains to make that connection clear. But it is also a serious inquiry into a woman's emotional distance from a disappointing husband. Marital resentment is transformed into Laura's resolve to do her part, not, as in Delafield, by leaving home, but by serving as its emotional center.

Aviator John Rhys's *England Is My Village*, a popular collection of closely linked tales of manly men and helpmeet women published in 1941, is in distinct contrast to the works studied here. In it, the wife of a Hemingwayesque flier acknowledges her inferiority to him and to fighting men in general. Describing herself as unable to withstand danger, despite the fact that she has just gone on a dangerous night flight, she finishes her self-deprecation by apologizing: "Your lives aren't in your bodies...You've jobs and comradeship and things" (46). The novels discussed in this essay challenge this sex stereotyping. Although male characters with war work or military rank are there in the background, they are not the principal ones with jobs and comradeship and things. It is women who emerge as able to do their part, see a task through, or, at the very least, act responsibly. One recent student of World War II fiction notes that only a "handful of women...allowed their insight[s] to lead them to overt feminism," whereas in most women's writings, "protest was more muted" (Higonnet, "Introduction" 16). Delafield, Gibbons and their contemporaries are no feminists. They do not, at least consciously, present women as an oppressed group or call for an alteration in gender relations. But neither are they sympathetic to war or its toll on the male combatant. In omitting praise of the fighting man, their works seem to extend the critique of masculine psychological remoteness to men at war as well. What these writers do create is a gallery of men who are, quite clearly, lacking, who range from passive to anxiety-ridden to unstable to suicidal.

In these works, the wartime ideal of the Englishman primed for the battle is a fantasy. In a famous comment, Virginia Woolf contended that men used women as ego-enlarging mirrors. As if to correct that situation, the writers here picture men at half rather than twice their normal size. Whether from disappointment with men or reluctance to empower them, writers as divergent as Delafield, Miller, Frankau and the others question a wartime code which enshrined men while relegating women at best to the status of those who also served. However such texts were accounted for in their day, rediscovering them we find that they replaced masculine with feminine strength, decisiveness and endurance. In so doing, they offered a significant challenge to the orthodoxies of wartime Britain.

Notes

[1]When one is discussing "male" and "female" war fiction, one must qualify the terms. Men wrote fiction about the homefront; women wrote about combat. See, for instance, Somerset Maugham's *The Hour Before the Dawn* (1942) and Edith Pargeter's *She Goes to War* (1942). But most male writers did focus on combat, just as most females did not.

[2]Their personal histories were rather different: Delafield married a military man with artistic connections; Gibbons, an actor; Bowen, an educator; Miller, a psychiatrist; Panter-Downes, a farmer. Frankau never married. But, all except Frankau led domestic lives which included a stable marriage to a solid provider, a home, children and community involvement—lives desired by or reflecting those of ordinary Englishwomen.

[3]The Wrens, or WRNS, stood for the Women's Royal Naval Service; the WAAF, for the Women's Auxiliary Air Force, the ATS, for the Auxiliary Territorial Service.

[4]ATS women had been present on gun sites since 1940. In the ATS, "the girls lived like men, fought their fights like men, and, alas, some of them died like men. Unarmed, they showed great personal bravery." Quoted in Jack Cassin-Scott, *Women at War, 1939-45* (London: Osprey Publishing Company, 1980) 7.

Works Cited

Bowen, Elizabeth. *The Heat of the Day.* [1948] New York: Avon, 1978.

_____ "Introduction." *Ivy Gripped the Steps.* New York: Alfred A. Knopf, 1945.

Campbell, John. *The Experience of World War II.* New York: Oxford UP, 1989.

Cassin-Scott, Jack. *Women at War, 1939-45.* London: Osprey, 1980.

"The Climate of Treason." *Times Literary Supplement.* 3 Mar. 1949: 152.

Costello, John. *Virtue Under Fire: How World War II Changed our Social and Sexual Attitudes.* Boston: Little, Brown, 1985.

Delafield, E.M. *Diary of a Provincial Lady in Wartime.* 1940. Rpt. Chicago: Academy Chicago, 1989.

_____ *The Way Things Are.* [1927] New York: Penguin/Virago, 1988.

Goldsmith, Margaret. *Women at War.* London: Lindsay Drummond, 1943.

Higonnet, Margaret. "Introduction." *Behind the Lines: Gender and the Two World Wars.* Ed. Higonnet et al. New Haven and London: Yale UP, 1987.

Miller, Betty. *On the Side of the Angels.* [1945] New York: Penguin/Virago, 1986.

Panter-Downes, Mollie. *One Fine Day.* [1946] Boston: Little, Brown, 1947.

[*Review of Diary of a Provincial Lady*]. *New York Times Book Review.* 7 Apr. 1940: 9.

Rhys, John. *England Is My Village.* New York: Reynal and Hitchcock, 1941.

Simmons, Judith. "Stella Gibbons." *Contemporary Novelists.* Ed. James Vinson. Vol. 55. London: St. James, 1972.

"Wartime Village." *Times Literary Supplement.* 10 Mar. 1945: 113.

"Some Classic Pattern"
Pens and Needles on the Home Front

Cecilia Macheski

Women have not only been knitting—they have been thinking.
Nellie McClung, 1915

In Edwin Muir's poem, "Telemachos Remembers," the boy sits at his mother's loom as "Half-finished heroes sad and mum,/ Came slowly to the shuttle's hum./ Time itself was not so slow." Muir's modern rendering of Penelope through Telemachos' innocent vantage point renews our stake in her as an emblem for wartime waiting. By World War II, women had taken up knitting rather than weaving as the measure of their time, but the link to the patient queen of Ithaca is potent in novels and autobiographies women wrote as well as in their sweaters and socks. Muir's Penelope reigns as a figure of wisdom and sadness, keeping her woman's secret from her son. He wonders, "How could she bear the mounting load,/ Dare once again her ghosts to rouse/." Telemachos thinks he finds the answer in the figures in Penelope's unfinished tapestry: "I wet them with my childish tears/ Not knowing she wove into her fears/ Pride and fidelity and love."

Telemachos' retrospective insight can teach us where to find answers to our similar questions about women's lives on the homefront in World War II. Not only in their texts, but in their textiles, women encoded those virtues Telemachos recognized. But women also recorded their anger and their frustration, often in a language the warlike Odysseus and his son would never understand.

Writing in 1915, Nellie McClung, a Canadian feminist, asked "What Do Women Think of War? (Not That It Matters)" and inevitably found her answer and her rhetoric in the click of knitting needles. "Since the war broke out, women have done a great deal of knitting. Looking at this great army of women struggling with rib and back seam, some have seen nothing in it but a 'fad' which has supplanted for the time tatting and bridge. But it is more than that. It is the desire to help, to care for, to minister.... The woman's outlook on life is to save, to care for, to help. Men make wounds and women bind them up, and so the women, with their hearts filled with love and sorrow, sit in their quiet homes and knit" (157). One can only guess at the futility she must have felt when the next war came. Useless though her wisdom was in stopping that conflict, McClung's recognition of the echoes in the regular clicking of needles as women crafted sweaters and socks for soldiers and sailors, helps us trace the lineage of Penelope and those we can call her daughters.

Now, as Muir reminds us, Penelope in Homer's story had no daughters, only the rather feckless Telemachos, too young to go to war, but no doubt old enough to trouble her with his acne, his dirty togas cast aside on the dining couches, his pleas to be allowed to borrow the chariot on Saturday night and, most of all, to take a ship and escape domestic responsibilities to go in search of his father. How she must have longed for daughters in whom she could confide her loneliness, her desires and the secret of her weaving. She had only the ancient Eurycleia and her handmaidens, one of whom finally betrays her greatest secret, the shrewd nightly unweaving of her tapestry, Laertes' shroud.

But Penelope did have her daughters, long after Odysseus' return. These were not conceived in the great bed that sent its roots down into the earth beneath the palace. They were, rather, drawn in the threads of the loom, in the weft of the tapestry, and, like long strands the Fates spun out but never cut, they claim their identity in every war when women pick up needles to knit for absent men.

The Penelope myth and the tasks of needlework are implanted in women's heritage as deeply as the secret of the bed in Penelope's marriage. By the Second World War, Penelope's loom, in the modern guise of knitting and sewing needles, becomes a pattern of imagery in women's writing and in the popular patriotic culture of the war years. This imagery is more complex than might at first appear, especially to those who do not sew or knit. On the surface level, a woman knitting is an icon of loyalty, patience, patriotism. She is deemed virtuous as she keeps her hands from falling into idleness. Second, but much more covertly, knitting connotes shrewdness, a virtuous guise like Penelope's for subversive activity, such as thinking, dreaming or harboring less than patriotic notions. Third, the seemingly innocent needles can become weapons to attack the results of war, and to make fiercely concrete and domestic the abstractions of wartime rhetoric.

In the popular culture of the films and novels of the war years, knitting was often ridiculed, or at least only superficially appreciated. A good example is the very successful film "Mrs. Miniver."

At the beginning of the film, Greer Garson represents the engaging pre-war heroine as a woman with few concerns beyond those of domestic bliss, as she hops first onto and immediately down from a bus in order to return to a millinery shop in quest of a hat that had earlier enticed her. Toward the end of the patriotic movie, after she has held a Nazi at gunpoint in her kitchen and before she loses her daughter-in-law in an air raid, the much altered Mrs. Miniver huddles with her family in their underground bomb shelter, vigorously knitting. So obsessive has this occupation become that her husband must remind her that he will not again risk his life to return to the house during a bombing raid in order to find her missing knitting needles. However much the tweedy squire-spouse may tease her, he is clearly proud of his wife, and the film argues that the adaptations Mrs. Miniver has made in trading in her frivolous consumerism for useful production is to be much admired. And while men, like Mr. Miniver, could mock and trivialize their women's work, many texts and popular images suggest that women themselves saw their knitting not only as a serious contribution to the war effort, but also as belonging to a realm men, in their eagerness for battle, would understand no more than the infant Telemachos could understand his mother's craft. Mrs. Miniver, after all, did not kill her Nazi pilot; she gave him milk and ham and bread, and, when she turns him over to the police, she does it sadly, assuring him it is for his own good. She sees him, finally, not as the enemy, but merely as a young man, another Telemachos, all too much like her own Air Force pilot son.

Through their knitting women like Mrs. Miniver send a covert message about the human price of war, as they earnestly construct whole cloth even as the fabric of society around them is being torn apart. If the first Penelope was patient, she was also shrewd. By her craft she defended and protected her family and her homeland, and it should not surprise us that in almost every war, but especially WWII, women cast on their stitches to protect and sometimes shroud their men, and themselves, with a combination of Penelope's patience and her shrewdness. The former virtue was, of course, socially promoted, but the latter began to worry those who saw danger in crafty women.

Mollie Panter-Downes and Mary Lee Settle share a common perspective on World War II, as both wrote works that recollect the war. Like Homer's *Odyssey*, *One Fine Day* and *All the Brave Promises* begin with a knowledge of the end and both, in a sense, are about the homefront as women experienced it, and the consequences of the men's coming home. In both works, images of Penelope and needlework are central, either overtly or covertly. Both heroines must wait, although Settle chose to do so by leaving her home in America and volunteering for the Women's Auxiliary Air Force in England in 1942. Still, even as a WAAF, she must wait, and knit, much like the civilian characters in *One Fine Day*.

Mary Lee Settle's autobiography of her experiences as "Aircraft Woman 2nd Class 2146391" is a narrative that opens with the wild adventure and promise of war excitement, but closes with the much sadder note of loss, disappointment, isolation. This shift from the patriotic to the disillusioned, the near pacifist, is reflected subtly in the way knitting is described throughout the book.

We see knitting first in the classic wartime symbol of oddly sized handknit socks. Lofty, a sort of Charon who ferries the young eager Settle across the wartime Atlantic is "a thin boy in the outgrown uniform of an apprentice in the merchant navy..." (6). His innocence is captured for us as "his wrists stood out beyond his jacket sleeves, and the heavy socks someone had knitted for him were a wide expanse between his trouser cuffs and his worn shoes, brightly polished" (6). These socks endear him to us, as, far from being stylish, they are a recurring wartime necessity. Paul Fussell's *Wartime* is dedicated, for instance, "To the memory of my mother and father, who sent socks and books."

Later, when Settle has joined the WAAF, she carries us through her war experience stitch by stitch, increasing our sympathy for the aging and tired women the war has left in England to wait for their men. Her landlady when she visits London for a few days begins as a creature seen only from the outside, reflecting the popular stereotype of the spinsterish war widow: "She wore...one of those heavy tweed skirts and long oatmeal cardigans that came from a whole world of common-sense uniformity, but are never seen in any shop" (84). Later, the eccentric Mrs. Mead takes on newer and far more sympathetic colors as Settle gets to know her better, through her knitting: "Mrs. Mead gathered up her tin helmet and her knitting bag to go on duty. I found out then where the cardigans came from—from ARP duty, in the shelters, at the R/T sets, waiting for the trains.... All across England there was a huge net of half-finished knitting—khaki-drab, navy-blue, Air-Force blue and civilian 'depot beige'—as the women waited in that stretched spacial time I knew so well for the war to end. Nostalgia has muted and softened the click of knitting needles...in the quiet of that tried waiting...I had forgotten the silence...as if we were all waiting in one vast depot for an interrupting train that never came but was always coming, so that nothing could be planned and carried through" (86-87). Here, as with Lofty's sock, the outsized knitted garment molds itself to human form. The common thread is the waiting, always the waiting. That "stretched spacial time" is Penelope's time at her loom, too, and soon Settle and Mrs. Mead have formed another women's community in its realm.

Later, Settle describes the women who, like herself, were radio listeners, who sat with headphones to receiver-transmitter sets in eight hour shifts listening for lost planes over the unceasing jamming noises of the Germans. Some women, she remembers, "turned down the sets to protect their brains from the jamming, got out knitting or books..." (60). Again, between the bursts of allied communications there were long maddening periods, "dead areas of animal waiting..." (60).

For Settle, the knitting begins to lose its wholesome quality and takes on an edge of growing impatience as the war progresses, and as the glamour and romance are replaced with cruelty and violence. A ground crew worker is decapitated by a propeller blade as the result of an administrative oversight; his head bounces from her foot like a soccer ball as she steps out of the radio room after her shift one night. A sadistic commanding officer punishes a young soldier unjustly and the women stand by helpless and frustrated against the injustice. Their response: "We got out our knitting, got on with the mechanics of our jobs, settled again to waiting through the gray days..." (151).

For some women, the waiting proved too long, and they turned to liaisons with the available allied forces personnel while their husbands were too far away to comfort them. Settle tells of one unlucky woman who finds herself pregnant while in the WAAF. Her husband has been in Africa for nearly a year. Unable to go to a doctor, as abortion is illegal, she feels she has no choice but to act for herself:

"How did you do it?" Viv asked, practically...
"Knitting needle." (108)

Thus the knitting needle becomes a tool, a weapon, to fight the effects of war. The frustrated young woman has instinctively seized the most familiar tool she has, the tool that once counted off minutes in stitches, to end her waiting when the authorities turn a blind eye to her need.

This gradual shift from Lofty's loving socks to the needle as cruel instrument reflects Settle's own changing attitude toward the war. The adventure with which the narrative begins has eroded by the end, as, fatigued and disillusioned, she leaves the WAAF, and must wait, as she says, until the 1960s before she can confront the experience in writing. Like the pregnant girl, Settle found the only instrument handy for her own emotional surgery when she took up her needles with her pen.

The image of Penelope is not far from Mollie Panter-Downes' mind either when she writes *One Fine Day*, her novel about recovery from the war years. Laura, the wife of a returned soldier, is a dreamy, somewhat impractical but sympathetic woman, who discovers, once the war removes her cook and maid, that she must make adjustments if she is to retain the gentility her husband (and her in-laws) expect. She is not sure these values interest her. She has spent the war happily eating off trays with her daughter, ignoring household chores and enjoying a female community from which her returned husband shrinks.

Although the novel is set shortly after the war has ended, it is structured with many flashbacks to the war years. Laura, quite a contrast to the diligent and disciplined English Women's Club type her mother-in-law manifests, is reminded at one point of the "working parties" held during the war. When asked if she attended these, her answer is vague, and she recalls to herself how the dust from lint bandages had made her sneeze. Yet Laura remembers:

"...She wouldn't go again. But she turned up next week all right. She enjoyed it. There was something soothing about it, Laura always felt, as though they were repeating some classic pattern which went on recurring for ever in different fancy dresses, the group of women sitting sewing round the lady of the house while their men were at the wars, fighting the Trojans or the Turks or the Nazis. Men must fight and women must sew— of course in this war women had fought too.... While you destroy, we build up, we stitch and fold quietly in the inner courtyard which is the true centre of the house." (112)

One is struck by the remarkable similarity between her words and those of Nellie McClung written during the previous war. Panter-Downes emphasizes more explicitly than the other women writers the link to Penelope, however, as Laura translates the scene in the manor house before her into a modern Ithaca: "...Mrs. Vyner, bending her damp-looking pale face over the Singer, all giving place to the loom and slowly growing greens and blues and greys of the tapestry forest" (113). The greens, blues and greys of military service issue are transformed by the romantic Laura into Penelope's tapestry as Trojans and Nazis merge into a single entity, as all wars become the same for women who wait.

Yet, like Settle, Panter-Downes recognizes the frustration women feel. We recall that, when Telemachos has been sent off to bed, the smooth pictures of the tapestry get ripped out each night by the crafty Queen, and something of woman's rage is manifest in another member of Laura's working party, Mrs. Cranmer. Here Panter-Downes, like Settle, offers a feminist reading of Homer. Laura wonders, when this domineering woman doesn't finish a thought about what might have happened if the Germans had gotten to London, "What would she have liked...To do something violently active, instead of sitting at the head of the long table, crying" (124). Here needlework reflects her frustration. "It was possible to imagine Mrs. Cranmer in another age, directing the heating of boiling water, heaving rocks over the battlements, even stumping out herself with the troops...But she had been tied helplessly to her corner of the big decaying house...She had never had even that taste of danger" (125). Thus, her anger takes the only outlet that is available: she turns her needle into a weapon, "And she had sewed so atrociously at her working parties...[that]...Mrs. Vyner would roll it up and pop it in her bag, to take home and unpick and remake Mrs. Cranmer's sampler of fury with the fates" (125).

Laura, though less angry, again turns to Homer to express her worry: "Ulysses had returned to a Penelope grown boring, commonplace, grey" (22). She is fortunate enough by the end of *One Fine Day* to recognize the irrelevance of such a concern to her happiness, and to see that it is a reflection of the myth that war is a glamorous adventure. Settle's narrative suggests that, even for those women given something warlike to do, the adventure soon reduced itself to more waiting, more knitting, and perhaps more serious anger and frustration.

Why knitting and sewing? What about these seemingly humble and repetitive tasks attracts women, especially wartime women and writing women?

There are simple answers, of course, as the wartime propaganda machine in the United States reminded citizens. As the wonderful *No Idle Hands: The Social History of American Knitting* by Anne L. McDonald attests, women, their fingers wrapped with yarn, sitting in so-called Stitch and Bitch clubs, were exhibiting loyal, patient and domestic behavior. They were less likely to get into trouble if they were busy. And, in a practical light, the nation needed knitters. The soldiers needed socks. But women, and especially women writers, looked more closely at the knitters' community both in Britain and in the United States, as the two works discussed here suggest. The war—this war and probably all wars—created women's communities on the homefront, the kind of groups Panter-Downes' Laura saw as part of a "classic pattern" that "went on recurring for ever." Such groups, of course, always exist, whether formally as convents of nuns or casually as wartime grocery queues. Knitting and needlework clubs merely continued the quilting bees and sewing circles where women had always shared words and patterns, and complained about men. But the Second World War added a new dimension, or at least stirred up old fears that women were crossing some dangerous line away from "femininity" as they began to work not only as nurses but as munitions manufacturers, radio operators, ambulance drivers, as they encroached on the male domain of genuine warfare.

Another glance at Hollywood suggests how Penelope's shrewdness could outweigh her virtue in the popular mind. In a 1943 Kay Kyser film, *Around the World*, for instance, the "girls" who have merrily and patriotically sung and danced their way around the globe to keep up troop morale gather for a quiet moment on the plane en route from New Delhi to China. They form a knitting and sewing circle and, trouser clad, stitch away the time. They are, however, interrupted by the master himself, who dances by to remind the hoofers that, while he likes them in trousers just fine, the "boys" they are here to entertain want women in skirts. He sings in slangy rhythms, "a boy in khaki thinks a girl in slacky is tacky." The girls cheerfully take the warning and agree to "let the soldiers wear the trousers" and that "dresses it shall be" on stage. Clearly, even the patriotic click of the knitting needles is inadequate disguise for the subversive intent of these insidious women who are trying to distract the ever-vigilant Kyser from their real treason, the trousers. It is a very brief scene, and the women's all-too-ready acquiescence to authority suggests patriotism as their only motive. But, to a reader familiar with the Penelope story as reinterpreted in the 1940s, this Hollywood fable reflects a genuine male concern that women's solidarity, made inevitable by the war, was still a threat if it went too far, or outlived the war.

While evidence of women's communities and women's attempts to deconstruct traditional male roles partly explains the appeal of knitting and needlework, knitting, in particular, offers an even deeper response to the war. We must understand exactly what the technique of knitting is to understand why it appealed so strongly to women both as a craft and as a literary symbol.

To knit, one needs two needles, and some yarn. There are, basically, two stitches: knit and purl. Knitting involves working combinations on the two basic stitches. Combinations must be worked both across a row and with an eye to the rows above and below. Thus, for example, a fabric worked with alternating rows of knit and purl stitches will be called stockinette, the familiar even fabric of crew neck sweaters. But alternating knit and purl stitches within a row can prepare the ground for the more elastic ribbing familiar from cuffs and sock tops, or for the nubbly textured fabric called moss or rice stitch, depending on whether the knitter repeats the knit one, purl one of the first row in her second row, or whether she switches to purl one, knit one. The variety of combinations possible grows enormous, as the knitter explores odd and even numbers, and tricks like twisting or dropping or adding stitches create elaborate lace, cables and textures. Finally, add the variable of color, and we realize that the knitter's task is little different from that faced by a computer programmer toying with infinite mathematical permutations and combinations.

To knit, then, is to see possibilities, to explore new combinations. The knitter is one keenly aware of the multi-faceted nature of things. It is no surprise, in this light, to recognize that Virginia Woolf's Mrs. Ramsay *knits* a stocking at the very center of *To the Lighthouse*. Woolf's modernist, multi-faceted style mirrors a knitter's way of knowing, a knitter's style. It is a pluralistic response to the world, one that offers many angles, denying a single strand toward truth. And it is no doubt this dimension that outsiders found so dangerous, and feared would grow with the second war. McClung's knitting, thinking women use their stitches to allow them to see beyond the single-minded, official (and largely male) view of war. While the propaganda bureaus hurtled rights and wrongs, the women translated these into knits and purls, put them on the needles of their consciences, and considered the permutations. K3, P2, K2, P2, K8, P2, K2, P2, K1, K2 tog., K1 might be a code, but it is, in fact, the pattern for a cable stitch from a pattern for "Service Woolies for Air, Land and Sea," illustrated with a handsome young man posed in front of a war plane, goggles in hand [Figure 1]. In working the intricacies of such patterns for the sweaters and socks they sent overseas, knitters coded no simple messages of truth, but something contemplative and questioning, as complex as the cables they twined. The very names of stitches recall the domestic pleasures curtailed by war: rice stitch, moss, basket cable, open star, bluebell, coral knot, sugar-stick ribbing, cat's eye, waffle, beech-leaf lace, bell-ringer's peal pattern. With so many paths to truth, who would settle for mere knit and purl? Would not a knitter see the world not

Fig. 1. Knitting for the Boys at War: "Service Woolies for Air, Land, and Sea," Knitting Pattern from Patons and Baldwins Ltd., Clackmannanshire, Scotland, 1942. Printed with their permission.

as flat but round, not as black and white but illuminated with the brilliant colors of a fair isle jersey?

But knitters are not the only ones to claim kinship with Penelope, and, of all the novels about World War II to use the "classic pattern," Beryl Bainbridge's *The Dressmaker* is among the most powerful, most wicked and most witty. Penelope, disguised here as Nellie, is transformed into a working class seamstress of near heroic proportions, whose stitching takes on tragic dimensions as she, like the ancient queen, must complete a shroud.

Nellie, her sister Margo, and their niece Rita form a close women's community in their tiny house on Priory Road, even sleeping in the same large bed both for warmth and to protect Rita from recurring nightmares. *The Dressmaker* is about what the war did to the moral values of a tough, hard working family, but Bainbridge is not one to draw on stereotypes of heroism for her characters. Behind the modest facades of Priory Road lurk the eccentricities, fantasies and epiphanies of women whose lives are caught between the poverty and desperation of wartime and the new freedoms wartime poses as alternatives to the confining conventions of neighborhood ethics. Rita lives with her aunts because Jack, her father, cannot be trusted to raise her since her mother's death. Precisely what his weaknesses are remains unspoken, but the aunts' contempt encourages us to read unimaginable perversity into his character. Jack is a butcher by trade, and an active black market trader, much to the patriotic Nellie's indignation. Margo, in contrast to the good, solid Nellie, is a "bad girl," who loves the beautiful dresses her sister makes and wants to dance, smoke cigarettes and enjoy the male company the war has cast her way with little respect for the prewar behavior Nellie advocates.

The novel develops with the thick, macabre texture at which Bainbridge is so expert, as young Rita falls in love with Ira, an American G.I. stationed at a nearby base. Around this crude, illiterate son of a white southern dirt farmer, the innocent Rita spins a web of romance, creating from the dumb clay of Ira a sensitive and gently platonic lover. Ira has little on his mind except a sexual liaison, however, and when he figures out that Rita will not oblige, he soon turns his attentions to the older and more experienced Margo. She obliges, taking him upstairs to a box room in which Nellie has secreted away her mother's furniture, her most cherished possessions. When Nellie returns home early and unwell to hear noises from the storage room, she discovers Margo and Ira making love. Leaving the room and dressing in haste, Ira drags his army jacket across the polished wood of a table, and rage that Nellie has accumulated and repressed throughout the story, the war, and even her life, finds its target:

He was no good, he was disgusting. She could feel the anger gathering in her breast. The whole house was loud with the beating of her outraged heart.

No passive Penelope, Nellie takes action:

She raised her arm and stabbed him with the scissors.... She strikes his neck, and he bashed his head on the curve of the umbrella stand...Opened his mouth in agony. Died before the air left his lungs. (154)

The sharp, beaky scissors that have trimmed dress fabric and snipped thread for so long join the ranks of the angry instruments like the WAAF's knitting needles and Mrs. Cranmer's "sampler of fury," but here they strike their human target, a real man, a soldier, a seducer. Margo, following him down the stairs, "was moaning, rocking herself back and forwards on her chair as if to ease some private grief," but Nellie is transformed by her action:

"We haven't had much of a life," cried Nellie. "We haven't done much in the way of proving we're alive. I don't see why we should pay for him."

Finally, Nellie "stood up and went into the hall. She pulled down the curtain from under the stairs" (156). Like Scarlett O'Hara, Nellie has an eye for the possibilities in yards of straight fabric in the heavy drapes. "'We best wrap him up,' she said. 'What for?' Margo asked. 'We don't want young Rita tripping over him.'" And Bainbridge draws Nellie into her web:

She was very capable, a dressmaker to her bones. She put the chenille curtains under the clamp of the sewing machine and made a bag for Ira. She made Margo drag him by the feet into the kitchen.... Nellie said they had to put him inside the curtain.... They slid him into the bag...Nellie made Margo hold Ira in her arms by the sewing machine so that she could sew the bag over his head. It had to be a proper shroud. (157)

The men in Bainbridge's odyssey are few and weak. Jack the butcher is called in to haul away the body before Rita returns and discovers what has happened. Against Nellie's strength, Jack is helpless, as he groans and tries to deny what has happened. He has failed in the role of father, surrendering his daughter to the care of aunts. Ira, poor, illiterate, an outsider, elicits little sympathy from the reader even as Nellie's shears strike his neck. The creature she has become is so much an avenging force that Ira shrinks to insignificance. She almost takes the story out of human proportions, except for the lowly murder weapon. The sewing scissors domesticate the near-epic rage, and, in the last paragraph of the book as she stands, "the tape measure still dangling from her neck" (160), she becomes a working class Penelope who has repelled the unwanted suitor from her home without the aid of son or husband. She has restored the women's community that the war years have made her domain. Young Ira is no Telemachos; Jack, no Odysseus. The men have been banished from this modern Ithaca on Priory Road, this wartime Herland. Nellie has found her daughter, but the secret of the shroud will be kept from her for a while longer. The classic repeated pattern, then, is not only the cable or the cat's eye—it is war itself. Trojan and Turk and Nazi, in the hand of Penelope's daughters, get woven into the same tapestry forest, so that they can secretly be ripped out and a new weft, a pattern of peace, may be worked in their stead. With characteristic wartime frugality, women writers unraveled the old yarn from Penelope's tapestry and carefully and covertly reworked it. In the vigils they kept not only with their sons but with their daughters, they cast on stitches for socks and ideas for stories. And, perhaps, long after the waiting was over, when the men sat back, rehearsed their war stories, and began polishing their weapons for yet another war, the women took their daughters aside, looped yarn around their hands, and told them, in the language of the needles Penelope had bequeathed them, the secret of the tapestry, and the shroud.

Works Cited

Dwan, Allan, dir. Kay Keyser in *Around the World*. RKO, 1943. Reissued on VHS by RKO Collection, 1990.

Bainbridge, Beryl. *The Dressmaker*. London: Fontana, 1973.

Fussell, Paul. *Wartime*. New York: Oxford, 1989.

McClung, Nellie. "What Do Women Think of War? (Not That It Matters)." From *In Times Like These*. 1915; rpt. 1972; excerpted in *Longman Anthology of World Literature by Women 1875-1975*, ed. Marian Arkin and Barbara Shollar. New York: Longman, 1989: 156-59.

McDonald, Anne L. *No Idle Hands: A Social History of American Knitting*. New York: Ballantine, 1988.

Muir, Edwin. "Telemachos Remembers." In *One Foot in Eden*. London: Faber and Faber, 1956: 30-31.

Panter-Downes, Mollie. *One Fine Day*. 1946; rpt. New York: Penguin Virago, 1986.

Settle, Mary Lee. *All the Brave Promises*. 1966; rpt. New York: Scribner's, 1988.

Wyler, William, dir. "Mrs. Miniver." With Greer Garson and Walter Pidgeon. Loews, 1942. Reissued on VHS by MGM/UA, 1969.

A Cry for Life:
Storm Jameson, Stevie Smith,
and the Fate of Europe's Jews

Phyllis Lassner

In their ongoing debate on the two World Wars, feminists have been focusing on whether women were besieged not only by the enemy but also by Allied propaganda.[1] There are British women writers of World War II, however, who engage in a different debate: whether anything, as Storm Jameson wrote in her memoirs, "is worth a fight" (*Journey II* 35). She concluded: "to accept, as genuine pacifists do, anything rather than war, total disrespect for freedom, the systematic crushing or deformation of the spirit, is to accept a death as final as the death of the body. Even in hell, one could not give up fighting for freedom of mind" (*Journey II* 38). Stevie Smith's three novels and the many novels and essays about World War II by Jameson complicate women's attitudes towards war in ways that the current feminist debate does not even begin to consider.

Years before Nazi Germany was officially recognized as a global threat, Jameson and Smith were assessing the costs of denying it. In 1934, Jameson wrote: "War, which modern ingenuity has made the collective suicide of nations, the last triumph of the irrational, is accepted by Fascists as the highest activity of the human spirit" and therefore a possibility we can no longer ignore. In 1936, Smith asks: "How many uniforms, how many swastikas, how many deaths and maimings" could be produced by a "Germany that cherishes everything...of the truest civilization" ("The Twilight of Reason" 16; *Novel on Yellow Paper* 118, 58).

The works of these writers are neither complacent nor uncritical of the war machine. For Jameson and Smith, what makes this second world war a unique assault on "the human spirit" is the unfettered "blood lust and ferocity" that drives Nazi Germany to a "vicious cruelty that isn't battlecruelty, but doing people to death in lavatories" (*NYP* 115, 118). Highlighting this cruelty for Jameson and Smith is the Nazi siege on the Jews, but what makes it particularly pernicious for these writers is its reflection in "the cruelty" of Britain's "outrageous aloofness" (*Over the Frontier* 266). Smith found public outcries distasteful, but her writing forcefully expresses her feeling that Britain's ambivalence towards the Jews is part of the hypocrisy and complacency that gives license to Hitler's world conquest. In her three novels, she confronts Germany's "modern hell" as a disease that doesn't stop at Dover, but is found festering in her own "mixed feelings towards the Jews" (Spalding 118). Expressing abhorrence of war, she denounces Chamberlain's campaign for peace at any price and, as Spalding concludes, asks not only of her heroine, but also of her readers: "And on whose side are you?" (138). Although Smith shares Vera Brittain's empathy for victims on both sides, she disagrees vehemently with her view of a "military caste" in which Britain and Germany are indistinguishable in their "desire for domination" (Layton 79). She forces herself and others to see that, with "no experience of war," it is easy to speak of "the bogy of nazi-ism" ("In the Beginning of the War" 29).

Jameson responded very differently to Hitler's threat than she did to the First World War, about which she "felt horror at each fresh evidence of the ruin begun in the War, and finished in the Peace" (*No Time Like the Present* 101). Many years after the Great War, Jameson recoils at her earlier belief in "those superb sentiments, and now see[s] what 'heroism' is sold for in the market and where patriotism banks its profits; not being able to spit in my own face I smile, with what assurance I can" (*No Time* 100-01).[2] Her despair at the wastes incurred by a war that only led to even greater losses in the next gives way, however, to the necessity for fighting to save the victims of the new reality of "Hitler's bloody harrow" (*Journey II* 18).

A prolific novelist, Jameson was president of British PEN during World War II and used her office to help save many writers and artists from Hitler's death camps. From her travels in central Europe, she saw early signs of the destruction of European Jewry, and many of her works of the thirties and forties argue for the recognition of this impending tragedy. Accepting politics as a writer's mandate, she called upon other writers "to grasp what, in 1937, is happening to human beings—in the world outside them and in their own minds and hearts..." (*The Novel in Contemporary Life* 25). If Stevie Smith felt unable to join Jameson's campaign, her novels crusade for a confrontation with the anti-Semitism latent in a culture that had claimed itself Germany's rival as the "highest civilization." It was Jameson who was "one of the few to discern...the relevance to the historical moment" of Smith's novels (Spalding 147).

The voices of Storm Jameson and Stevie Smith remind us that, at a time when "the present was an insoluble riddle and the past a kaleidoscope of fears, anguish, and the death of friends," it was nonetheless "very difficult for anyone to believe in the reality of evil men" (*Journey II* 45, 21). Caught between the tragic follies of a war to end all wars and the excruciating possibility of repeating it, Jameson and Smith confront their readers and themselves with the possibility that the death of body and spirit may result from not waging war to save those besieged by "evil men."

In several of Jameson's novels, most notably *The Black Laurel*, and in Smith's *Novel on Yellow Paper* and *Over the Frontier*, it is the Jew who tests all the characters' contradictory attitudes towards war. Appropriately paradoxical, the Jew in these novels brings out both the best and worst of European civilization. Like a Rorschsach test, the figure of the Jew is painted as amorphous, an object waiting to be filled in with ink blot representations of the desires and fears of his friends and enemies. His craggy and inconsistent outlines, suggesting a strange amalgam of man, beast, and insect, always produce disturbing responses, as though he represents some evolutionary mistake which calls into question other people's most basic sense of being human and upholders of civilization. A conversation about Jews in Jameson's novel, *Before the Crossing*, illustrates how these responses begin in the very notion of a civilization worth more than the lives who built it:

'Isn't their crime just that they infected the deliciously egotistical civilization of Greece and the vulgar egoism of Rome with the idea, so corrosive, too, of individuality?' 'They did something infinitely worse, they exalted the individual.' (98-99)

It is the sense of a coherent, uniformly satisfying culture and civilization that casts the Jew as the alien so that everyone else can feel secure in their own citizenship. But, of course the Jew also mirrors the fear that we may be cast out simply by dint of being ourselves and being, as we feel ourselves, to be different. In both Jameson's and Smith's work, it is not the Rorschach silhouette which is grotesque and terrifying, but the hatred and aggression which defend us from seeing ourselves reflected in it, and which lead to war.

A model for the development of this argument can be found in Jameson's story from her 1940 work, *Europe to Let*, "Between March and April." Here the English narrator, who is visiting Prague as it is about to fall to the Nazis, is presented as being on the liberal, humane side of the issues. He finds himself trying to figure out how "one could be sure" a man he meets is a Jew: "Possibly it was his mouth, too mobile and delicate: or the too eager intelligence in his brown eyes" (69). Unable to reach a satisfying evaluation, he finally parodies his own test: "Yes, his forehead was ugly. There was the Jew, the man with too much intellect, the man to be envied, despised, stoned" (*Europe* 69). Standing for all of us, the sensitive, cultured, civilized Englishman incriminates himself along with the Jew. For what is called into question is the paradox of an English culture that prizes the individual so long as he or she is English. Any other definition of individuality threatens the coherence of English culture. To characterize one's individuality as different is to be unEnglish, "envied, despised" and therefore unworthy of British protection from the stones of "evil men."

If any of Stevie Smith's three novels, *Novel on Yellow Paper*, *Over the Frontier*, and *The Holiday* could be said to have a plot, it is a woman's struggle to identify her individuality in her threatened but dominant civilization. Through non-stop monologues, her heroine argues with herself about how to feel her way through a world she experiences as alien and hostile, even though it is hers. Smith creates a canny and zany heroine to challenge the cultural myths on which her world and consciousness rest. Exploring the history of the British Lion and the German Fatherland, Pompey Casmilus questions anyone who universalizes moral and political issues as a way of silencing and making others vulnerable to Hitler's "stones." She parodies the lofty words of both German and British politics and then turns against herself to challenge her own assumptions about women's desire to disengage themselves from patriarchal politics.

Pompey Casmilus finds it convenient to identify with the male gods of an ancient underworld for whom she is named. For her, aggression expresses the joy of overcoming her feelings of vulnerability and helplessness; it enables her to feel a surge of power over someone else. Near the beginning of *Novel on Yellow Paper*, Pompey is elated at being "the only goy" and, indeed, "shot right up" at the thought that "a clever goy is cleverer than a clever Jew" (11).

Expressing feelings we might wish she would keep to herself, Pompey's tone and language disturb us with their uncensored and malicious glee.[3] She affronts us with not just a lack of civilized delicacy, but with the evidence that, although words and acts are different, they represent a process by which we can see the evolution of oppression into destruction. As the "only goy," she mirrors the condition of the alien. But she also overcomes the problem of feeling isolated by outsmarting the insiders. Appropriating the cleverness which stereotypically distinguishes her Jewish hosts, she protects herself by refusing to join them with any kind of camaraderie. Instead, she imagines herself as the incarnation of their worst fears about powerful insiders.

Do all goys among Jews get that way? Yes, perhaps. And the feeling you must pipe down and apologize for being so superior and clever: I can't help it really my dear chap, you see I'm a goy. It just comes with the birth. It's a world of unequal chances, not the way B. Franklin saw things. But perhaps he was piping down in public, and apologizing he was a goy. And there were Jews then too. So he put equality on paper and hoped it would do, and hoped nobody would take it seriously. And nobody did. (*NYP* 11).

Smith's technique here and in *Over the Frontier* is to double back on everything Pompey says to question her words as formative acts: "Hatred and contempt, what harm they have done to me and how gladly I would quit of them" (*OTF* 27).

Smith shocks herself and her readers by breaking the silence of pre-war anti-Semitism and predicting its consequences.[4] As Tony Kushner points out, despite British liberalism, Jews were considered not just aliens but "a malevolent power" in this xenophobic society, an image which persisted even through their expulsion (9). From World War I when many Jews were deported and interned, throughout the thirties, anti-Semitism, according to Malcolm Muggeridge, "was in the air" (Kushner 12). Pompey merely echoes the widespread feeling that Jews were exclusionary, a quality which offended even the most tolerant, such as Jameson's narrator in *Europe To Let*. It shouldn't surprise us, therefore, that even Leonard Woolf, Jew and ethical socialist, dismissed anti-Semitism as "just another of those ludicrous manifestations of nationalism that plagued the world," and "described Judaism as the primitive beliefs of desert savages" (Annan 28). George Orwell, who criticized both his fellow socialists' anti-Semitism and the conservatives' claim that Jews were "weakening national morale and diluting the national culture," nonetheless objected to Jewish refusal to assimilate; indeed, by 1940, he said he had heard enough about concentration camps and Jewish persecution (*Collected Essays* 3, 375-6).

Stevie Smith's relationship with George Orwell, which began in 1941, is analogous to her literary confrontation with anti-Semitism. "[N]ever regard[ing] him uncritically," she had already exposed the dangers in his kind of ambivalence towards Jews in her 1936 portrait of Pompey, who, as Spalding points out, comes to realize "the full danger in her pride at being a goy, for it is 'as if that thought alone might swell the mass of cruelty working up against them [the Jews]'" (154, 120).[5] In the figure of a woman who is struggling to find a reason for living, Smith shows the birth of destruction in complicity with "the thoughts and actions, the jealousy and greed that led to war" ("Mosaic"

107). For, however fragile she may be, Pompey, the "only goy," is a citizen in good standing in a society which prides itself on its xenophobia. If she feels left out by her hosts' unEnglish, ethnic coloring, she is also glad of it, for, though she struggles to thrive in a world of male domination, she shares the power of feeling an English superiority.

In both *Novel on Yellow Paper* and *Over the Frontier*, Pompey is repelled by and attracted to Jews. In both novels, she seeks refuge from her hostile feelings about Germans with a Jewish friend in Germany. Talking to herself and to us, Pompey involves us in her "januslike, double-faced" feelings towards "Jew-friends" (*NYP* 13). Identifying with the ethos that launched the empire as a civilizing and protective shelter, she admires those qualities in her Jewish friends that mirror English pragmatism. But, of course, these very attributes perpetuate the myths that seal the fates of her Jewish friends. Thus, in *Over the Frontier*, Pompey's beloved Mr. Aaronson, "sweet sweet cultured [and] sentimental" also makes Pompey happy by making money for her, albeit in mysterious international dealings (*OF* 197).[6]

The issue of anti-Semitism, already inflammatory in 1936 when *Novel On Yellow Paper* was published, explodes with gunfire in *Over the Frontier*, when Pompey assumes the mantle of the war gods in a fantasied midnight ride across a frontier that is literally no man's land as it is held by friends who are also enemies. As war creeps up on her idyllic vacation in Germany, the Jew represents what Pompey admires and detests about herself. As though she is responding to her aggression in the earlier novel, she faces the "racial hatred that is running in me in a sudden swift current, in a swift tide of hatred" (*OF* 159). First she acknowledges her hostility as a way of distinguishing between herself and the persecuted "other" with whom she would rather not identify. She then recognizes that she uses moral judgments to justify her hostility. In a classic set-up, she judges others according to abstract principles so that they are bound to fail her test of their good character. They thus deserve the enmity she bears them: "None but the Jews would have survived their persecutors...The Would points to pride and death in honorable suicide, the Would of history..." (*OF* 159). Regardless of the disparity between Pompey's behavior and her ideals, she must isolate herself from those whose behavior calls the ideals on which her identity is based into question. In this way, she mirrors the relationship of Jews to the British society that prided itself on rescuing Jewish refugees but also held them responsible for the anti-Semitism they engendered.[7]

Pompey's friendships with various Jews confront her anger at the alien who mirrors her own difference and vulnerability. Her actor friend, Igor Torfeldt, reflects back on his audience the contempt for one whose difference challenges a society's deepest beliefs. A member of his audience comments: "he is, I think, a Jew, but my dear, the very best type of young Jew—like *Our Lord*" (*OF* 73). Ironies abound here. For the Christian God of Jewish birth is none other than the alien; but he is also "one of us," "the god of our hope" (*OF* 267, 268). Self and other, powerful and powerless, he embodies the danger of identifying with power as an instrument of self-protection. In Smith's last novel, *The Holiday*, her heroine still ponders this query: "Can resistance pass to government and not take to itself the violence of its oppressors, the absolutism and the torture?" (*H* 10). This work was written during the war, but revised because her publisher felt that readers were tired of the subject. *The Holiday* thus reads uncannily as it talks about the "post-war" but really refers to the war. The heroine, teary, vulnerable Celia, finds herself complicit with "my dear country" about which she "think[s] with pride, aggression and complacency. I tie up my own pride and advantage with England's, I have no integrity, no honesty, no generous idea of a better way of life than that way which gives cream to England" (*H* 84).

Smith confronts pragmatic England with the temptations of cultural myths. In her ride over the frontier, Pompey finds that deeply held beliefs can produce the weapons of war when they justify fears of the unknown—of the alien. Coming full circle, her ride is no escape, either from her own warring spirit or from the hideous realities that war produces but yet sometimes make it worth a fight. Expressing both the anger and the resistance of the victim, the mocking voices of women in Smith's novels pit "the weapons of [English] strength, insularity, pride, xenophobia and good humour" against the "mad and bad philosophies" of "pan Germanism and Naziism" (*H* 82, *NYP* 56, "Germany in Poland" 164). Despite its history of imperial infamy, England, which has "no national Ideology . . . to be expressed in a word and impressed upon a people," is different from "the dotty idealisms" of Germany that will result in "a calamity in event we know too well" (*OF* 258-59). On Christmas eve, celebrating the birth of the Prince of Peace, Pompey decides that, despite the "cruel cynical flippant frivolous pragmatical English of the upper governing classes . . . we are right" and "we shall win" against "Germany and her infection of arrogance and weakness and cruelty" that "has brought us all to this pass, and me to a hatred that is not without guilt, is not, is not a pure flame of altruism" (*NYP* 56, *OF* 259).

Set at the end of the war, Storm Jameson's novel, *The Black Laurel*, argues that the ethos of the victors will be tested not only as it decides the fate of the enemy, but as it responds to the face of the victim. As a military and political delegation convenes in Germany, its determination of truth and justice becomes dependent on discovering the relationship between self and other as it is embodied in the figure of a Jew. Living on the margins of European civilization, neither a bad man nor good, serving all his masters, Heinrich Kalb survives so long as no nation has to claim him as theirs. Once the victors become the judges, however, he is sacrificed to the frustrated need to make distinctions between "murderers and blackguards," especially at a time when the equally strong need for order makes expediency so necessary. The refugee, who one character points out is, by definition, a "bad citizen," is easy to dispense with (*BL* 316). Typifying what Colin Holmes reports came to be known in Britain as "a race without a country," he is reviled as a "sojourner and deficient therefore in patriotism" (171). With no stable national identity, he defies the order of a civil society. But when he is sacrificed, so is justice. Bringing each of the major characters into contact with Kalb reveals the misalliance of justice and order. Taking the same risk as Smith, Jameson deploys anti-Semitism to show how the need for order begins as a defense against one's own chaotic and contradictory feelings. Kalb is composed entirely of Jewish stereotypes. Small and frail, his eyes nervously "frisking behind" thick glasses, he is also obsequious, secretive, and self-incriminating (*BL* 191). He uses his knowledge of art, not to disseminate learning, but to make deals and ingratiate himself into circles closed to him. Like Sadinsky, the Jewish exile in *Cloudless May*, he incurs the wrath of his customers by providing them with the opportunity to indulge and therefore confront their vanity and greed. But, in another sense, it is less important what the Jew is than how others react to him.[8] Basically inept and pathetic, Kalb arouses only revulsion, never compassion. One character finds that Kalb irritates him because "[h]e resented the little creature's friendliness, and yes, his innocence. Who in this world has an excuse for being so simple-minded, so resolute in believing in goodness? In its way it was a provocation" (*BL* 107). One of the novel's most sympathetic characters, Colonel Brett, sees Kalb as "a friendly insect," while the noble German philosopher, Lucius Gerlach, acting as Kalb's defense lawyer, cannot bring himself to touch his client, repelled by the Jew's grimy and shaking hand (*BL* 191).

As the novel is shaped, when no one can find reason enough to save the Jew, the fate of Europe is sealed.[9] Failing to see oneself in the other, as enemy or as victim, threatens to perpetuate an endless cycle of war. Near the end of *The Black Laurel*, a woman who supervises an internment camp in Czechoslovakia speaks from the heart of Europe:

What has happened to Europe is so terrible that no one believes it.... It's all our faults, not only the Germans', and especially your English fault—you wouldn't believe that horror was being born in Germany.... We are in history to our necks...from crime to punishment, and from punishment to vengeance for it. Yet there must be punishment for Terezin. There must be justice. The wounds made by justice are frightful. I know it, and I consent to them. And they will be avenged.... the next war, is the end. It doesn't matter, I tell you. We shall smile at it in its face. Until the last minute—until we are all dying of remorse for being ourselves—we can live! (*BL* 300-01)

For Stevie Smith and Storm Jameson, seeing the other in ourselves means to recognize that Germanic ruthlessness turns up in English history and that responsibility is both individual and collective. Thus, in *Over the Frontier*, Pompey tries to locate herself as she examines her cultural history through a German military memoir of a battle with Britain. In *The Holiday*, Smith shows how Germany is not the only nation which invokes universal forces of nature to justify an instinct for violence:

What is the dog within us that...tears and howls...It is the desire to tear out this animal, to have our heart free of him...and for the innocent happiness, that makes us cry out against life, and cry for death. For this animal is kennelled close within, and tearing out this animal we tear out also the life with it (*H* 57-8).

Smith's own experience shows how deep within us lies the tearing dog. In 1949—the same year that *The Holiday* was published and years after the horrors of the Holocaust—Smith lost her friendship with Betty Miller because she failed to understand the Jews' lasting anxiety about being outsiders. Smith had published a story, "Beside the Seaside: a Holiday with Children," whose main characters are easily recognizable as the Miller family. The Betty Miller character expresses "profound uncertainty" over "a strong growing anti-Jewish feeling in England" and then asks about her children: "when they get a little older, will they also be in a concentration camp here in England?" (13). However powerfully the novels confront anti-Semitism, Smith's use of the Miller's anxieties is blatantly unsympathetic—testament to the recalcitrant antipathy she admits is potentially dangerous.

The fate of the Jews complicates Smith's and Jameson's debates about the justness of World War II. If the Nazi plan to exterminate the Jews is beyond the English imagination, so is the representation of a tolerable Jewish difference. Even in the sympathies of Smith and Jameson, the Jew remains an unassimilable "other" whose separateness represents a test of English moral imagination and therefore an uncomfortable presence for which no narrative space can be found. Mourning the failure to save the Jews marks the apocalyptic moment when a new beginning is imagined for European civilization. In *The Black Laurel*, at the moment the Jew is sacrificed, the English political policeman, Renn, adopts a child: "With something between self-mockery and a painful joy, unexpected, he understood that he had attached himself again to the world by this child...[t]o begin to learn existence from the beginning" (*BL* 349). At the end of *Over the Frontier*, Pompey identifies a just equilibrium by facing two enemies: those masked as friends and those within herself. "Power and cruelty are the strength of our life, and in its weakness only is there the sweetness of love" (*OF* 278).

Years after the war, Stevie Smith and Storm Jameson still debated the merits of the devastating tactics which brought victory to the Allies. Jameson's novel, *The Green Man*, depicts the years 1930-1947 from the perspective of progressive leaders, intellectuals, artists, industrial barons and a Jewish survivor, and concludes that anti-Semitism, self-interest and self-justification are too deeply rooted in European culture to have led to anything but a passive role in the Holocaust. This is not to say that either writer justifies the war solely to save the Jews, but rather that they saw the prevailing anti-Semitism in England as symptomatic of cultural values which depend on a mission of superiority and dominance that all nations and all their men and women share to some degree. As Pompey sits out her imprisonment at the end of *Over the Frontier*, she confronts her own complicity with her captors:

But you see it is my fault I am in this galere...I may say I was shanghaied into this adventure, forced into a uniform I intuitively hated. But if there had been nothing in me of it...should I not now be playing, in...boredom,but safely and sanely enough, with those who seem to me now beyond the frontier of a separate life? (*OF* 272)

If Pompey is guilty of a defensive contempt of others and a resulting warring spirit, she is also vindicated. She understands her role in a culture where, as Colin Holmes reports, "hostile literary stereotypes of Jews were unlikely to have been presented if readers were unable to identify with them" (219).[10] Like the debates Jameson's novels dramatize, Smith gives her heroine the courage to violate the deadly silences of a passive aggression which makes war and destruction seem like the evil that others do. Jameson reminds us:

Our enemies are not the men and women of another country. They are ourselves...they are the interested persons...they are the 'realists' who accept a disorder which exists; they are the romantically-minded...they are women who commit the indecency of assenting to wars which others will fight; they are all of us in those moments when, losing faith, we think of a war as something other than it is—the blasphemous betrayal of the future of man." ("The Twilight of Reason," 19-20)

Notes

[1]See Gilbert and Gubar, *No Man's Land* and *Sexchanges*; Gubar, "This is My Rifle;" Higonnet, *Behind the Lines*; and Tylee, *The Great War and Women's Consciousness.*

[2]In her criticism of Jameson, Tylee considers neither the writer's self-criticism nor her changing views.

[3]Oates describes Smith's narrative voices as: "quirky, rambling, ingenuous, stubborn, funny-peculiar" (11). Garnett sees them as a "device for telling the truth which couldn't be told otherwise..." (321).

[4]Lee notes that Pompey "has no patience with pacifism in the face of the Nazis but knows that war brings out the darkness in people" (320).

[5]See also Barbera and McBrien, 138-139.

[6]Kushner sees the Shylock figure persisting in music halls during the war, even among Jewish entertainers, 111.

[7]Holmes discusses this phenomenon, 219.

[8]Balakian sees "the helpless, gullible Jew" not as an ironic use of a stereotype, but "as the distilled essences of Miss Jameson's clear and humane reasoning" (16).

[9]Harrison Smith's view of the novel as "haunted with...the sense that civilization is in peril" (22) is confirmed by Jameson's fear of an evil even greater than Belsen— "megadeath" (*Journey II* 313).

[10]Holmes shows that British anti-Semitism in fascist and professional circles did not lead to serious force and Jews were not targeted for discriminatory legislation 219.

Works Cited

Annan, Noel. "The Best of Bloomsbury." *New York Times Book Review* 29 March 1990: 28-30.

Balakian, Nona. "Portrait of Our Time." *New York Times Book Review* 16 May 1948: 16.

Barbara, Jack and William McBrien. *Stevie: A Biography of Stevie Smith.* London: Heinemann, 1985.

Garnett, David. *The New Statesman and Nation* 12, 5 September 1936: 321.

Gilbert, Sandra and Susan Gubar. *No Man's Land: The Place of the Woman Writer in the Twentieth Century.* I: *The War of the Words.* New Haven: Yale UP, 1988. II: *Sexchanges.* Yale UP, 1989.

Gubar, Susan. "This is My Rifle, This is My Gun": World War II and the Blitz on Women." *Behind the Lines: Gender and the Two World Wars.* Ed. Margaret R. Higonnet et al. New Haven: Yale UP, 1987: 227-259.

Higonnet, Margaret R. et al. *Behind the Lines: Gender and the Two World Wars.* New Haven: Yale UP, 1987.

Holmes, Colin. *Anti-Semitism in British Society 1876-1939.* New York: Holmes and Meier, 1979.

Jameson, Storm. *Before the Crossing.* London: Macmillan, 1947.

—— *The Black Laurel.* London: Macmillan, 1947.

—— *Cloudless May.* New York: Macmillan, 1944.

—— "A Crisis of the Spirit," *The Writer's Situation.* London: Macmillan, 1950.

—— *Europe to Let: The Memoirs of An Obscure Man.* London: Macmillan, 1940.

—— *The Green Man.* London: Macmillan, 1952.

—— *Journey to the North II.* London: Virago, 1984.

—— *No Time Like the Present.* London: Cassell, 1933.

—— "The Twilight of Reason." Philip Noel Baker et al. *Challenge to Death.* London: Constable, 1934.

Kushner, Tony. *The Persistence of Prejudice: Anti-Semitism in British Society During the Second World War.* Manchester: MU P, 1989.

Layton, Lynne. "Vera Brittain's Testament(s)." *Behind the Lines*: 70-83.

Lee, Hermione. "Stevie Smith." *British Modernist Fiction: 1920-1945.* Ed. Harold Bloom. New York: Chelsea House, 1986: 309-20.

Oates, Joyce Carol. "A Child With a Cold, Cold Eye." *New York Times Book Review* 3 October 1982: 11, 26-7.

Orwell, George. *Collected Essays. Vol. 3: My Country Right or Left: 1940-1943.* Ed. Sonia Orwell and Ian Angus. New York: Harcourt, 1968.

Smith, Harrison. "Berlin Tragedy." *The Saturday Review.* 1 May 1948: 22-3.

Smith, Stevie. "Brittain and the British." *Me Again: Uncollected Writings.* Ed. Jack Barbera and William McBrien. New York: Vintage Books, 1983: 176-77.

—— "By the Seaside: a Holiday with Children." *Me Again*: 12-26.

—— "Germans in Poland." *Me Again*: 174-75.

—— *The Holiday.* New York: Pinnacle, 1982.

—— "In the Beginning of the War." *Me Again*: 128-30.

—— "Mosaic." *Me Again*: 105-107.

—— *Novel on Yellow Paper.* New York: Pinnacle, 1982.

—— *Over the Frontier.* New York: Pinnacle, 1982.

Spalding, Frances. *Stevie Smith: A Biography.* New York: Norton, 1988.

Tylee, Claire M. *The Great War and Women's Consciousness: Images of Militarism and Womanhood in Women's Writings, 1914-1964.* Houndmills: Macmillan, 1990.

Cannibalism and Anorexia, or Feast and Famine in French Occupation Narrative[1]

Michael J. West

When one thinks of the "German" occupation of France, the example which comes to mind most readily is the Second World War. It is easy to go further back in history, of course, to the German advances into French territory during World War One, or even the occupation of northern France and the siege of Paris during the Franco-Prussian War. Many of the narratives of German Occupation during the Second World War bear a strong formal resemblance to these earlier narratives of Prussian/German advances and occupations. Even among themselves, many of the fictional and autobiographical representations of Nazi occupation display a remarkable homogeneity.

Three 20th century texts, Simone de Beauvoir's *La Force de l'âge* (published for the first time in 1960), the Louis Malle film *Au revoir, les enfants* (1987) and Michel Tournier's novel *Le Roi des Aulnes* (1970), display an obsession with food, which comes as little surprise considering the extreme lack of it during the period. The competition for food produces an intense antagonism among the French to the point where food becomes not only the principal form of mediation among individuals but also the means by which others are judged, criticized and even condemned. Food ultimately serves a narrative function as either a catalyst for the *récit* or the vehicle which produces its *dénouement*.

The works by de Beauvoir and Malle are generally considered autobiographical, while Tournier's novel presents a fictional account of the Occupation as seen through the eyes of an anti-hero accorded near-mythic status. The two more recent texts (Tournier and Malle) introduce a less frequently explored theme in Occupation narrative, that of children and the depictions of the Occupation through the eyes of children.[2] Both Tournier and Malle manage to avoid overly sentimental portrayals of children as victims of Nazi aggression, however. While Malle demonstrates that children can be just as cruel, duplicitous and anti-Semitic as their parents, Tournier's protagonist goes even further, ultimately becoming the mythic ogre of the novel's title. In both narratives, adults and children face the same hardship brought on by the lack of food. Malle and Tournier work out different solutions to this "crisis of scarcity" in the same narrative economy which describes a tragic and occasionally gruesome intersection of competition and self-sacrifice. All owe a great deal to an important 19th century precursor, Guy de Maupassant.

191

Two Maupassant short stories, "Deux amis" (1882) and "Boule de Suif" (1880), established the parameters for depictions of "self" and "other" which characterize Occupation narratives throughout the First and Second World Wars. While "Deux amis" presents a clear-cut opposition between a heroic (and starving) Paris and a voracious Prussian adversary (embodied in the officer who gives the order to execute the two friends), "Boule de Suif" problematizes the previously positive French identity by introducing French characters who are as duplicitous and ultimately as despicable as their Prussian enemies.

The inscription of the occupying force as Other in "Deux amis" represents little more than an overdetermined variant of a narrative like "Boule de Suif," which foregrounds the enemy within through a *dédoublement* of the national self. Significantly, both narratives display an obsession with eating. The first description of Boule de Suif inscribes her not only in reified terms but specifically as an *edible* commodity.[3] Food, or the lack of it, is also present from the very first line of "Deux amis": "Paris était bloqué, affamé et râlant. Les moineaux se faisaient bien rares sur les toits, et les égouts se dépeuplaient. On mangeait n'importe quoi" (209) ["Paris was sealed up, starving and howling. The sparrows were rare indeed on the rooftops, and the sewers were being rapidly depopulated. People ate anything they could get their hands on."]

Both narratives inscribe what could be designated a "revenge narrative," one in which the main characters lose either their lives or their self-respect, around the theme of food. Variations of this kind of narrative reappear again and again in 20th century narratives of the German occupation. For the *deux amis*, the inspiration of two glasses of absinth on an empty stomach (!) produces the fatal plan to sneak behind enemy lines to fish "for old times' sake," while Boule de Suif's ample *panier*—a metaphorical extension of her personal "abundance"—provokes not only the envy but ultimately the revenge of her fellow travelers, who encourage her to give herself over to the Prussian officer characterized by a purportedly insatiable sexual appetite. While the Prussian officer in "Deux amis" represents the fear of being overwhelmed and physically devoured by the enemy, the officer in "Boule de Suif" represents the sexual threat of the Other or the threat of being "devoured" sexually. In the last scene of "Deux amis," the officer orders his cook to prepare the fish that the two friends have taken from the stream, the same stream into which their bodies have just been dumped. In so doing, the officer places himself symbolically at one end of a food chain which posits the two friends at the other. While "Boule de Suif" displays none of the metaphoric cannibalism of "Deux amis," the brutality of rape constitutes an even more violent devouring of one human being by another. The duplicity of the other French travelers, first in convincing Boule de Suif to surrender herself to the Prussian officer's advances and then totally ignoring her after the fact, constitutes a less direct, though equally violent, aggression which borders on a symbolic cannibalism.

Representations of German occupation during the Second World War inflect the models put forth by Maupassant in "Deux amis" and "Boule de Suif." Simone de Beauvoir's autobiographical *La Force de l'âge*, dedicated to Jean-Paul Sartre, presents graphic scenes of life in Paris and the rest of France during the Occupation. Her concerns for Sartre's safety and welfare are never far from her obsession with finding enough to eat. The few descriptions of Germans in the work are much less harsh than one might expect, and considerably more even-handed than the views expressed by de Beauvoir's friends and even her own father: "il [mon père] les haïssait en tant que 'Boches': je ne pus jamais utiliser ce mot dont le chauvinisme me heurtait; c'est en tant que nazis que je les détestais" ["he (my father) hated them as *Krauts*. I could never use this word because of its offensiveness; it was the Nazis I hated"] (474).

Rather than criticize the Nazi occupiers, de Beauvoir would rather direct her scorn at collaborators, of which there was no lack, even in her own beloved Café Flore. With understated disdain, she recalls her reaction at overhearing two collaborationist journalists seated near her: "C'était leur nullité même qui les rendait dangereux" ["It was their own uselessness which made them dangerous"] (546).

Most often, though, her preoccupation with Sartre's well-being and her usually futile attempts to find enough to eat dominate her description of life during the Occupation. When Sartre has been transferred to a German POW camp in Silesia, de Beauvoir despairs and imagines him succumbing, not to torture but to hunger: "Je vois vaguement une carte d'Allemagne, avec une noire frontière barbelée, et puis il y a quelque part le mot Silésie, et puis des phrases entendues comme: Ils meurent de faim" ["I vaguely remember a map of Germany with a dark, barbed-wire border, somewhere on which was written the word 'Silesia,' and then muttered statements such as 'They're dying of hunger'"] (476). Even after Sartre's return, however, the two still very nearly die of hunger in Paris, where food becomes increasingly difficult to find, and that which is available becomes increasingly less edible. At one point she writes: "La révolte de nos estomacs prouvaient qu'un grand nombre des marchandises qui se donnaient pour comestibles ne l'étaient absolument pas" ["Our sickened stomachs told us that goods which were supposedly ready to eat were in fact inedible"] (534-5).[4] More than the reader's heart is wrenched at the descriptions of de Beauvoir's attempts to disguise spoiled meat which she receives through the mail from a well-meaning friend. Most often her attempts are successful, although she is mortified when Sartre occasionally pushes away his plate in disgust. At one point Sartre is present when she receives a package containing half a rabbit. Before she has even finished unwrapping the package, however, Sartre grabs it and runs downstairs to throw it in the trash (525).

When the two leave Paris for one of their occasional bicycle excursions between the Occupied and "Free Zones," they find little improvement. Sartre in particular has great difficulty finding enough to eat, either through absent-minded neglect or through his refusal to eat things like tomatoes, which happen to be all that anyone has to eat in Marseille on one occasion. At times, the two simply run out of money. The situation reaches a critical point in La Pouèze during one trip when Sartre passes out for three days and de Beauvoir notices that she has lost 16 pounds and her body is covered with pustules (536).

More interesting than her description of collaborators or even of her own misfortunes, though, is her mention of Sartre's lack of appetite and his refusal to eat. Of course, it is quite obvious that Sartre simply has a weaker stomach than most of his friends—we might find it hard to blame him—, and it is also very likely that anyone who smoked as much as Sartre did would have had less of an appetite than most people. For whatever reason he refuses, though,

Sartre's behavior begins to describe what could be designated as an "anorexic" mode, that is, a pathological absence of appetite. In a revealing footnote, de Beauvoir remarks that Sartre "refusait d'habitude les plus minimes privilèges ["Sartre would normally refuse even the slightest indulgences"] (536). This refusal marks an important development in Occupation narrative.

The notion of a French character who refuses food represents a relatively recent development in narrative terms. It is somewhat surprising, given the high value placed on gastronomy in French culture, where talking *about* food is often as important as eating itself. The refusal of food (without the corresponding refusal to talk about food, curiously enough[5]) is taken up in another autobiographical representation of the Occupation, Louis Malle's film *Au revoir, les enfants*. In this story, food fulfills several important narrative functions. It is partly in observing Jean Bonnet's eating habits that the character based on Malle, Julien Quentin, realizes that Bonnet is Jewish. During the scene in which Bonnet refuses pâté and offers it to someone else, Julien asks him why. When Bonnet replies that he is not hungry, Julien asks him if it is not rather because it is pork.

The parallels between Malle and Maupassant are striking, but we find an even more important similarity between the film and de Beauvoir's memoirs in the way in which Jean Bonnet/Kippelstein refuses not just pâté but the *biscuit vitaminé* as well, for no other apparent reason than a basic generosity. In another scene, Bonnet and one of the other boys receive the last helpings of what appears to be a *cassoulet*. There is only one piece of chicken left, and Bonnet insists that the other boy take it, leaving only the lentils for himself.

One scene in the film makes an important link not only with de Beauvoir but Maupassant as well. At the film's center, Malle places the "bonding" scene between Julien and Jean in which the two become lost in the woods and are discovered by Nazi soldiers who bring them back to the school wrapped in blankets. Immediately after their return, there is a pause during which the other boys greet Jean and Julien and ask them various questions about what they've been doing and how they've been treated by *les Boches*. One of the German soldiers is in the process of reprimanding the priests for not being as careful as they ought to have been when he overhears himself and his men referred to as *les Boches*. The soldier then asks one of the priests, in excellent French, whether *les Boches* may have their blankets back. It is an awkward and a revealing moment at the same time: not only are the Germans capable of speaking quite fluent, idiomatic French, but they are also capable of at least a certain degree of humanity by looking after the two boys and bringing them back unharmed. At the same time, they are even capable of irony. This capacity for irony, combined with advanced linguistic competency, are traits which go back to Maupassant's "Deux amis." When Morissot and Sauvage are brought before the Prussian officer, Maupassant writes: "Une sorte de géant velu [. . .] leur demanda, en excellent français: Eh bien, messieurs, avez-vous fait bonne pêche?" ["A kind of hairy giant...asked them in impeccable French, 'Well, messieurs, how was the fishing today'?"] (217).

The film's formal narrative devices show more of an affinity with Maupassant than with de Beauvoir, in fact. The denunciation of the school, which comprises the film's turning point, is the product of another "revenge narrative," this one, as in "Boule de Suif," centered around food. The discovery of the kitchen helper Joseph's black market scheme provokes the closing denunciation, arrest and deportation of Jean Bonnet, the other Jewish children and the pastor. As in "Boule de Suif," we have a duplicitious *bonne soeur* in the film, who denounces one of the children hiding in an infirmary bed. In contrast to Maupassant, however, nearly *every* character has its opposite number in the Malle film: there are bad *religieuses* and good priests (the opposition male/female seems only coincidental), decent Germans and evil Germans, and, more importantly, good French and bad French: from "bad" children who refer to the Germans as *Boches* and who repeat the antisemitic insults they have learned from their parents, to "good" children like Jean Bonnet who stay out of the black market (unlike Julien) and willingly offer their own portions of food to others.

The difference between "good French" and "bad French" becomes most apparent in the restaurant scene—yet another narrative function centered around food—in which the Milice make their appearance to harass the restaurant's sole Jewish patron (after Jean Bonnet). This is a crucial moment in the film, since it is only through the intercession of the group of Nazis seated next to the Quentin entourage that the Milice are called off and "put in their place." Of course, the primary motivation for the Nazi officer to remove the Milice is to impress Julien's mother, but, as Marcel Ophuls' *Le Chagrin et la Pitié* and *Hôtel Terminus* have shown, we also see just how the French themselves could prove to be even more vigorously anti-semitic than the Nazis.

In spite of the more sophisticated narrative structure found in *Au revoir, les enfants* which splits "the French" into "good" French and "bad" French and "Nazis" into "evil" Nazis and "not-so-evil" Nazis, in this film we still have little difficulty identifying heroes or villains. We may be surprised at Joseph's sudden re-entry into the narrative as a collaborator, but this only serves to remind us of de Beauvoir's comment on collaborators.[6]

Far more problematic and more interesting are the questions posed by Michel Tournier's novel *Le Roi des Aulnes*, in which the main character, Abel Tiffauges, functions rather as an anti-hero. In opposition to nearly all the elements of Occupation narrative examined thus far, here we have a first-person narrative told from the "wrong" side. Falsely accused of raping a young girl, the would-be pedophile is saved from prison when war breaks out. Rather than being sent to jail, Tiffauges finds himself dispatched instead to the Eastern Front, where he is almost immediately captured and becomes a collaborator. With Tournier we enter the domain of the mythic, and the novel's title is intended to guide us. Tiffauges *is* "le Roi des Aulnes," *l'ogre* in its original sense of "géant des contes des fées, à l'aspect effrayant, se nourrissant de chair humaine ["terrifying fairy-tale giant which feeds on human flesh"] (Le Petit Robert), not too far removed from the Prussian officer in "Deux amis," originally described as "Une sorte de géant velu..." ["A kind of hairy giant..."] (217). "Food" in the context of Tournier's novel, however, becomes not just any human flesh but particularly children's flesh.

Tiffauges' evolution from child to child-eater or ogre is marked by certain stages. During the first stage, under the tutelage of his grotesque and sinister classmate Nestor, Tiffauges tastes human blood for the first time when he is forced to lick the wounded knee of the class bully, Pelsenaire:

The thigh, the knee and the upper calf were covered evenly by a dark, black silk which would have been otherwise undisturbed except for a gaping wound just above the knee-cap. Out of the wound flowed a dark crimson liquid which turned first to ochre and then to brown as it mixed with the mud. My tongue circled the wound and traced a grey halo. Several times I had to spit out bits of earth and cinders. The wound, with its swollen mass and pale ridges of torn skin folded in on themselves, welling with blood, unfolded in its own distinct geography. I passed my tongue over the wound once quickly but still clumsily enough to provoke a twitch around the kneecap. Then a second, longer pass. Finally I placed my lips on the gaping wound and left them there for a time too long to remember.

What happened next I can't recall. I believe I was overcome by shivers and even convulsions before being taken to the infirmary. I seem to recall being ill several days. My memories of those days at Saint-Christophe are all rather confused now. What I do recall, though, is that my teachers decided to alert my father of my illness and, eager to find some plausible source, they suggested a case of indigestion caused by an overindulgence in sweets. The irony of their diagnosis was of course lost on them. (31)[7]

The overtly sexual nature of this first taste of blood is revealed in phrases like "mes lèvres se sont posées sur les lèvres de la blessure et y demeurèrent un temps que je ne mesurai pas" ["I placed my lips on the gaping wound and left them there for a time too long to remember"] and "je fus pris de frissons, de convulsions même" ["I believe I was overcome by shivers and even convulsions"] (31).

The transformation of the kneecap into an erotogenic zone and the generally sadistic nature of the scene recall Freud's discussion of infantile sexuality in "Three Essays on Sexuality":

Children who distinguish themselves by special cruelty towards animals and playmates usually give rise to a just suspicion of an intense and precocious sexual activity arising from erotogenic zones ... (93)

We shall give the name of 'pregenital' to organizations of sexual life in which the genital zones have not yet taken over their predominant part. We have hitherto identified two such organizations, which almost seem as though they were harking back to early animal forms of life.

The first of these is the oral or, as it might be called, cannibalistic pregenital sexual organization. Here sexual activity has not yet been separated from the ingestion of food; nor are the opposite currents within the activity differentiated. The object of both activities is the same; the sexual aim consists in the incorporation of the object—the prototype of a process which, in the form of identification, is later to play such an important psychological part. A relic of this constructed phase of organization, which is forced upon our notice by pathology, may be seen in thumb-sucking, in which the sexual activity, detached from the nutritive activity, has substituted for the extraneous object once situated in the subject's own body. (198)

Given his reaction of shivers and convulsions, Tiffauges' licking of the kneecap might be and in fact should be read as part of the "cannibalistic pregenital sexual organization" mentioned by Freud.

This pregenital stage lasts even into Tiffauges's adult life. During the physical examination which precedes his military service, he is characterized as a *microgénitomorphe* or having abnormally small genitalia (110). Likewise, the "incorporation of the object" to which Freud refers should be interpreted as the collapsing of the two different processes of ingestion and sexuality. The arrival of puberty coincides with a voracious appetite for fresh red meat: "mes dents, comme l'avait prophétisé Nestor, se sont mises à grandir, je veux dire, un appétit d'une exigence peu commune a commencé à me tenailler quotidiennement l'estomac" ["My teeth, as Nestor had indeed predicted, began to grow, accompanied by an unusually large appetite which began to gnaw at my stomach daily"] (110). In an almost comically grotesque parody of vegetarianism, Tiffauges explains how his love for meat is really an expression of love for animals:

When I say 'I love meat, I love blood, I love flesh,' the verb love alone is important. I am all love. I love to eat meat because I love animals. Sometimes I think that I could even kill the animal myself, with my own hands, before eating it with an almost affectionate appetite, this animal that I've raised myself and with which I've shared my life. You might say that I would eat it with a more enlightened sensibility than I would with some other *anonymous, impersonal* meat. This is what I vainly tried to explain to that stupid Miss Toupie, who's a vegetarian out of disgust for slaughterhouses. (112) (emphasis added)[8]

Tiffauges reveals his own cannibalistic urges through the implied opposition of "anonymous," "impersonal" meat to the "personal" meat he would prefer. Every reader of Grimm's fairy tales, and especially Perrault's "Le Petit Chaperon Rouge" (Little Red Riding Hood), knows how often children are devoured by various wolves, ogres and trolls.

In exploiting the mythic register of the legend of "le Roi des Aulnes," Tournier illustrates Roland Barthes' definition of myth in the chapter of *Mythologies* entitled "Myth Today" as "a second-order signifying system," in which the sign of the first-order system, "language," becomes the signifier of the second, "myth."[9] Tournier replaces the pedo*phile* Tiffauges with the "pedo*phagic*" Roi des Aulnes, who is nothing but a mythical representation or allegory of the Vichy government, which assumed power in June 1940 under the leadership of Philippe Pétain. In becoming head of state, Pétain insisted on qualifying his action as *le don de sa personne*, a *don* both to the French people as well as Nazi Germany. As self-sacrifice, Pétain's gesture was necessarily figurative rather than literal, though. The German authorities realized the need for a legitimate (and legitimized) French head of state, and the choice of the benign, de-sexualized Pétain reflected the twin strategic imperatives of finding a figure who could command the respect of the French people without being strong (or "potent") enough to pose a serious threat to the Reich. Neither the Germans nor the French would accept the literal self-sacrifice of "le Maréchal." Even after the War, the French could not bring themselves to "eat their own" and execute Pétain, but rather punished him with a prison term instead.

Twentieth-century representations of the German Occupation, particularly Malle's *Au Revoir, les enfants*, work to refute Pétain's *don de sa personne* and, in fact, portray just the opposite: an insatiable Vichy government which fed on its own population—a population which, when faced with the inevitable prospect of its own sacrifice, in some cases slowly starved itself nearly to death. Like Maupassant before them, Malle and Tournier skillfully exploit the deliberate confusion of eating and sexual functions. In the 20th century, post-Freudian and post-Second World War context, however, this confusion focuses not on adults but rather on children. More recent modern narratives raise some rather frightening, if not gruesome, implications of the Brillat-Savarin's dictum "Dites-moi ce que vous mangez et je vous dirai qui vous êtes" ["Tell me what you eat and I'll tell you who you are"].[10] This is not meant to portray cannibalism as some sort of ultimate recuperation of national identity, or even less as a variation of the relentless pursuit of some mythic fountain of youth, but rather a questioning of the limits of introspection during historical moments as complex and dangerous as those experienced during wartime.

Notes

[1]Many of the ideas in this paper came about as a result of a course I taught on Occupied France in the Fall of 1989. For that reason, I would like to dedicate it to the students in that course. All translations from the French are my own.

[2]This is not to say that the theme was totally ignored before Tournier and Malle. René Clément's film *Les Jeux interdits* (1950) comes immediately to mind as one of the better known examples of war narratives which take children as their main characters.

Likewise, the theme of cruelty to children is hardly a modern one and even predates its frequent exploitation in 19th century melodrama, including Dickens. Prior to the Second World War, many Surrealist works portrayed or at least broadly suggested the killing of children. Three examples come to mind immediately: 1) the "rhapsodic" sequence between the two lovers near the end of *L'Age d'or* (1930), during which the female character says to the male, to the strains of the Liebestod from *Tristan und Isolde*, "Quelle joie d'avoir assassiné nos enfants!" ["How wonderful to have killed our children!"]; 2) The opening line of Roger Vitrac's *Free Entry* (1922) in which the Man in Formal Dress says, "They invited me to strangle the children,"; and 3) André Breton's recounting in *Nadja* (1928) of the play *Les Détraquées*, during the course of which the bloodied body of a young girl falls out of an armoire.

[3]"Petite, ronde de partout, grasse à lard, avec des doigts bouffis [...] pareils à des chapelets de courtes saucisses, avec une peau luisante et tendue, [...] elle restait cependant appetissante et courue, tant sa fraicheur faisait plaisir à voir" (19). ["Small, as round all over as a barrel, with swollen fingers...like a string of sausages with glistening, taut skin,...she was a delight to behold in all her freshness."]

[4]The word-play on the term *comestible*, which functions grammatically in French as both an adjective and in the plural as a noun, is, unfortunately, lost in translation.

[5]We might be tempted to infer that, in a certain sense, talking about food becomes a way of eating vicariously, as if discourse were trying to serve as an admittedly poor substitute for food itself.

⁶The full quote from *La Force*: "Je ne détestais pas les entendre [les collaborateurs]; il y avait dans leurs visages, dans leurs propos, quelque chose de si dérisoire que, pendant un instant, la collaboration, le fascisme, l'antisémitisme m'apparaissaient comme une farce destinée à l'amusement de quelques simples d'esprit. Et puis, je me ravisai, avec stupeur: ils pouvaient nuire, ils nuisaient; leurs confrères, dans *Je suis partout*, indiquaient les retraites de Tzara, de Waldemar George, de beaucoup d'autres, et réclamaient leur arrestation; ils réclamaient qu'on déportât le cardinal Liénart qui avait tenu en chaire des propos anti-allemands. C'etait leur nullité même qui les rendait dangereux" ["It wasn't unbearable to listen to them (the collaborators); there was something about their faces and their speech which was so ridiculous that for a moment it seemed that collaboration, fascism and anti-semitism were all part of some simple-minded farce. And then suddenly I realized that these people could be and were in fact dangerous; their colleagues at *Je Suis Partout* revealed [Tristan] Tzara's whereabouts and demanded his arrest, as they did to Waldemar George and so many others; they were also demanding that Cardinal Liénart be deported for preaching a sermon which was supposedly anti-German. It was their own uselessness which made them dangerous"] (546).

⁷The original quotation is: "La cuisse, le genou et le haut du mollet étaient uniformément sculptés dans un limon noir, [sic] vernissé qui eût été impeccable sans la plaie centrale, complexe et pourpre, ouverte au-dessous de la rotule. Il en suintait une coulée vermeille qui tournait à l'ocre, puis à un brun de plus en plus sombre en se mêlant à la boue. Ma langue fit le tour de la blessure qu'elle entoura d'une auréole grise. Je crachai à plusieurs reprises de la terre et des residus de machefer. La plaie d'où le sang continuait à soudre étalait tout près de mes yeux sa géographie capricieuse avec sa pulpe gonflée, ses élevures blanchâtres de peau excoriée et ses lèvres roulées en dedans. J'y passais la langue rapidement une première fois, pas assez légèrement cependant pour ne pas provoquer un tressaillement qui souleva en rictus le bourrelet de muscle arrondi coiffant la rotule. Puis une seconde fois plus longuement. Enfin mes lèvres se posèrent sur les lèvres de la blessure et y demeurèrent un temps que je ne mesurai pas. Je ne saurais dire exactement ce qui se passa ensuite. Je crois que je fus pris de frissons, de convulsions même, et qu'on dut m'emporter à l'infirmerie. Il me semble que j'y fus malade plusieurs jours. Mes souvenirs sur cet épisode de ma vie à Saint-Christophe sont assez confus. Ce dont je suis sûr en revanche, c'est que mes maîtres crurent bon d'avertir mon père de cette indisposition et qu'alléguant n'importe quoi, ils firent allusion, avec une ironie dont l'énormité leur échappa, à une indigestion due à un excès de friandises.

⁸In the original French, Tiffauges writes: "Quand je dis J'aime la viande, j'aime le sang, j'aime la chair, c'est le verbe aimer qui importe seul. Je suis tout amour. J'aime manger de la viande parce que j'aime les bêtes. Je crois même que je pourrais égorger de mes mains, et manger avec un affectueux appétit, un animal que j'aurais élevé et qui aurait partagé ma vie. Je le mangerais même avec un goût plus éclairé, plus approfondi que je ne fais d'une viande *anonyme, impersonnelle*. C'est ce que j'ai tenté vainement de faire comprendre à cette sotte de Mlle Toupie qui est végétarienne par horreur des abattoirs."

⁹Roland Barthes, "Myth Today," in *Mythologies*, trans. Annette Lavers. New York: Hill and Wang, 1972, 115. Originally published as *Mythologies* by les Editions du Seuil, 1957. The influence of Barthes' work and of semiotics in general on *Le Roi des Aulnes* cannot be overemphasized, from the opening pages of the novel—"Tout est signe" (15)— to the description of the hero's mentor, Nestor: "Mais ce n'était encore que la face manifeste de Nestor. Sa face cachée, que je fus seul a soupçonner, c'était les signes, le *déchiffrement des signes* (italics in the text). [. . .] Les signes, le déchiffrement des signes…De quels signes s'agissait-il? Que révélait leur déchiffrement? Si je pouvais répondre à cette question,

toute ma vie serait changée, et non seulement ma vie mais—j'ose l'écrire assuré que personne ne lira jamais ces lignes—le cours même de l'histoire" (40).

[10]The post-modern identity has been, in fact, already shaped by such works as Peter Greenaway's recent *The Cook, the Thief, his Wife, her Lover* (New York: Miramax Productions, 1989), in which a kitchen serves as the setting for lovers' trysts and where a young boy who works—significantly—as kitchen help is brutalized by being threatened with an act of auto-cannibalization, having to eat his own navel. The shocking series of revenge narratives which close the film begin when the lover is similarly brutalized and, in fact, killed by being forced to eat pages from books, which function metaphorically as extensions of his own genitalia. In the film's final scenes, the thief's wife exacts her revenge by forcing her husband to eat her lover, beginning with his penis, before she shoots him.

The recent re-emergence of cannibalism as a theme is also reflected in another film, *The Silence of the Lambs* (Los Angeles: Orion Films, 1990), in which the cannibalistic anti-hero is portrayed with as much, if not more, ambiguity as Abel Tiffauges in *Le Roi des Aulnes*.

Works Cited

Barthes, Roland. *Mythologies*. Annette Lavers, trans. New York: Hill and Wang, 1972.

de Beauvoir, Simone. *La Force de l'âge*. Paris: Gallimard, 1960.

Freud, Sigmund. "Infantile Sexuality," in "Three Essays on Sexuality," *Complete Works*, trans. James Strachey. London: Hogarth P, 1961. Vol. VII, 173-207; "Jokes and Their Relation to the Unconscious," Vol. VIII, 42.

Malle, Louis. *Au revoir, les enfants*. Paris: Nouvelles Editions de Films, 1987.

Maupassant, Guy de. *OEuvres complètes*. Tome IV: *Boule de Suif, Correspondence, Etude de Pol Neveux*. Tome XIII: *Mademoiselle Fifi*. Paris: Louis Conard, 1924.

Tournier, Michel. *Le Roi des Aulnes*. Paris: Gallimard, 1970.

Contributors

James Rodger Alexander is an Associate Professor of Art at the University of Alabama at Birmingham. He has exhibited both sculpture and photography throughout the eastern United States and western Europe. His scholarly research and publications have focused primarily on the conceptual cross pollenization of art and culture. A long-time student of poster art from both World Wars, he has drawn upon images from his large personal collection in developing this current study.

Marilyn Fain Apseloff is Professor of English at Kent State University where she is a specialist in Children's Literature. The former president of the Children's Literature Association, she has written widely in that field and currently is the ongoing writer of the "Literature for Children" article for the annual *The World Book Year Book*. The study that appears in this book combines her expertise in writing for youth with her deep interest in the Holocaust and the World War II Polish experience in particular.

Lynn Z. Bloom is Professor of English and Aetna Chair of Writing at the University of Connecticut, Storrs. She is the author of *Doctor Spock: Biography of a Conservative Radical*, co-author of *American Autobiography 1945-1980: A Bibliography*, and editor of the two World War II diaries discussed in her article. Her recent research on autobiography, supported by the National Endowment for the Humanities, includes such works in progress as *Telling Secrets: Autobiographies of American Childhoods* and *Our Stories, Our Selves: Reading, Writing, Researching Autobiography*.

Carol Burke is an Associate Professor in the Humanities Center and Assistant Dean of the School of Arts and Sciences of Johns Hopkins University in Baltimore, Maryland. She has published widely in a number of areas including an examination of accounts of supernatural and supernormal experiences (*Vision Narratives of Women in Prison*), a collection of family folklore (*Plain Talk*) and a book of original poetry (*Close Quarters*). A volume on creative writing which she co-authored with Molly Tinsley, *The Creative Process*, will be appearing shortly.

Laura Hapke is Professor of English at Pace University in New York City. The author of a number of articles on women in literature in journals such as the *Victorian Newsletter* and the *Journal of American Culture*, she published *Girls Who Went Wrong: Prostitutes in American Fiction, 1885-1917* in 1989. She is currently completing a work on wage-earning women in American literature.

Sue Hart was born in Detroit but went west to do graduate work in literature at the University of Montana and never left the state. She is currently Professor of English at Eastern Montana College in Billings where she specializes in Women and the Frontier Experience, Montana authors and creative writing. The author of many essays in scholarly journals, she also has published poetry and short stories. Her 1987 PEN Award winner, "Star Pattern," is set during the years of World War II..

M. Paul Holsinger is Professor of History at Illinois State University. The founder and chair of the Popular Culture Association's World War II area of study, he has published widely in a number of fields including American children's literature. Two of his articles looking at the impact of popular fiction on the growing Boy Scout and Camp Fire Girls movements appeared recently in the *Children's Literature Association Quarterly*. He is currently completing work on a definitive bibliography of all English-language children's and juvenile works dealing with the Second World War era.

Rose Kundanis, Associate Professor of Journalism at Keene State College (New Hampshire), has worked as an editor for a local newspaper in Tennessee and as the director of television for Marietta College in Ohio. She currently supervises all broadcast journalism for both WKNH-FM and Keene State College Television. Her research on the image of child care in popular magazines has been presented at numerous Popular Culture Association meetings.

Philip Landon is Professor of English at the University of Maryland—Baltimore County. He is a student of the various ways in which the ideology of the Progressive movement has influenced the evolution of American film genres. The article appearing in this volume has grown from his research for a forthcoming book-length study of the Hollywood war film as it evolved in the early 1930s to the present. An essay focusing on the period immediately before his current scope, "From Cowboy to Organization Man: The Hollywood War Hero, 1940-1955," was published in *Studies in Popular Culture* (XII:1, 1989).

Phyllis Lassner teaches women's studies and composition at the University of Michigan. In addition to numerous articles on feminist theory and literature, she has authored two books on Elizabeth Bowen—a feminist reassessment of her major fiction and the first book-length study of her short stories. She is deeply involved in examining the World War II writing of British women and, in addition to her chapter in this work, has published studies on many aspects of that theme.

Cecilia Macheski is Professor of English at LaGuardia Community College, City University of New York. She has co-edited two recent books: *Fetter'd or Free: British Women Novelists 1670-1815* and *Curtain Calls: British and American Women and the Theater 1660-1820*. In 1988, and again in 1991, she served as Fulbright Scholar in Women's Studies and American Literature in New Zealand. An avid knitter and needlework enthusiast, she is completing work on a book about those subjects in literature which is scheduled for 1993 release.

Robert L. McLaughlin is Assistant Professor of English at Illinois State University. His primary research focuses on the writings of Thomas Pynchon and especially on that author's *Gravity's Rainbow* with its context of 1960s ideology and vision of alternative organizations of reality. In addition, he has published and presented research findings on the works of Ernest Hemingway, Sinclair Lewis, Norman Mailer, T.S. Eliot, Marjorie Kinnan Rawlings and Stephen Sondheim.

Jennifer E. Michaels is currently Professor of German at Grinnell College in Grinnell, Iowa. The author of three books: *D.H. Lawrence: The Polarity of North and South, Anarchy and Eros: Otto Gross' Impact on German Expressionist*

Writers, and *Franz Jung: Expressionist, Dadaist, Revolutionary and Outsider,* she has also published numerous articles on such important German writers as Heinrich Boll, Bertolt Brecht, Gerhart Hauptmann, Hermann Hesse and Hertha Pauli. She is presently working on a book-length manuscript about Franz Werfel.

Sally E. Parry is currently an Assistant Professor of English at Illinois State University in Normal, Illinois. A specialist on twentieth-century American literature, she has, during the past several years, written and presented papers dealing with such well-known authors as Sinclair Lewis, Margaret Atwood, Dylan Thomas, Upton Sinclair and Marjorie Kinnan Rawlings. She is presently working on a book about Sinclair Lewis as a social critic.

Mary Anne Schofield, Professor of English, is a specialist in 18th-century English literature as well as a student of World War II; she has authored three books: *Quiet Rebellion* on the fiction of Eliza Haywood; a biography of Haywood; and *Masking and Unmasking the Female Mind: Disguising Romances in Feminine Fiction 1713-1799.* She has also edited nine other books including *Cooking By the Book: Food in Literature and Culture* for Popular Press in 1989. A study of the wartime writings of British and American women from 1939 to 1945, is forthcoming.

David K. Vaughan directs a graduate-level technical communication course at the Air Force Institute of Technology in Ohio, where he also teaches courses in military ethics and the literature of armed conflict. He has published articles on technical writing, juvenile series fiction and the literature of flight. He is the author or editor of two books, one describing the writings of Anne Morrow Lindbergh and a second presenting the diaries and letters of a World War I American Air Service pilot.

Michael J. West is currently Senior Lecturer in French at Carnegie Mellon University in Pittsburgh, "the spiritual capital of the Rust Belt." He is interested in issues of gender and sexuality, has written and published about the works of Paul Nizan and Drieu la Rochelle and has translated interviews with Michel Foucault. Presently he is preparing a manuscript on the *Expositions Universelles* in Paris as part of the 'spectacle of ideology' and the *mise en scéne* of technology.

Margaret Wintersole is a doctoral candidate in the English Department of Texas Christian University, Fort Worth, Texas, where she is completing a study on *film noir.* Her special research interest combines the study of modern rhetorical theory with the interpretation of visual images especially in regard to entertainment films. A related article on British wartime movie-making, "The British Hero in Feature Films of World War II" appeared in *Studies of Popular Culture* (XXII:2, 1989).